About the Author

Rajub Bhowmik is an adjunct faculty of Police Science and Criminal Justice, in the Department of Law, Police Science and Criminal Justice Administration at John Jay College of Criminal Justice of the City University of New York (CUNY).

He also teaches Psychology in the Department of Behavior and Social Science at Hostos Community College of the City University of New York (CUNY). Rajub Bhowmik is an active law enforcement officer in the Critical Response Command (CRC) at Counter-Terrorism Bureau (CTB) of the New York City Police Department (NYPD).

Dedication

This book is dedicated to those in law enforcement who have altruistically sacrificed their lives in betterment of our society. And to those who have gone beyond the call of duty, often without fanfare or recognition. This book is specifically dedicated to Sergeant Paul Tuozzolo of New York City Police Department, a dear friend and a mentor who made the ultimate sacrifice on 11/04/2016.

Rajub Bhowmik

LEADING THEORIES OF DELINQUENT BEHAVIOR AND CRIMINOLOGY

AUSTIN MACAULEY PUBLISHERS™

LONDON · CAMBRIDGE · NEW YORK · SHARJAH

A CIP catalogue record for this title is available from the British Library.

ISBN 9781788236249 (Paperback)
ISBN 9781788236256 (Hardback)
ISBN 9781788236263 (E-Book)
www.austinmacauley.com

First Published (2017)
Austin Macauley Publishers Ltd™
25 Canada Square
Canary Wharf
London
E14 5LQ

Acknowledgements

I would like to express my sincere gratitude to Dr. Oliver Crespo (Hostos College-CUNY), and Dr. Maki Haberfeld (John Jay College-CUNY) for believing in me and guiding me to the academic arena.

Contents

Chapter 1
Theory and Criminological Theory

Understanding Theory and Its Implication

It's really a daunting task to comprehend the actual meaning of the word "*Theory*" since a never-ending list of criminal justice practitioners, politicians, and pundits termed this word an absurd opposite of the word "*Fact*". Just like the field of criminology is very difficult to study with respect to the causes of crime, the same goes true for the word 'Theory' as well. The reason being, theories are particularly based upon articulation of an idea whist the facts provide us with tangible results exactly opposite of the impractical mental maneuvers (Hirchi & Gottfredson, 1993). Apparently, it seems true but as a matter of fact, this is a distorted image of theory since theory is not a fancified image of the fact; theory is a reality. Roshier (1989) argued that theory is not just made merely by presuming an idea; theory is born out of sufficient merit in an idea that's why theory is explored further in a bid to investigate the real facts. An effective theory is factually based on an idea, or series of ideas which is deeply rooted in the thinking of general population that pops up in human behavior, experience, feelings, and real situations. That's why an effective theory is reliable enough to be tested on empirical findings as well as against the new facts.

Consider an idea of a young child's condition of child molestation during infancy and later his involvement in child trafficking business or making a prostitution gang. Consider a situation where minority groups and immigrants in a country get caught in majority of crimes. Why there is discrimination between a legally defined criminal behavior and other behaviors which might be odd but don't fall in the category of criminology. The criminology theories provide concrete explanations about the deviant behavior of criminals, which further corroborate the relationship between certain events referring to a set of events (Akers, 1977). In other words, theories define and explain why a set of certain events are connected to each other. For instance Van de Ven & Poole (1995) explained different theories which serve as building blocks for explaining change processes in an organization. Similarly, an empirical ground for a theory of personal victimization has been explained by Hindelang, Gottfredson & Garofalo (1978). Curan and Renzetti (2001) explained theory as a series of propositions or statements interrelated with each other.

It's a kind of *'what is'* and *'what will be'* relationship that doesn't straightforwardly provide answers to 'what ought to be' and they don't perfectly fall in the category of religious and philosophical values and beliefs about crime and society as well. One can assume that criminology theories are theoretical and a bit intangible, but they are not mere speculations. They hold more than armchair speculations in a bid to comprehend and unfold human behavior and society on a broader perspective. If somebody wants to dig deep into deviating social norms, they need to identify why people choose the paths other than socially and legally accepted etiquettes. In the light of aforementioned facts, studying criminology theories is pivotal not only for legal professionals and law enforcers, but for ordinary citizens as well because people commit crimes and people become crime's victims (Reiss, 1986).

Exploring Criminological Theories

Criminology is regarded as a specific branch of knowledge that entails the processes of law making, law breaking and the reaction to it. This provides us with a vantage point from where we can explore the criminological theories with all our might and understanding. Despite that some people know the consequences of breaking law yet they persist on committing crimes (Sutherland, Cressey and Luckenbil, 1992). So, we can divide it into two main parts i.e. the *law making and its enforcement* AND *law breaking*. The first part put an impact on why do we have legal laws and why the criminal justice system is in place. The later part accounts for delinquent behavior of people for which they are subjected to legal intervention, punishment, and prevention. This research is all about investigating the later part i.e. delinquent and criminal behavior of people which lead them to violate social norms and etiquettes outlawed by the legal system, society, and the state alike. How to account for the existence of human evil and how can we mark people who are harmful to others because the most ill human acts are committed by ordinary individuals (Waller, 2002). This is where we need to foresee the facts considering criminology theories in a bid to realize how, why, and what ought to be done to identify and curb the human evils polluting the minds of ordinary citizens. It is an attempt to systematically analyze social psychology of criminal mind with respect to the sociology of crime. It includes but not limited to the social, political, and economic conditions in which mind is susceptible to crime and criminality even in the oddest of circumstances. There are certain types of theories which can be sort through to find evidence on law and the criminal behavior such as Marxist, Feminist, and Conflict labeling theories (Simpson, 1989).

Theories of Law and Criminal Justice

"Theories of law and criminal justice" provide with a clear insight about what marks the certain behavior of people as crime in society and what action ought to be taken as a reaction from the legal system. Who defines and takes the decision that a certain action is illegal and falls in the category of crime. The three variables which affect the implementation of law in criminal justice system, the enforcement decisions, and legislations are social, political, and economic variables.

It is worth mentioning here that nor do they reflect the philosophies of what type of legal system our society should be having, not either it is a hypothetical statement to endorse an argument in favor of effective criminal justice system. Because philosophies and theories can offer desirable objectives of a criminal justice system but they don't unearth any concrete scientific reasoning behind law and criminal justice. The philosophies and hypothetical statements might support relevance with criminal justice system i.e. what should be and how should be BUT they cannot form the basic grounds upon *"why laws are formulated and enforced"*. Theories do not help us in totality; for instance, they would help us in formulating a hypothesis about the behavioral triggers that are directly linked with the criminal justice actions and decisions BUT they won't feed the system with proper, correct, and exemplary values which the system needs.

An interesting fact is that one cannot weed out the theorists from philosophies altogether. The theories of crime are interrelated with philosophies and criminal justice system in a bid to reach out some tangible goals of an effective criminal justice system. For instance, if we consider the importance of *conflict theory* in criminology, we would find out that there is a strong relevancy between conflict theory theoretical propositions regarding system's operation with the moral and political debate over the fairness of the system. From neutral eyes, a fair system is deemed as a system where every single criminal is treated impartially on legal grounds keeping in consideration only the legal laws and the nature of criminal act. On the flip side, the conflict theory instigates a hypothetical moral and social debate that criminal justice system is polluted to such an extent that apart from relevant laws and the nature of criminal act, it focuses on other factors such as gender of criminals, their class, race, and position (Hindelang, 1978). Even at times, analysts deem that gender equality with respect to nature of criminal act falls short of what is needed in the justice system. Covington and Bloom (2003) argued the same that women's' imprisonment should be reduced if the society really wants to grow positively. At the face of it, it looks nice upon hearing but can literally fret eyelids when it comes to defining an impartial / just criminal justice system. Hence, research evidence needs to be investigated with regards to conflict theory and the fairness of the criminal justice system for the sake of providing a better system to the citizens.

Theories of Delinquent Behavior and Criminology

These theories try to dig deep into the basic questions behind a delinquent and deviant mindset. For instance, why people breach the legal and social customs? This question stretches out two more questions interconnected with each other:

Why the group rates of crime and deviation show variations on different locations?

Why do some ordinary people instigate to indulge in delinquent and deviant activities?

The first question unfolds the scenario if the group crime rates have to do anything with specific locations or groups in the societies. For example, why less people fall prey to criminal activities in Great Britain and Japan as compared to United States? Why the ratio of males in committing violent crimes is much high than the females? How do we give a reason to justify the dissimilarities in drug use and homicide in a single society?

So, we have two set of questions i.e. focusing on societal and group patterns whilst second one pointing towards differences in individual personalities. The former that points towards broader questions is called "*Macro Theory*" (Liska, 1990) whilst the later which point towards individual personalities is referred as "*Micro Analysis*" (Groff, Weisburd and Yang, 2010). Many other analysts described the same analysis using different terms for instance Cressy (1960) named macro theory as "*epidemiology*" while individual crimes as "*Individual conduct*". All these terms relate both to the questions as well as to the answers each theory presents. For example, if a theory is investigating about the differences in crime rates with regards to the gender differences, it might investigate micro level biological differences between the two genders thus operating on the micro level analysis (Sampson and Wooldredge, 1987). Either way, the micro and macro theories are interconnected with each other; one theory might be explaining the other or vice versa. Most of the macro level theories grasp direct and indirect statements about the conditions such as societal or structural make-up, which trigger the low or high crime rates in a certain group of population. The individual conduct theory emphasizes that the criminal act committed by an individual is directly or indirectly linked with their life history, individual attributes, or due to a specific situation.

Then there are *"biological theories"* which takes the combination of both macro and micro level analysis and digs deep into several layers of explanation to draw upon explanatory variables. It includes numerous physiological, neurological, chemical, or genetic variables (Rafter, 2008). The *"psychological theories"* revolve around certain personality traits including a specific personality, emotional disturbance and inability to appropriately react to one's environment, psychological imbalance, and mental retardation (Pacheco and Barnes, 2014). Many analysts defined *"sociological theories"* which accounts for a criminal or deviant behavior through investigating the socio-demographic, structural, and cultural variables (Lynch, 2002; Rock, 2006). There are several other theories in the list which we will discuss in the later chapters. This book takes the reader towards numerous criminological theories thus discussing what it offers and evaluating its strength and validity.

Standards for Examining Theory

How can we conclude that a specific theory is the best in explaining a criminal justice or crime scenario? The reason being, at times, one theory might be befitting the air of correction for a scenario, but using another theory in the same scenario might provide conflicting explanations of crime. We cannot justify a crime scenario if we select a theory that is at odds with the situation. How do we pluck out the best preferable theory among a congregation of criminology theories? The weakest way or the very wrong way for welcoming or refraining from a theory of crime is how good it fits into your own preferences, principles, or beliefs.

If the nature of these theories is scientific, then they should be evaluated by scientific standards. Determining its empirical validity by gathering evidence is *"the very important factor"* when putting a theory to test. But cultivating a justified opinion about a theory involves numerous other major standards by which theories can be evaluated such as:

Internal logical consistency (Barnea, Rahav and Teichman, 1987)

Scope and parsimony (Vito and Maahs, 2015)

Testability (Gibbs, 1985)

Empirical validity (Baumer and Gustafson, 2007)

Usefulness and policy implication (Burke, 2013)

Learning Scope and Parsimony of a Theory

The very basic essentiality for a well-defined theory is that its hypotheses and concepts are logically sound and internally consistent every step of the line. For instance, if a theory states that criminals fall prey to biological deficiency that accounts for their deviant behavior cannot state that socialization in family is the primary reason behind criminal behavior. The *scope* of a theory determines its range or capacity to which it offers its propositions. For example, a check forgery case isn't broad in its scope. Likewise, a case of juvenile criminality without adult delinquency is also limited in its scope when compared with a theory that accounts for both these phenomena.

Parsimony is also a very important attribute in a scientific theory, which focuses on the briefness and compactness of a set of hypothetical propositions. The scope and parsimony are interconnected with each other in the sense that wider the scope, with a few abstract and concise statements is likely to remove the claptrap and make use of as few propositions as possible in a bid to express the broadest range of facts, which is also the primary principle of parsimony (Whiteside, 1994). For instance, if a theory proposes that all types of juvenile crimes are directly linked with hormonal changes in juveniles, then this theory is much more parsimonious when compared with some other theory which lends a number of hypothetical propositions to express crime and deviant behavior. Parsimony, in a sense, confines the set of options for investigation and sets out a small but precise path to reach out the triggers of criminal behavior. While evaluating a theory, the parsimony factor needs to be thoroughly analyzed in a bid to clutch concrete evidence behind the deviant behavior. That's why many analysts choose parsimony over comprehensiveness (Cornish et al., 2008).

Justification Against Empirical Findings

A scientific theory that cannot be tested and justified against empirical findings is just a piece of claptrap, and nothing else. According to Gibbons (1979), "*in the final analysis, the acid test of a scientific theory is testability; that is, the extent to which it can either be verified or disproved by appropriate empirical evidence*". Merely fitting a theory with regards to empirical evidence compatible with its propositions won't make it enough to be justified. The reason being, a theory can also be prone to empirical manipulation thus falsifying the accuracy of theory in return. In other words, a theory must be open to testability against evidence that might oppose or invalidate its propositions based on the negative findings. A theory couldn't be taken as testable if it is not *falsifiable* and a good theory must be always practical in the sense that it should corroborate the knowledge in a scientific discipline (Van de Ven, 1989).

Tautology refers to a proposition or statement that involves circular reasoning OR in which the same thing is repeated twice using different words / propositions. Tautology is what makes a theory untestable because it holds useless restatements for the sake of proving its authenticity. For instance, if a theory proposes that the deviant behavior is due to biological deficiency in a person and then reiterates that biological deficiency is what makes a person to commit crime is tautological. It has been observed that circular reasoning is being used to validate a certain behavior and then the same reason is reused to express the same behavior.

A theory can also be regarded as untestable if its statements are so much broad and wide that the statements can easily be supported by conflicting empirical evidences. For instance, a theory might propose that male bank robbers are overwhelmed by unconscious childhood guilt with regards to their sexual attraction towards their own mothers during some stage of their infancy. Since this proposition isn't true by definition, it would be considered as a testable explanation of male bank robbery. This said theory can only be considered as a well thought-out and well supported theory if considerable numbers of male bank robbers are found who fit this description. On the flip side, the theory would be stated as false if enough evidence is found against this proposition such as male robbers disclose that the lack of education tempted them to clutch the money easy way through bank robbery. At the same time, the theory can clutch a support if the latter findings about male bank robbers are disapproved on the score that it was their unconscious impulse which they are again denying of their true criminal behaviors.

If a theory is not measurable by reportable and observable events, it falls in the category of untestable theory. If the system cannot find observable events that can be stated as objectives behind crime thus repeatable measures of these concepts cannot be made, it would again be taken as untestable even for a non-tautological theory. For example, Felson and Clarke (1995) stated in their book *Criminology and Public Policy*: "*In the end, these theories become untestable in practice and thus unverifiable, leaving out for the moment the evidence and arguments against them in the first place.* Likewise, if a theory states that people fall prey to criminal activities because they are possessed by some invisible spirits, it gives no way to prove this theory because nobody would be able to make the spirits come and state the truth or nobody can hold them accountable for such criminal wrongdoings. The fact is, it might not be possible that every theory is measurable but at least a theory should be able to connect itself with measurable outcomes in a logical way. For example, a branch of social learning theory proposes that the juvenile and children copy their elders which might be their immediate family members or the screen stars which they adore by watching them on big screens or other social media platforms. In this case, "*imitation or copying*" is measurable and testable since one can closely observe their elders or peer models to figure out how much their criminal or deviant behavior copies their models. Hence the said theory is logically measurable and testable. Winfree, Backstrom and Mays (1994) also argued that punishments and enforcements persuade the young people to see delinquency behavior as the right thing rather than perceiving it unfavorable such as the gang's honor or defending the neighborhood by whatever means necessary. This theory is also measurable thus testable also.

Stipulation of Empirical Validity and Deterrence Theory Explanations

Empirical validity is "*the necessary*" factor for cultivating a just judgment about a theory. Simply put, Empirical validity reflects if a theory is backed by research evidence or not. If a theory has no empirical validity, it would be judged as false, even with the attributes of being parsimonious, logical, and non-tautological. For judging the empirical validity of a theory, the main thing is, what degree of empirical evidence the theory supports? Do the research based findings fall in the category of strong or weak support? Does the research evidence lessen its effectiveness or broaden its support? Can its empirical validity be comparable with the other theories? For instance, Baumer and Gustafson (2007) investigated the empirical validity of the classic anomie theory pronounced by Robert Merton using such standards.

Let's consider the case of "*deterrence theory*" which states a proposition that offenders, if given severe legal punishments, will be deterred from their crimes forever. Suppose if evidence based research reveals that severity of legal punishment only tends to deter a small group of offenders OR the severity of punishment has just less probability of repeating crimes from the punished offenders when compared with the unpunished offenders then the theory is likely to have some empirical validity but not significant enough to prove its worthiness. On the flip side, "*labeling theory*" labels the offenders as criminals if they are caught or processed by the criminal justice system. Hence that deviant label sticks with them as a stigma and motivates them in a negative manner to repeat their crimes (Becker, 2008; Lemert, 1972). If the evidence based research finds it fit in various circumstances and the chances of recidivating for a caught criminal are more than those who haven't been caught yet, then this theory would be having an upper edge over deterrence theory.

Evaluating Criminological Theories: Causation and Probability

When it comes to evaluating theories in criminology, one should be assured about the concept of causation and probability. The concept implies that the theory will always bear the factor of probability of occurrence but a theory must not 100% identify the variables that always instigate the deviant behavior OR the theory must not be used explicitly to decide to arrest a wrongdoer. In fact, science gives us a conventional concept of causality using X and Y as variables. Y would only produce effect if it is preceded by variable X which is a *necessary condition* i.e. absence of X would void the occurrence of Y, and a *sufficient condition* i.e. Y would always occur when X is present there. In this regard, the criminology theories do not play on the same level of harmonization between X and Y i.e. they never meet the same causation criteria of necessary and sufficient conditions. The empirical validity of criminology theories bears a concept of probabilistic causality. If it is viewed in term of X and Y then it would be like "the occurrence of Y is more probable in the presence of X. In other words, the changes or variations in a criminal or deviant behavior are connected with the changes or variations in the explanatory variables discovered in the theory. Simply put, the variations in the associated explanatory variables would predict the probability of the occurrence of crime or deviant behavior. From the explanatory variables, one would be able to judge when the crime is more likely to occur or re-occur. Likewise, the empirical validity of the theory will be stronger if the probability is stronger or vice versa.

The explanation of correlation between the explanatory variables in shape of causation even in the probabilistic scenario becomes an unintelligible crisscross because the connection between two correlated variables might be different than described in the theory. For example, a theory might propose that the probability of a juvenile's criminal behavior is directly proportional to his connection with other juveniles who are already criminal minded. Hence the theory can be supported by a correlation between one's own criminal behavior and the deviant behavior of his friends. On the flip side, this connection might be occurred conversely i.e. it might be possible that the juvenile might be indulged in criminal activities first, and then he reached out his delinquent friends. Thus, the dependent variable becomes his association with criminal minded friends. Hence further research will be required in a bid to figure out the actual direction of the association.

The probabilistic causality concept supports the stance that the external forces do not determine a human behavior completely; likewise, the human behavior is not completely determined by an unrestricted activity of freewill choices. More accurately, "*soft determinism*" is what determines a behavior from the middle ground viewpoint (Matza, 1967). It elucidates about the unpredictable behavior of human mind that can never be completely 100% predicted. It also shows the authoritative factors together with limitations, yet leave space for human choices at the same time. Soft determinism stance is almost universally accepted by criminologists across the globe. "*The fundamental assertion of soft determinism is that human actions are not deprived of freedom because they are causally determined*" (Matza, 1967).

When we speak about soft determinism, we take humans as free agents; free agents who were not compelled or forced to perform a certain action or a set of actions. For instance, a person cannot be called as a free agent if he took some action under the influence of drugs or a threat since the person's action was influenced by the factor of either drug or threat. On the flip side, if he is not under those influences then his action as a free agent would be deemed as he has chosen to act in that way as a free agent. Despite their actions are not deemed as completely free since we don't strive to point out the absence or presence of causes but try to point out the type of causes that are present (MacIver, 1942). A universally accepted theory of soft determinism states that "...*Biological, sociocultural, and developmental factors may influence-but not determine-behavior because the systematic processes underlying criminal behavior are complex, dynamic, and self-reinforcing. A key reason for the effective unpredictability of these and similar nonlinear systems is their extreme sensitivity to initial conditions* (Vila, 1994).

Usefulness and Policy Implications of Criminological Theories

The usefulness of a theory in criminology in terms of its effectiveness and applicability on criminal justice system and practice is extremely important. While evaluating a theory, non-usefulness is a sure sign of its ineptness to fit in the system. In other words, the better the theory fits in the system by providing a well-thought-out explanation of the problem, the better it would strive to solve the problem rather than just being a gross inconvenience in shape of a useless theory. Digging deep into the theories reveal that almost all the major criminology theories have propositions that have been well utilized and explained in the criminology practice. Either explicitly or implicitly, each theory is backed up by reasoning for or against the human nature, particularly the criminal mindset and occupies its place in the formation of a well-thought-out police policy, criminal justice practice, prison regimen, treatment program, and therapy. These are the theories which are being investigated consistently by evaluators thus bringing in new recommendations to be incorporated in our legal and criminal justice system. Every single recommendation is based on some underlying theory evaluations and findings that's how the laws are enacted, redefined, and enforced. That's how the system operates under fundamental hypothetical but logical systems and that's how the limitations of the people are defined in our justice system.

Hence the hurdle isn't that which theory is backing a certain policy, the question is, how well a policy is guided and backed by a theory to the best of its requirement, and how good the ground on which the policy is established is. When a policy is explained in theoretical form, most of the time, people misunderstand it due to the complexity of its mixing theoretical strands. Even it seems like an ill-stated or obscure policy just made or adopted for the sake of justifying its economic, bureaucratic, or political reasons. The hybrid mixture of such ill-stated policies about criminal justice system raises several questions by the public. This consistent mode of rationalizing a theory or a mixture of theories for a policy in criminal justice system instigates the criminologists to try any number of things to figure out what works and what doesn't. Again, the theoretical purity of a theory becomes secondary thing if its utility and effectiveness is deprived of its practical implementation. Making a theory's usefulness and effectiveness also leads to adopting theories without checking the nitty-gritty about how well a theory establishes itself as a good theory. This implies that even if a theory is non-tautological, empirically valid, to the point, parsimonious and clear, yet it has to sustain the crossroad of usefulness and effectiveness. The theory gains more validity if it can be implemented for guide programs and practices at large. On the contrary, this can also be deemed as a theory lacking its exactness and accuracy on the score if the adopted program adopted it poorly on the grounds of its theoretical principles rather than accurately counting on the actual circumstances. No doubt theories are made in a bid to make the criminal justice system better than its former state, reduce recidivism, and to change the delinquent behavior, but at the same time, theories are vulnerable to ethical or practical roadblocks. Even at times, theories are manipulated by political forces or some other influential parties who have their own interests rather than keeping the validity of the theory. Criminologists also argue about the effects of political manipulation of crime prevention in the criminal justice system since its practical application lessens its usefulness to a considerable extent (Gilling, 1997). All these factors make crime prevention a difficult beast to tame. These issues which consistently impinge upon a theory's effectiveness should be given a broad attention if a society wants to frame crime prevention on a broad-ranging canvas.

2. Summary

The main thread of an argument regarding the creation of criminology theories revolve around either *breaking the law* OR *making and enforcing* it. The making and enforcing of law holds the distinct set of practices with regards to contents of the laws and the conduct of criminal justice system alike. Breaking the law defines and elaborates the different forms of deviant criminal behavior with respect to its origination, occurrence and patterns. When it comes to analyzing individual behaviors, we focus on micro level theories; on the contrary, addressing delinquency among different target groups based on societies groups and their locations, we count on structural or macro level criminology theories. Gaining an insight of crime and criminal justice system is the primary aim behind a criminology theory. Theories don't provide us an absolute path regarding what ought to be done but they do provide us with probabilistic causality based on research based empirical evidence.

3. References

Akers, R. L. (1977). Deviant behavior: A social learning approach.

Barnea, Z., Rahav, G., & Teichman, M. (1987). The reliability and consistency of self-reports on substance use in a longitudinal study. *British journal of addiction*, *82*(8), 891-898.

Baumer, E. P., & Gustafson, R. (2007). Social organization and instrumental crime: Assessing the empirical validity of classic and contemporary anomie theories. *Criminology*.

Becker, H. S. (2008). *Outsiders*. Simon and Schuster.

Burke, R. H. (2013). *An introduction to criminological theory*. Routledge.

Cornish, D. B., & Clarke, R. V. (2008). 2. The rational choice perspective. *Environmental criminology and crime analysis*, *21*.

Covington, S., & Bloom, B. (2003). Gendered justice: Women in the criminal justice system. *Gendered justice: Addressing female offenders*, 3-23.

Cressey, D. R. (1960). Epidemiology and individual conduct: A case from criminology. *The Pacific Sociological Review*, *3*(2), 47-58.

Curran, D. J., & Renzetti, C. M. (2001). *Theories of crime*. Pearson College Division.

Felson, M., & Clarke, R. V. (1995). Routine precautions, criminology, and crime prevention. *Crime and public policy: Putting theory to work*, 179-90.

Gibbons, D. C. (1979). *The criminological enterprise: Theories and perspectives*. Englewood Cliffs, NJ: Prentice-Hall.

Gibbs, J. P. (1985). The methodology of theory construction in criminology. *Theoretical methods in criminology*.

Gilling, D. (1997). *Crime prevention: Theory, policy, and politics*. Psychology Press.

Groff, E. R., Weisburd, D., & Yang, S. M. (2010). Is it important to examine crime trends at a local "micro" level? A longitudinal analysis of street to street variability in crime trajectories. *Journal of Quantitative Criminology*, *26*(1), 7-32.

Hindelang, M. J. (1978). Race and involvement in common law personal crimes. *American Sociological Review*, 93-109.

Hirschi, T., & Gottfredson, M. R. (1993). Commentary: Testing the general theory of crime. *Journal of Research in Crime and Delinquency*.

Lemert, E. M. (1972). Human deviance, social problems, and social control (2™" Ed). *Englewood Cliffs, NJ.*

Liska, A. E. (1990). The significance of aggregate dependent variables and contextual independent variables for linking macro and micro theories. *Social Psychology Quarterly*, 292-301.

Lynch, M. (2002). The culture of control: Crime and social order in contemporary society. *PoLAR: Political and Legal Anthropology Review*, *25*(2), 109-112.

Matza, D. (1967). *Delinquency and drift*. Transaction Publishers.

MacIver, R. M. Social Causation (Boston: Ginn & Co., 1942), 209.

Pacheco, D., & Barnes, J. C. (2014). Psychological theories of crime. *The Encyclopedia of Theoretical Criminology.*

Rafter, N. (2008). *The criminal brain: Understanding biological theories of crime.* NYU Press.

Reiss, A. J. (1986). Why are communities important in understanding crime? *Crime and Justice, 8,* 1-33.

Rock, P. (2006). *Sociological theories of crime.* Oxford University Press.

Roshier, B. (1989). *Controlling crime: The classical perspective in criminology.* Milton Keynes: Open University Press.

Sampson, R. J., & Wooldredge, J. D. (1987). Linking the micro-and macro-level dimensions of lifestyle-routine activity and opportunity models of predatory victimization. *Journal of Quantitative Criminology, 3*(4), 371-393.

Simpson, S. S. (1989). Feminist theory, crime, and justice. *Criminology, 27*(4), 605-632.

Sutherland, E. H., Cressey, D. R., & Luckenbill, D. F. (1992). *Principles of criminology.* Rowman & Littlefield.

Van de Ven, A. H. (1989). Nothing is quite so practical as a good theory. *Academy of Management Review, 14*(4), 486-489.

Van de Ven, A. H., & Poole, M. S. (1995). Explaining development and change in organizations. *Academy of Management Review, 20*(3), 510-540.

Vila, B. (1994). General paradigm for understanding criminal behavior: Extending evolutionary ecological theory, A. *Criminology, 32,* 311.

Vito, G. F., & Maahs, J. R. (2015). *Criminology.* Jones & Bartlett Publishers.

Waller, J. (2002). *Becoming evil: How ordinary people commit genocide and mass killing* (p. 240). Oxford: Oxford University Press.

Whiteside, L. (1994). Structural equation model of adolescent delinquency.

Winfree, L. T., Bäckström, T. V., & Mays, G. L. (1994). Social learning theory, self-reported delinquency, and youth gangs a new twist on a general theory of crime and delinquency. *Youth & Society.*

Chapter 2

Social Bonding and Control Theories

1. Introduction

The field of criminology has remained active on the issue of motivations that encourage or influence people to commit crimes or engage in delinquent behavior. Over the years, different criminology theories have been given that aim towards explaining the human behavior of delinquency and attempt to understand the factors that contribute to criminal behavior. Different theories of criminology and delinquent behavior have made different assumptions about contributing factors as well as the reasons that lead to people committing crimes (Cote, 2002). Some of the most popular and well-known theories of delinquent behavior include the theory of social bonding and theory of control. Both theories are based on different assumptions yet there is some conceptual level integration between these theories that links the concepts with each-other. There are some similar concepts present in both theories as well as presence of some other factors that contradict each-other.

In this research report, the conceptual approach of social bonding theory and social control theory are examined. The approach in this project taken is to emphasize the similarities and differences that exist in both theories to have a more comprehensive and integrated form of criminology theory of delinquent behavior. In addition to this, this report will also examine the structural and conceptual approaches taken by the earlier control theories and modern control theories.

1.1 Internal and External Theories and Three Social Control Factors

A popular sociological concept of delinquent behavior is based on social control element and this involved the socialization process, the environment in which an individual learn self-control, and control that is applied on the individual by various types of social norms based sanctions. These social control sanctions provide a reward for affirming to the norms and punishment upon deviating from the norms. The concept of social control was examined in early studies by Reiss who provided defining aspects of the social control factor in respect to criminology applications (Anderson, 2014). According to this theory, an individual engages in delinquent behavior if there is a failure in social controls or self-control aspects. In this theory, an individual learns personal self-control ability from the social norms and feels a controlling pressure from the society to follow the customs and social expectation. The personal level of control is defined as 'internalized control', while the social control aspect of it is perceived as external application of control through means of sanctions and lawful punishments.

This theory that was proposed by Reiss was later explained and expanded by Nye (Miller, 2014) and he identified that all the social control factors and elements can be divided into three separate categories, which are described below:

Direct Control: this refers to the direct form of achieving control over behavior by means of imposing some punishment or threatening with sanctions for any violation of misconduct. Additionally, complying with the code of conduct is rewarded.

Indirect Control: this is an indirect way of influencing an individual regarding delinquent behavior. This control prevents an individual from engaging in delinquent behavior because his or her criminal behavior may lead to disappointment or emotional pain to parents, family members or friends.

Internal control: this control factor refers to the element of guilt and self-consciousness in an individual that prevent him or her from engaging in any kind of delinquent behavior.

1.2. Techniques of Neutralization and Drift and Delinquent Behavior Explanations

The theory that introduced various techniques of neutralization and drift was proposed by Sykes and Matza (Jacobs & Copes, 2014) and this theory used the neutralization techniques as a way of explaining the delinquent behavior among individuals. The neutralization techniques refer to various justification methods and excuses that are offered by criminals for their act of committing a crime. In most cases, these excuses are illogical and unreasonable extensions of various commonly present rationalizations that exist in the society. Having belief in the definitions of neutralization of committing a crime does not mean that the delinquent behavior having person does not approve of the traditional social values in all aspects or that such people believe in values that have complete contradiction to normal social values (Pratt & Cullen, 2000). Having such beliefs only represents that these people have a set of 'subterranean principles' that either make use of or rationalize criminal activities by means of extending the traditional social values in some manner. In explanation of their theory, Sykes and Matza made it clear that the various techniques of neutralization as proposed by them are different types of 'definition favorable' to criminal activities and delinquent behavior. Despite the approach taken by Sykes and Matza is not viewed as a control theory by the researchers themselves, many scholars and researchers in criminology consider the 'techniques of neutralization' theory a control theory.

Skyes and Matza based their theory on their interpretation of the various principles of delinquency behavior and social norms. Later, these two researchers also used their neutralization propositions in development of 'drift' theory of criminal behavior. This theory makes the proposal that the various neutralization techniques proposed in the previous theory present a way of 'episodic release' for the criminals and delinquents from the traditional moral and social restrictions (Liska, Sanchirico, & Reed, 1988). The major cause of delinquent behavior presented in this theory is the ability awarded to delinquents to periodically evade the traditional moral obligations, allowing for the adolescents to drift towards criminal behavior and out of criminal activities. If the presence of traditional social values is perceived as social control factors then neutralization of these factors can be easily seen as a weakening in the social control on individuals.

2. Containment Theory of Criminal Behavior

Around the same time as Nye proposed the control theory based on social control factors, Walter Reckless (Flexon, 2014) also proposed a control theory that is more commonly known as the Reckless's 'containment' theory of criminal behavior. The foundation of this theory was also based on the familiar concept of internal and external factors of control and these factors were given names 'inner' and 'outer' containment factors by Reckless. The theory given by Reckless did not remain limited to just this approach as he also included various factors that encouraged or influenced young individuals to engage in delinquency behavior, which are factors that 'pulls' and 'pushes' an individual towards criminal behavior (Nagin & Pogarsky, 2001). The most root conceptual proposition of the Reckless' containment theory is that the presence of inner or outer pushes or pulls will develop some degree of delinquency behavior in an individual unless there is another containment that counteracts it. In cases where the motivation to delinquent behavior is stronger in comparison to the containment, it is expected that a criminal behavior will take place.

It is possible for a young individual to get pushed towards criminal behavior due to presence of some strong inner psychological drives such as aggressiveness, anger and hostile behavior. In addition to this, there exist two different types of environment based factors that impact delinquency behavior, which are- 'pushes,' environmental conditions that put pressure on an individual to engage in crime (poverty, presence of opportunity and deprivation); and 'pulls,' various positive environmental factors that influence an individual towards criminal behavior (delinquent friends and involvement in gang activities). There exist several different outer containment factors that prevents an individual from engaging in criminal activities and these factors also influence a crime-free life; factors in outer containment category include family supervision, schooling guidance and strong positivity in the social group (Bernard, 1992). The inner containment factors that counteract criminal behavior influences mostly include own concept of good behavior as well as self-consciousness.

3.   Exploring Hirschi's Social Bonding Theory

Nearly all the earlier criminology theories of social control were replaced by the social control theory proposed by Hirschi (Krohn, Massey, Skinner, & Lauer, 1983). This theory of criminology that is given by Hirschi remains of the most renowned and practiced theory of control in modern times. This social control theory is more commonly known as the social bonding theory. The popularity of the social bonding theory and its acceptance in criminology has reached so high that from last few decades, the earlier theories of social control is included in text books and criminology researchers as only an introductory background information to the social bonding theory (Colvin, Cullen, & Ven, 2002). In many aspects, Hirschi's social bonding theory has become the modern equivalent of social control theory for many criminology experts. In current state of criminology sciences, social bonding theory is certainly a well-regarded and center place having theory of criminology. Social bonding theory has become the most discussed as well as most tested of all the criminology theories in the world.

The position achieved by the social bonding theory in the criminology field is a well-deserved position by this theory. This theory presents a comprehensive conceptual understanding of the theory of social bonding in a way that is consistent, coherent on logical aspects and explains the criminology aspects of an individual in a precise manner. In this theory, a social control conceptual mode is developed that integrates the important aspects of all the previously popular control theories.

3.1 Theory Explanations and Four Key Components

The theory of social bonding that is given by Hirschi (Cassino & Rogers, 2016) begins with the introduction of a common proposition of this theory that 'an individual engages in delinquent behavior or activity in situations where the social bond of the individual with the community has either weakened or completely broken.' According to this theory of social bonding, the social bond is a combination of four different components that serve as the building blocks for the social bonding (Warr, 1998). These components include attachment, commitment, involvement and belief. The higher the strength of these components is for a person with his or her parents, family members, colleagues, peers, friends and school teachers, the more that person is likely to have a controlled behavior and less likely to take part in delinquent behavior. The weaker these components in the social structure of an individual become, the higher is the probability of that individual taking part in delinquent activity (Elliott et al., 1979).

The theory of social bonding relies heavily on these four components to represent an individual's social bonding and relations with society. Hirschi has suggested that these four factors have a very high degree of correlation with each-other and have high influence of other components as well (Allatt, 1984). If there is weakening in one of the components, it is likely that similar level of weakening will be observed in other components as well.

3.1.1 Social Bond: Commitment

Commitment is an important part of the social control theory of criminology and delinquency behavior. Commitment refers to the degree to which an individual has developed a feeling of investment in traditional social value or has gained a 'stake in confirming to social norms.' If an individual has commitment to traditional norms and social values of non-delinquency types, he or she also believes that the commitment will be at risk of breaking or lost completely if engaged in an activity that either directly violates the law or deviates significantly from commonly accepted social norms. Making investment in the traditional means of education and engaging in conventional occupational activities also provide strength to this kind of commitment towards the social norms and values (Elliott, Ageton & Canter, 1979). In a way, our society expects this kind of commitment from all members of the community as a way of developing a positive non-delinquent environment. Majority of conventional social activities and values generally refer to development and nourishment of this commitment among individuals. For example- social norms, family values, morality, social responsibility and laws; all refer to the process of developing a commitment towards the society among individuals.

According to the social control theories, the greater degree of commitment present in a person, the more that person has to lose from engaging in tasks that are violating the laws or social norms. The aspect of social commitment develops an environment where an individual loses his or her investment in the commitment if he or she violates the social norms or obligations. The cost of losing all investments relating to the commitment prevents an individual from committing a crime of engaging in an activity that is deemed delinquent by the society. Due to this reason, the whole

53

proposition of commitment refers to a rational element of thought process that goes through the mind of an individual before engaging in a criminal activity. This commitment is relative yet important as it may impact an individual's decision to engage in delinquent behavior or not to a significant degree.

3.1.2 Social Bond: Attachment

Attachment to others refers to the degree to which an individual feels close affection towards other individuals in his or her life, have some admiration for them, have concerns about their expectations or identify with them. The more insensitive a person is to the various attachment factors to other people, the more that person is likely to feel less constrained by the social norms and expectation of others. As these people are not feeling many restrictions to meet some positive expectations from others, it is highly likely that such people will engage in activities that do violate the social terms and norms in some respects.

According to Passanisi, Gensabella and Pirrone (2015), the whole concept of self-control, having an inner control on self-actions and awareness of self-consciousness are all too subjective to consider for criminology theory. This is not possible to effectively measure or observe these factors. It is argued by the author that the proposition of self-control is most commonly used by the earlier theories of social control in a way that can be described as tautological, suggesting that most theories simply assumed that the social internal control factors were weak in a situation where an individual took part in delinquent behavior (Thornberry, 1987). To this end, attachment provides a much better alternative to the proposition of self-control concept as it simply eliminates the always present tautology with self-control and all self-control concepts can be subsumed in the proposition of attachment.

The proposition of attachment in the theory of social control states that the attachment of an individual towards parents and other people in life is a highly important factor that control delinquency behavior in a person and helps maintain conformity. Additionally, this theory also emphasizes the argument that the attachment factor with peers can also play a vital role in encouraging delinquent behavior activities. In this manner, the attachment proposition of control theory can result in prevention from delinquent behavior as well as engaging in delinquent activities.

3.1.3 Social Bond: Involvement

Involvement is a proposition that is commonly associated and linked to in different criminology theories that are based on social control or social bonding approach. The whole concept of involvement concept refers to any individual person's interest or obsession in the traditionally socially accepted activities. Examples of such activities include studying, giving quality time to the family, taking part in extra-curricular tasks at school and engaging in activities that are designed to empower the society. According to this proposition, if an individual is already occupied with many different activities that are not delinquent in any way, that person becomes less and less likely to take part in criminal activities or offensive behavior (Hale, 1996). Taking part in social activities that require constant involvement develop a scenario in which the individual members of society are too busy with their involvement in social activities or have high time consumption to pursue any kind of delinquent activity in any way. In this manner, involvement is a proposition that restricts ability of individuals to take part in activities that are non-conforming by simply reducing the opportunities that people might have to pursue such an activity.

3.1.4 Social Bond: Belief

Belief is one of the key concepts in the theory of social bonding and plays a very vital role in criminology theories of social bonding. According to the social bonding theory, belief is defined as the validation of common traditional social values and norms. A higher emphasis is on endorsement of different social rules and laws in general as the morally right thing to do and obeying such laws and policies. The very fundamental of the 'belief' concept does not specify having validation about some specific type or law or social norm and it also does not mean that individuals hold deviant belief that 'motivates' them to engage in criminal activities (Laub, 2006). On the contrary, the social bonding theory suggests that if there are deviant beliefs present in the society or in an individual committing crime, then there remains nothing to explain further.

The primary objective that this concept aims to address is trying to explain the reason for which people violate social norms and laws that go directly against the beliefs that they already have. The answer to this is given by Garland & Sparks (2000) in the argument that people take part in activities that are inherently against the beliefs they already have because the extent of belief has weakened in the social structure of that individual or that person no longer shares the same beliefs. The less a person starts to believe that he should be obeying the laws developed by the society as part of social norms, the more likely that person becomes to commit the criminal activities that violate the same beliefs.

3.2 Analyzing of Social Bonding Theory and Its Reliability

The theory of social bonding relies entirely on four core components of the theory, attachment, commitment, beliefs and involvement. The theory offers clearly defined measures of evaluating the effectiveness or influence of social bonding on basis of these four principle factors. Since introduction of the social bonding theory, majority of research studies have focused on using either these four measures or measures that are like these. Performing a thorough review of these measures enables better understanding the results that are offered by the social bonding theory in criminology.

A teenage individual's attachment with his or her parents can be measured by use of a supervision technique of parental activities as well as verifying the discipline in the individual along with other factors like communication level with parents and relationship depth. On basis of these observations, it can be identified whether or not the teenager has some affection for parents or not and the extent of affection. Towards the measure of commitment, there are many different components that help in understanding commitment extent in a person, such as the performance of adolescent in school. The same process of evaluating performance in school is also helpful in measuring all four components of social bonding theory by tools like analyzing grades in school, checking scores in tests and perception of scholastic behavior (Tittle, 1995). An individual's attachment for school is easy to measure as it is directly reflected in the way individual might have positive attitude towards school activities and have motivations to perform good at school. It is possible to have a measure of attachment with colleagues and peers by validating the respect the person has for opinions given by peers and friends.

An individual's commitment to the traditional lines of action reflects on the desire and objective of the individual to follow peruse traditional goals in life. If a teenager is getting involved in activities closely linked with adults (gambling, drinking and smoking) in a pre-mature age then it reflects on lack of commitment in the teenager as well as attachment for standard social norms. In such a situation, it can be expected from the teenager to have very little regard for the social norms and law, making it more likely that the teenager will engage in delinquent behavior.

3.3 Empirical Strength of Social Bonding Theory

The theory of social bonding was proposed by Hirschi and the research conducted by Hirschi certainly provided good support for the concepts pitched in the theory. In his research studies, it was found that the weaker a social bond (except for the involvement component of social bonding) with the component is, the more likely it becomes for the individual to take part in behavior that can be categorized as delinquent. However, it is also found the studies that the strongest relation with delinquent behavior is present relating to the association with friends or peers who are engaged in criminal activities. This is a finding of empirical research that is not well anticipated by the theory itself. In similar fashion, later studies on the theory of social bonding also found that higher level of attachment with peers can link to conformity only in cases where the peers and friends are themselves traditional and followers of social norms (Sampson & Laub, 1993; Farrington, 2005). In contrast with the original theory argument of Hirschi, it is found by empirical evidences that an individual who is attached to friend how are into delinquent activities is also likely to be delinquent (AGNEW, 1985).

It is also found that many deviant teenagers have social relationship with other people who are on the same level of conforming as other young individuals (Ozbay & Ozcan, 2007). Another research study that focused on use of empirical data found out that in contrast to the theory of social bonding that argued that attachment to parents always leads to positive attitude towards social norms irrespective of the behavior adopted by parents is a false statement (Akers, 2013). According to this empirical study, if the parents are involved in criminal activities and teenager has high level of attachment with parents then this attachment is likely to work as a motivator for the teenager to become delinquent.

On overall analysis of validity of social bonding theory on basis of empirical data suggests that the theory has gained some verification from the empirical evidences. However, the degree to which various relationships between delinquent behavior and social bonding theory has varied from a moderate value to low values. It is rarely the case that very high degree of correlation was found in the bonding theory and empirical research. Additionally, presence of high variance is also very rare between the social bonding theory and results of empirical research.

4. Analyzing Gottfredson and Hirschi's Self-Control Theory

4.1 Self-Control Justifications and Suggestions

In recent studies, the focus of research studies performed by the Hirschi, the focus has certainly shifted from the traditional social bonding theory that is the pinnacle of social control theory in modern times. Along with Gottfredson, Hirschi has proposed a different criminology theory that is entirely based on the self-control aspect of social control theory. This self-control theory that is presented describes the theory as a central theory that is able to explain all of the different theories and criminal behavior characteristics among individuals (Cullen & Wilcox, 2010). The argument made by the researchers who proposed this theory is that this enables explanation of crime and criminal intent in all cases, across all ages and in all of the different situations of crime.

The theory of self-control suggests that any individual who has high level of self-control would be able to control own behavior in difficult situations and therefore, is significantly less probable across all stages in life to engage in criminal activities. On the other hand, a person who has low self-control is more probable to commit criminal activities and engage in delinquent behavior. Presence of low self-control does not guarantee occurrence of criminal activity as circumstances may create counteracting element to the low self-control aspect. This mechanism indicates that the lack of self-control or low self-control can lead to a crime only if the circumstances are also favorable to criminal behavior. It is not specified by this theory whether the various counteracting factors present in the environment are positive motivators to avoid criminal activities, stronger positive motivators to engage in criminal activities or external factors that specifically counteract the lack of self-control in a person (Thornberry et al., 1994). There can be several different sources that lead to presence of low self-control in a person such as weakening of socialization process or ineffectiveness of relationships within the community.

4.2 Self-Control Theory Vs. Social Bonding Theory

The low self-control theory has some concepts that are quite like the concept used in the social control theory, namely the concept of vulnerable self. To a large extent, the internal control factor is also representative of the social control theory. In majority of the earlier theories of social control criminology, the concept of self-control is present at the center of the theory. However, as discussed before, the concept of self-control does not exist as an independent separate entity in the social bonding theory. In the social bonding theory, the concept of self-control is rejected entirely as it is deemed unobservable and therefore, all characteristics of the self-control concept are subsumed in the attachment concept of social bonding theory. Contrary to this, the theory given by Gottfredson and Hirsch has the concept of self-control as its only core principle and the while theory revolves around this concept. Yet, all the four core elements that are present in the social bonding theory (commitment, belief, involvement and attachment) remain nearly absent from the theory of self-control as given by Gottfredson and Hirsch.

It is not made clear by the Gottfredson and Hirsch's theory of self-control that how this theory relates to the theory of social bonding or to any other prominent theory of social control. There is no explanation or argument about why there is a heavy contradiction present in the two major theories of social control given by Hirsch. While the social bonding theory eliminates use of self-control concept, the theory later proposed in collaboration with Gottfredson is entirely based on the self-control concept for explanation of delinquency and criminal behavior. The most reasonable explanation is that the self-control theory is a general theory and the concept of self-control in this theory subsumes all the four core principles that are present in the social bonding theory.

4.3 Self-Control Theory and Criminality

Presence of low self-control is not just helpful in explaining criminal activities, it is also able to provide an explanation to the phenomenon that Gottfredson and Hirschi referred to as 'analogous behavior.' Various examples of analogous behavior include acts like violent accidents, use of drugs, developing drinking habits, smoking and unlawful acts of sex. These acts are seen by the theory of self-control as the representation and realization of low self-control presence in an individual. In measures based testing of the original social bonding theory, similar factors like smoking and drinking were used to identify lack of commitment in an individual. In that scenario, lack of commitment was presented as a major source of delinquent behavior. The self-control theory suggests that there is a wide variety of different activities that can be deemed crime and analogous behavior, but the theory does not provide a clear explanation for the contradictions present in the self-control theory and social bonding theory.

The claim of self-control theory is that it explains delinquent behavior among people across all races, genders, age-groups and cultures; essentially, providing explanations for all types of crimes in all circumstances. This is certainly a very significant and large claim to make for a theory and Gottfredson and Hirschi do attempt to provide support for this aspect of the theory. They support the theory by identifying the policy related implications of self-control and validating it with help of empirical data showing distribution of crime and its various correlating data factors (Cornish & Clarke, 2014). As per the theory of self-control, it is not much likely that any kind of actions taken by the officials in adulthood of a person would have much impact. This theory argues that the ability of have strong self-control comes from the effectiveness of early childhood and socialization interactions in family.

4.4 Monitoring Self-Control Theory and Examples

Many researchers have made efforts to identify or develop some measures of monitoring self-control aspect of an individual that are not directly linked with the propensity towards committing crime. However, majority of these research studies have not succeeded in devising a direct measure of monitoring or evaluating self-control. Instead, such research studies make assumptions of low self-control on basis of involvement in some certain types of behavior or some other kind of behavior indicators. For example- a study that would focus on cases of DUI (driving under influence) would assume that any offenders who were drinking alcohol a week prior to the incident of DUI have low level of self-control. In such a scenario, it would not be a surprise that the result of this study would correlate drinking of alcohol with the instances of DUI offenses (Krohn, 1986). What this kind of research approach does is link one behavior characteristic of alcohol with other type of alcohol behavior. Other researchers have attempted to use different indirect measures for measurement of self-control. For example- examining the extent to which there is a change or consistency in the behavior of an individual towards delinquent behavior. There have been mixed results obtained from the studies that focused on establishing measures of self-control. In most cases, it is found that the theory of low self-control is very stable and consistent and people having low self-control are indeed more likely to engage in criminal activities.

The theory of low self-control has a logical consistency to it and it also functions in a wide scope of explanations. In the very short time of existence in criminology field, this theory has gained a lot of attention and interest and has the potential of surpassing the theory of social bonding in popularity to become the principal theory of social control.

4.5 Hirschi's Contradictions of Both Theories

Hirschi has contributed heavily in the theories of criminology as he proposed the theory of social bonding, which is one of the most well-known theories of criminology. In addition to this, Hirschi also collaborated with Gottfredson in proposing the theory of self-control. The theory of social bonding was based on four core principles of socialization, which included commitment, involvement, attachment and beliefs. According to the theory of social bonding, there is no place for the self-control concept in the theory as this factor is not observable and cannot be measured.

The concept of self-control is rejected entirely as it is deemed unobservable and therefore, all characteristics of the self-control concept are subsumed in the attachment concept of social bonding theory. Contrary to this, the theory given by Gottfredson and Hirsch has the concept of self-control as its only core principle and the while theory revolves around this concept. Yet, all the four core elements that are present in the social bonding theory (commitment, belief, involvement and attachment) remain nearly absent from the theory of self-control as given by Gottfredson and Hirsch. It is not made clear by the Gottfredson and Hirsch's theory of self-control that how this theory relates to the theory of social bonding or to any other prominent theory of social control.

There is no explanation or argument about why there is a heavy contradiction present in the two major theories of social control given by Hirsch. While the social bonding theory eliminates use of self-control concept, the theory later proposed in collaboration with Gottfredson is entirely based on the self-control concept for explanation of delinquency and criminal behavior (Liska, 1992). The most reasonable explanation is that the self-control theory is a general theory and the concept of self-control in this theory subsumes all the four core principles that are present in the social bonding theory.

5.   Policy Implications of Social Bonding and Control Theories

5.1 Policy Implications of Social Bonding Theory

Social bonding theory provides a lot of policy implications for a sustainable social development model. The theory of social bonding is certainly one of the most popular and tested theory of criminology and this theory suggests that criminal behavior among individuals become more prominent due to lack of any of the following four core principals of the social bonding theory – attachment, commitment, beliefs and involvement. These factors are representative of the way an individual socializes in the community and collaborates with other people in own social groups, which would include family members, friends, people at school and peers.

Any effective social development model that aims to reduce delinquent behavior in the community would address these four factors to develop a strong social environment. For most effective results, it is imperative that an integration of the social bonding theory is performed with other social learning theories. According to the social development model, most emphasis should be on development of various components of society like family, schooling system and community activities. These components lead to a sequential improvement in the behavior of individuals within the community. The main objective should remain on influencing positive change among the adolescent people in the society to develop a strong sense of belonging among them. Inclusion of community support activities and an effective rehabilitation program is also very important.

5.2 Policy Implications of Self-Control Theory

According to self-control theory, all the crimes and criminal behavior can be explained on basis of low self-control among people. As per this theory, the root cause of every delinquent behavior is present in low self-control and without it, non-delinquent behavior remains dominant. It is also suggested by this theory that presence of low self-control does not result in crime automatically as it also requires favorable circumstances. Unfavorable circumstances or positive circumstances can function as counteracting actors to the low self-control and prevent occurrence of delinquent behavior.

The arguments and concepts of self-control theory can be implemented in policies for higher effectiveness of policies in preventing criminal behavior. This theory suggests that most optimal practice that helps develop a strong self-control among individuals is the attachment to family in early years. Towards this goal, policies should be implemented that encourage positive socialization. It is possible to achieve the goal of positive socialization by giving youth the opportunities to engage in various types of community support activities and conforming activities (Hawkins & Weis, 1985). Engagement in such activities develops skills among individuals that are necessary for successful involving in the community and having the ability to interact effectively with the community. Promoting such activities should inherently increase attachment level among individuals which directly correlates to the self-control theory. Prominently increasing such activities and participation in community support activities also results in increased commitment, social bonding and positive beliefs.

6. Summary

The control theory of criminology considers motivations to engage in criminal activities as inherent factors and focuses on explanation of conformity as the real problem. In taking this approach, the theory of social control differentiates from all the other theories of criminology that always focus on the motivations that a person might have for committing a crime. However, this difference exists in form of extent of consideration and emphasis on the motivation rather than differences in opposing assumptions. Ultimately, all of the different criminology theories that focus on law-violating criminal behavior are attempting to answer the same question of why people engage in criminal behavior or stay away from such acts.

This report examines the various theories of social control that have existence since the very early theories of social control. Theory of social bonding and self-control is discussed in detail and validity of each theory is verified on basis of empirical research. It is found that the self-control theory is significantly different from the social bonding theory and has a lot of contradictory aspects to it.

7.   References

Agnew, R. (1985). Neutralizing the impact of crime. Criminal Justice and Behavior, 12(2), 221-239. http://dx.doi.org/10.1177/0093854885012002005

Akers, R. (2013). Criminological theories (1st ed., pp. 80-88). Hoboken: Taylor and Francis.

Allatt, P. (1984). Fear of crime: the effect of improved residential security on a difficult to let estate. The Howard Journal of Criminal Justice, 23(3), 170-182. http://dx.doi.org/10.1111/j.1468-2311.1984.tb00504.x

Anderson, J. (2014). Criminological theories (1st ed., pp. 178-180). Jones & Bartlett Publishers.

Bernard, Y. (1992). North American and European research on fear of crime. Applied Psychology, 41(1), 65-75. http://dx.doi.org/10.1111/j.1464-0597.1992.tb00686.x

Cassino, P. & Rogers, W. (2016). Hirschi's social bonding theory nearly 45 years later: A comparison of a traditional, contemporary and hybrid model. Theory in Action, 9(2), 21-44. http://dx.doi.org/10.3798/tia.1937-0237.16009

Colvin, M., Cullen, F., & Ven, T. (2002). Coercion, social support, and crime: an emerging theoretical consensus*. Criminology, 40(1), 19-42. http://dx.doi.org/10.1111/j.1745-9125.2002.tb00948.x

Cornish, D. & Clarke, R. (2014). The reasoning criminal: rational choice perspectives on offending (1st ed., pp. 168-170). Transaction Publishers.

Cote, S. (2002). Criminological theories (1st ed., pp. 169-171). Thousand Oaks, CA: Sage Publications.

Cullen, F. & Wilcox, P. (2010). Encyclopedia of criminological theory (1st ed., pp. 201-202). Thousand Oaks, Calif.: Sage.

Elliott, D., Ageton, S., & Canter, R. (1979). An integrated theoretical perspective on delinquent behavior. Journal of Research in Crime and Delinquency, 16(1), 3-27. http://dx.doi.org/10.1177/002242787901600102

Farrington, D. (2005). Childhood origins of antisocial behavior. Clinical Psychology & Psychotherapy, 12(3), 177-190. http://dx.doi.org/10.1002/cpp.448

Flexon, J. (2014). Containment Theory. The Encyclopedia of Theoretical Criminology, 1-5. http://dx.doi.org/10.1002/9781118517390.wbetc023

Garland, D. & Sparks, R. (2000). Criminology, social theory and the challenge of our times. British Journal of Criminology, 40(2), 189-204. http://dx.doi.org/10.1093/bjc/40.2.189

Hale, C. (1996). Fear of crime: a review of the literature. International Review of Victimology, 4(2), 79-150. http://dx.doi.org/10.1177/026975809600400201

Hawkins, J. & Weis, J. (1985). The social development model: An integrated approach to delinquency prevention. The Journal of Primary Prevention, 6(2), 73-97. http://dx.doi.org/10.1007/bf01325432

Jacobs, B. & Copes, H. (2014). Neutralization without drift: Criminal commitment among persistent offenders. British Journal of Criminology, 55(2), 286-302. http://dx.doi.org/10.1093/bjc/azu100

Krohn, M. (1986). The web of conformity: A network approach to the explanation of delinquent behavior. Social Problems, 33(6), S81-S93. http://dx.doi.org/10.2307/800675

Krohn, M., Massey, J., Skinner, W., & Lauer, R. (1983). Social bonding theory and adolescent cigarette smoking: A longitudinal analysis. Journal of Health and Social Behavior, 24(4), 337. http://dx.doi.org/10.2307/2136400

Laub, J. & Sampson, R. (1993). Turning points in the life course: Why change matters to the study of crime*. Criminology, 31(3), 301-325. http://dx.doi.org/10.1111/j.1745-9125.1993.tb01132.x

Lechin, F. (2001). Asthma, asthma medication and autonomic nervous system dysfunction. Clinical Physiology, 21(6), 723-723. http://dx.doi.org/10.1046/j.1365-2281.2001.0382a.x

Liska, A. (1992). Social threat and social control (1st ed., pp. 103-105). Albany: State University of New York Press.

Liska, A., Sanchirico, A., & Reed, M. (1988). Fear of crime and constrained behavior specifying and estimating a reciprocal effects model. Social Forces, 66(3), 827-837. http://dx.doi.org/10.1093/sf/66.3.827

Miller, J. (2014). The encyclopedia of theoretical criminology (1st ed., pp. 144-146). Chichester: Wiley Blackwell.

Nagin, D. & Pogarsky, G. (2001). Integrating celerity, impulsivity, and extralegal sanction threats into a model of general deterrence: Theory and evidence*. Criminology, 39(4), 865-892. http://dx.doi.org/10.1111/j.1745-9125.2001.tb00943.x

Ozbay, O. & Ozcan, Y. (2007). A test of Hirschi's social bonding theory: A comparison of male and female delinquency. International Journal of Offender Therapy and

Comparative Criminology, 52(2), 134-157. http://dx.doi.org/10.1177/0306624x07309182

Passanisi, A., Gensabella, A., & Pirrone, C. (2015). Parental bonding, self-esteem and theory of mind among locals and immigrants. Procedia - Social and Behavioral Sciences, 191, 1702-1706. http://dx.doi.org/10.1016/j.sbspro.2015.04.547

Pratt, T. & Cullen, F. (2000). The empirical status of Gottfredson and Hirschi's general theory of crime: A meta-analysis. Criminology, 38(3), 931-964. http://dx.doi.org/10.1111/j.1745-9125.2000.tb00911.x

Thornberry, T. (1987). Toward an interactional theory of delinquency*. Criminology, 25(4), 863-892. http://dx.doi.org/10.1111/j.1745-9125.1987.tb00823.x

Thornberry, T., Lizotte, A., Krohn, M., Farnworth, M., & Jang, S. (1994). Delinquent peers, beliefs, and delinquent behavior: A longitudinal test of interactional theory*. Criminology, 32(1), 47-83. http://dx.doi.org/10.1111/j.1745-9125.1994.tb01146.x

Tittle, C. (1995). Control balance: Toward a general theory of deviance (1st ed., pp. 112-114). Boulder: Westview Press.

Warr, M. (1998). Life-course transitions and desistance from crime*. Criminology, 36(2), 183-216. http://dx.doi.org/10.1111/j.1745-9125.1998.tb01246.x

Chapter 3

Social Learning Theory and
Conflict Theory

1. Introduction to Social Learning Theory

The social learning theory borrowed its initial breath from the works of Burgess and Akers (1966) *differential association reinforcement theory* which was a fine effort to combine the sociological approach of Sutherland's (1947) *differential association theory* alongside the principles of behavioral psychology within the differential association theory. The backdrop of these works with a longish style of interpretation, made the very foundation of further developments by Akers new theory referred commonly as *"Social Learning Theory"*. For all the praise that this theory received, it secured enough reason to be cited and empirically tested in the research literature to date. To be very honest, the discussion of social learning theory with respect to criminal delinquent behavior has become a standard norm all around (Akers, 1973).

It is worth mentioning here that the *"Deterrence Theory"* unfolds criminal behavior by investigating only one part i.e. direct positive punishment through certainty, severity, and celerity (Hollinger & Clark, 1983). On the flip side, the social learning theory encapsulates both positive and negative punishments alongside positive and negative reinforcement. Let's try to comprehend it now on the backdrop of Sutherland's differential association theory formulated under 9 suggestions:

9 Propositions of Sutherland's Differential Association Theory:

The behavior of criminal is learned.

Communication and interaction with other persons is how the criminal learns the behavior.

The fundamental part of learning criminal behavior happens due to his communication and interaction with closest personal groups.

As soon as the criminal learns the delinquency, he learns:

Different ways and means of committing the crime, at times with extremely simple techniques while at times very complicated

The course of his motivation, modus operandi, rationalization, and his approach of looking at things.

The legal codes, both favorable and unfavorable, imprint the direction of his motives and drives.

In the backdrop of an abundance of definitions encouraging to law violation over the definitions not encouraging to the law violation, a criminal person chooses to become delinquent.

This process of learning the criminal behavior through connecting with both anti-criminal patterns and the criminal patterns is much the same process as we see in any other forms of learning.

A criminal behavior cannot be interpreted by the general values and needs despite that it is a turn of phrase of the general values and needs at large. The reason being, the same values and needs are intended to express a non-criminal behavior as well.

The differential association is not same in frequency, duration, priority, and intensity. In fact, the determinant and effectuality of the learned behavior will be the outcome of the longish cycle, the most frequent, and the closest and earliest influences.

Sutherland (1947) *marked the 6th point as the main "principle of differential association"*. According to him, criminal tries to drive a hard bargain from the prevailing definitions towards committing a crime in a society. He will either praise the favorable definitions of violation of law which would increase the probability of committing a crime OR he might praise and learn the unfavorable definitions that would decrease the probability of engaging in a delinquent behavior. Simply put, *"when it comes to committing a crime, all bets are not off since the prevailing excessiveness of the type of definitions will set the trajectory of criminal behavior"*. In a way, the criminal tries to balance the favorable definitions against the unfavorable definitions in a bid to choose his own route to either go for or go against the delinquent behavior. It is thus logical to postulate and empirically tested that he learns the crime-favorable definitions from the bad persons (criminals) and the unfavorable definitions from the good folks (non-criminals). However, here comes a moot point i.e. it's not impossible that a criminal is boxed-in a pro-criminal act due to an influence towards crime propagated by law-abiding good persons as well (Cressy, 1960). Similarly, *"the pattern of exposure of a person towards different factors put an impact on the characteristics, nature, and balance of the differential association towards committing a crime"*. For instance, to the contrary of unfavorable definitions, if he is exposed towards favorable definitions of crime first (priority determinant), and these definitions would act like pouring fuel on fire due to their frequency and strength (intensity) alongside its consistent occurrence (duration), the criminal is likely to get indulge in the delinquent acts exactly opposite of the societal etiquettes and norms.

Despite that Sutherland's (1947) differential association had never been consigned to the bin years after its emergence, Burgess and Akers (1966) *postulated that there is an information fog in the said theory that's why it doesn't suffice a substantial empirical support thus needs modification in a bid to make it more visible, fill the void of information fog and its empirical validity against the criticisms and shortcomings.* The reason being, all the praise and accolades do not take this theory out of the woods due to the opposing criticism regarding the difficulty of operationalizing concepts. Hence, Burgess and Akers (1966) rekindled its luster by modifying it in the shape of "*Differential Association-Reinforcement Theory*".

Burgess and Akers Differential Association-Reinforcement Theory in 7 Steps

The principles of operant conditioning set the route of how criminal behavior is learned (*This modifies the Sutherland's 1st and 8th principle*)

Either the criminal learns through social conditions in which the other persons' behavior is discriminative or reinforcing to incline him towards delinquent act OR he learns the ins and outs of criminal behavior by getting influenced in non-social conditions that are discriminative or reinforcing (*This modifies the Sutherland's 2nd principle*).

The primary component of the criminal's learning behaviors happen in those settings / groups which encompass the chief source of reinforcements (*This modifies the Sutherland's 3rd principle*).

The subsisting reinforcement contingencies alongside the availability of effective reinforces make up the learning of criminal behavior which includes avoidance procedures, attitudes and techniques (*This modifies the Sutherland's 4th principle*).

Actually, the affectivity and availability of reinforces make the possibility of particular class of learned behaviors and they also determine the frequency of their occurrence as well as the norms and rules by which these reinforces are applied (*This modifies the Sutherland's 5th principle*).

The delinquent behavior is nothing short of an application or working model of the norms that are discriminative for delinquent behavior and under circumstances when such behavior is reinforced to a higher degree as compared to the non-criminal behavior, it instigates the learning of criminal behavior (*This modifies the Sutherland's 6th principle*).

The strength or power of a criminal behavior is directly proportional to the amount, rate of recurrence, as well as the likelihood of its reinforcement (*This modifies the Sutherland's 7th principle*).

Akers Social Learning Theory and Social Behavior

Akers Social Learning Theory encapsulates the following main points:

In social behavior, the fundamental learning technique is instrumental to an individual's own stimuli i.e. how he perceives his environment and draw conclusions to shape up his behavior. Hence, this would vary from person to person, that's the key point this theory has underscored many times.

Social behavior can be learned in two ways 1) from imitation i.e. copying other's behavior OR 2) from direct conditioning.

The reward (positive reinforcement) will strengthen the behavior whilst the punishment (negative reinforcement) will weaken it. The same goes true for positive and negative punishment i.e. behavior is weakened by positive punishment and strengthened by the loss of reward in shape of negative punishment.

The conforming and deviant behavior is formed and continues to stick based on present and past punishments and rewards as well as the punishments and rewards for the alternative behavior.

People learn according to the contacts and relations with those groups in which they communicate and spend their lives. That's how an individual develops his orientation, attitude, and norms (*definitions*) both as bad or good behavior.

The more an individual perceives the definitions as good (*Positive definition*), or the very least perceives the definitions as justified (*neutralizing definition*) exactly opposite to the delinquency (*negative definition*), there would be a higher chance for him to be involved in conforming attitude.

The best example towards Akers Social learning theory is the research conducted by a few theorists who were trying to research the behavior on substance use. They drew upon a conclusion that the individuals who were holding negative attitude or intolerant attitude towards a substance are much more likely to refrain from the substance as compared to those individuals who were holding positive attitude (Fejer & Smart, 1973; Kendall, 1976; Jessor & Jessor, 1973; Calhoun, 1974; Johnston, 1973). These examples also favored the notion that parental and peer influence were important variables in setting the behavioral trajectory of the respondents. Social learning theory also second this very important factor (Pearce & Garret, 1970; O'Donnell et al., 1976; Akers, 1977).

Albert Bandura's Social Learning Theory

Albert Bandura (1977) gained the same opinion of Akers social learning theory in almost all manners except that he added two important ideas to it:

The mediating processes takes place between the stimuli and the responses

Observational learning is the key through which behavior is learned all the way through environment.

The children see people around them with varying behaviors and they observe them accordingly (Bandura, Ross & Ross, 1961). Children are surrounded by parents, brothers and sisters within the family and teachers, friends, media as influential models outside the family. While paying attention to their models, they encode the behaviors and use their observation to imitate that behavior later.

In this regard, the child is likely to imitate the behavior of the same sex first.

Then the people around the child are likely to give him a response with either punishment or reinforcement.

Suppose the consequences are punishing, the child is likely to stop that imitation. If the consequences are rewarding, he is going to continue the imitation (reinforcement).

The child would also observe the other persons that how do people react when they perform the same behavior and would learn that behavior based on consequences (*reward or punishment*). This creates the "*identification*" i.e. when the observer adopts / identifies some behavior from the model. Identification is different from imitation in the sense that imitation involves copying a single behavior while identification includes copying more than one behavior / numerous behaviors from the model.

Bandura also took the concept that people are *"active information processers"* (Bandura, 1977). This implies that the cognitive mental processes work together to decide whether a new response is needed or not. Simply put *"humans do not observe and imitate the behavior automatically, there is a meditational process involved prior to imitation only then the subject (child) decides whether the behavior (stimulus) should be imitated or not (response)*. In this regard, Bandura proposed 4 meditational processes between observation and imitation as follows:

Attention: reflects the degree of extent to which we note the behavior. Obviously if the behavior is to be imitated later, it must grab our perception and attention to a great degree. Simple exposure towards a certain behavior doesn't confirm that the observer is going to imitate the behavior. In this regard, TV modeling is the best medium where viewers do observe the models without any further incentives to grab their attention (Bandura, Grusec & Menlove, 1966).

Retention: shows how good the observer remembers the behavior. If the retention is weak, the observer is not likely to imitate the behavior later. Hence, long term retention is essential. Bandura performed empirical testing on adults in this regard also (Bandura and Jeffery, 1971).

Reproduction: implies the skill and capacity to perform the observed behavior. The reason being, an individual might want to imitate a certain behavior but didn't find the courage to perform it or because of some physical disability. Reproduction is a strong meditational observation which is likely to make or break the process of imitation.

Motivation: reflects the punishment and rewards which would motivate the observer to perform a certain behavior.

Social Learning Theory: Analysis and Explanation

Previously, the theory presented by Sutherland was in difficult situation without a paddle BUT Akers modifications put it back in the saddle. It is worth mentioning here that Akers modifications were by no means a competitor or rival to Sutherland's differential association theory. No doubt that it eases its empirical and theoretical interpretations in literature with an obvious air of correction in response to the criticisms bombarded by the theorists, still Akers kept the central tenet the same. *Akers modifications were a bit like putting the game settings on easy mode.* Akers didn't wave off the Sutherland's postulations altogether, instead, he built his modifications on the foundations of Sutherland's theory thus broadening its horizon so that it is able to provide valid answers to other scholars' principles with regards to the behavioral learning theory primarily the acquisition of behavior, its continuation, and its termination (Akers, 1985).

In 1998, Akers gave his theory another voice by commenting that how the cognitive learning theories like those postulated by Albert Bandura (1977) are aligned more closely with his social learning theory. He hypothesized that the mechanism of the learning process is primarily grounded upon the differential reinforcement or the operant conditioning (Akers, 1973, 1977, 1985, 1998). *Stating more clearly, the voluntary actions of a person or his operant behavior are affected by a system of punishments and rewards which ultimately influence his decision for either going for or against the conforming behavior.*

Key Point: *The differential theory of Burgess and Akers (1966) had to be taken with a grain of salt because they presented 'imitation' entity of behavioral learning process simply as an entity of behavior itself and not a distinct behavioral mechanism. On the flip side, Akers theory of social learning closed down this loophole by describing imitation itself as a vicarious enforcement or observational learning.*

The central concept of social learning theory states that **"*the same learning process*"** that coincides with the situations, interactions, and social structure, generates both deviant as well as the conforming behavior. The key difference is dependent upon the direction of the balance of influence on behavior. Similarly, when a person differentially associates himself with other bad people (depicting criminal behavior) and takes up the definitions of criminal behavior favorable to it, he is likely to get indulge in criminal behavior with an assumption of comparatively greater reward in delinquent act than the potential punishment for the said behavior (Akers, 1998).

Why the social learning theory has turned all tides in its favor? There are numerous reasons to back its validity and successful existence:

Without any unintelligible twists, it explains why people do not prefer to commit crime as well as why they do not choose to desist from criminal act.

Why people continue to get indulged in offending behavior, why they choose to deescalate / why they escalate, why do they initially take leverage of criminal act, why do they opt for only conforming behavior and why do they opt for only non-conforming behavior?

The Concept of Differential Association, Definitions, Differential Reinforcement and Imitation (*4 Dimensions of Akers Social Learning Theory*)

Differential association remains a very important factor in describing Akers social learning theory. He explains that the early childhood years within the family as well as the association developed in school, free time, and in close groups during the period of teenage years mark the key learning part of the differential learning process. The learning process takes further strides in the later years through the behaviors, attitudes, beliefs, and norms of the group of individuals including school teachers, religious leaders, and neighbors or even through *"virtual groups"* like internet, print and electronic media and so on (Warr, 2002). Amid a longish cycle of interpretations towards a person's decision to be part of either conforming or non-conforming behavior, social learning theory reiterates that early associations (priority factor), as well as their duration alongside the closest, intimate or most vital groups (intensity factor) are the important factors to be considered. The following lines secure the same reasons stated by Akers & Sellers (2004):

"The groups with which one is in differential association provide the major social contexts in which all of the mechanisms of social learning operate. They not only expose one to definitions, but they also present one with models to imitate and differential reinforcement (source, schedule, value, and amount) for criminal or conforming behavior."

"Definitions" are like rolling the dice on one's own attitudes, and compass reading towards a certain behavior. These definitions play their distinguishing role contrary to the other differential associations described above. Akers subdivided these definitions into 2 groups i.e. *general and specific*. General beliefs surround one's own personal interpretation and definitions grounded upon moral, religious, and other relevant traditional values (Akers, 2013). On the contrary, the specific beliefs are personal definitions which instigate a person either for committing a crime or going against it. Akers also introduced the concept of *"positive*

belief" and "*neutralizing belief*" where positive belief is a definition embraced by an individual that "*committing a crime is wholly permissible and morally desirable*". For instance, a person holds strong belief that it's completely fine to get indulged in sexual intercourse with girls' other than his life partner. The neutralizing belief also holds true for the same favoring of a criminal act, yet it is wholly influenced by the excuses and justifications (Bandura, 1990; Sykes & Matza, 1957, Cressey, 1953). For instance, a person justifies to himself that "because my life partner is unable to satisfy my sexual desires; I am helpless to indulge in prohibited sexual activities OR I'm an alcoholic, that's why it's fine to beat up somebody under the influence of alcohol."

Akers and Silverman (2004) also fueled concerns over the intensity of some definitions such as the ideologies hold by terrorist groups and militants that these definitions are ingrained into their belief system and they alone are more than a match for persuading them to commit a criminal act.

"*Differential Reinforcement*" resembles the differential association but it creates another point of tension i.e. the imbalance or disproportion of attitudes, value, and norms toward engaging in a criminal act enhances the likelihood that the individual would indulge in such behavior. What's more! The probability of either committing a crime or refraining from criminal act or continue doing it is also affected by the individuals' calculation about already experienced or anticipated past, present, and future rewards and punishment. *Higher the reward and greater in number is likely to increase the probability of committing a crime and continue repeating it.* Hence, differential reinforcement operates according to the quantitative law of effect rather than either-or-mechanisms i.e. most frequently occurring behaviors that are highly enforced are normally selected and likely to be repeated accordingly.

Imitation is the simplest rule which expresses the same explanation as the name "Imitation" i.e. when an individual simply copies another individual (models, film stars, politicians etc.) by viewing and observing them directly or indirectly (through media etc.) Bandura (1977) marked this behavior as "*vicarious reinforcement*"

Social Structure and Social Learning (SSSL) and Four Domains

It's obvious that Akers social learning theory didn't draw a red line against the differential association theory, yet he moved back and forth and gave Sutherland theory a new lifeline. Ultimately, Akers social learning theory proved to be more than a match for differential theory in every sense of the word. Akers social learning theory has provided with a significant amount of variation in criminal behavior at individual level (Akers & Jensen, 2006). Akers (1998) also commanded the attention of theorists by positing another avenue of variation by explaining crime at the macro level in shape of *Social Structure and Social Learning (SSSL)*. As explained in the previous chapters, it's literally next to impossible to produce a water tight rule for delinquent behavior, the new theory proposes that certain types of "*social structural factors*" put an indirect impact on individuals' behavior; and the impact of these social factors works all the way through the following social learning variables all of which put a direct impact on his decision making for committing a crime.

Theorists hammered out an agreement that there are 4 domains of social structure through which the social learning process works (Akers, 1998; Akers & Selling, 2004):

Differential social organization
Differential location in the social structure
Theoretically defined structural variables
Differential social location

"*Differential social organization*" is nothing short of structural associations of crime in the society which put an impact on the rate of criminality. While taking a hawkish view of these correlates, one can point out the population density, age composition and a few concrete attributes which have a considerable propensity to persuade a society or a community and the relevant social systems towards comparatively low or comparatively high crime rates.

"*Differential location in the social structure*" points toward the socio-demographic attributes of social groups and individuals which reflect their position / role inside a bigger social structure. They become the fragments of overall social structure where age, marital status, ethnicity, race, gender, and class defines the standings and positions of the individuals as well as their social categories, groups, and their roles in the larger overall social structure.

"*Theoretically defined structural variables*" commands attention of theorists toward the theoretical concepts which had been induced in the old and new literature to pinpoint the criminogenic conditions of groups, communities, and societies at large. The continued strength of theoretical concepts coupled with a longish cycle of interpretations paved the way to pluck out the theoretically defined structural variables like patriarchy, group conflict, social disorganization, class oppression, and anomie.

"*Differential social location*" reflects the membership of an individual with regards to his association with the primary groups, secondary groups, and the reference groups like work groups, colleagues, leisure groups, friendship and peer groups, and the family.

The variables became more visible when Akers and Sellers (2004) argued that differential social organization of community and society as well as the differential locations of individuals inside the social structure (religious connections, class, race, gender etc.) provide the circumstances which amounts to nurture the process of learning. In other words, one couldn't help saying that environment is the main catalyst where learning occurs, and an individual's decision for committing a crime is heavily decided based on his possession of definitions swinging towards deviant acts, his exposure to criminal attitudes and peers, and his dealings with the different models. With regards to Akers novel idea about explaining social learning theory with social structure, a few theorists managed to test its validity and perfectly saddled the unanswered questions with the attributes like binge drinking by students of college, violence, rape, elderly alcohol abuse, and substance use (Akers & Jensen, 2006).

At the same time, theorists argue that these are just preliminary findings with fragments of partial solutions coupled with bunch of empty words. At the face of it, one can say that it's too early to make a definitive statement for or against the said theory none the less, these initial findings would serve as a stepping stone for more better and authentic solutions in the future.

Empirical Testing and Reliability of Social Learning Theory

No doubt that crime stands tall to find the loopholes in the system and no theory can predict 100% propensity of crime even using all corners of its might and understanding. That's why empirical testing of social learning theory doesn't fill the void of its criticism to date. This is surely worthy of comment that the full empirical testing of social learning theory doesn't fill the literature works till late 1970's. However, the preliminary research support was offered to second its empirical testing in shape of "*qualitative study of professional theft*" by Sutherland (1937) and a famous research regarding "*apprehended embezzlers*" conducted by Cressey (1953). The social learning theory enjoyed varying level of support for the numerous components during the past 5 decades and the evidence is quite visible and convincing (Akers & Jensen, 2006).

Outranking the old theory in power, privilege, and capacity to fight back, Akers himself worked with various scholars across numerous samples over a wide range of delinquent behaviors, from simple criminal behaviors to serious offences. His process of beefing up the logics pertaining to the very delinquency can be summed up into 4 key projects:

The boys town study

The Iowa study

The elderly drinking study

Rape and sexual coercion study

In case of *boys town study*, Akers collected the data of 3000 students in 8 communities in Midwest who fall in Grades 7 through 12 (Akers & Jensen, 2006). Akers and his colleagues could completely test the 4 components of social learning theory whilst most of the questions put up in the survey on the instances of substance use and abuse in adolescence (Akers et al., 1979). Akers could discharge the powers and empirical validity of four main components of social learning theory primarily the imitation, differential reinforcement, differential association, and definitions. It exhibited that the social learning variables could explain about the multivariate results i.e. more than ½ of the total variance with regards to the frequency of alcohol drinking (R^2 = .54) and greater than two 3rd of the variance with regards to the use of marijuana (R^2 = .68) were shown. The social learning variables also showed that the adolescent who was prone to use the substance were vulnerable to step forward with alcohol and drugs. An interesting fact about the "*imitation*" was that this variable was only able to gain strength in the process of initiating the use i.e. first time attempt as compared to the maintenance or frequency of use. Socia*l learning theory gave a vantage point from where the theorists could understand more with a lot less.* For instance, Lanza-Kaduce et al. (1984) drew up an interesting result that the correlation of social learning variables was considerably visible with respect to stopping hard drug use, marijuana, and alcohol, the immediate credit of which was given to the predominance of the unfavorable definitions, exhibition to self-denial models, negative social sanctions, aversive drugs, and the efforts of non-using associations.

The *Iowa Study* Project was composed of longitudinal examination spanning across 5 long years with regards to smoking among the juniors and the students of senior high school at Iowa, Muscatine (Akers & Jensen, 2006). The first-year data was provided by Spear and Akers (1987) in an effort to reproduce and compare the findings with those of boys town study project. Interestingly, the results were same with an added demonstration later by Akers (1998) that the adolescents' behavior would be strongly influenced by their parents and peers. For instance, if their friends and parents don't smoke, they would be showing higher probability of not smoking as well. The longitudinal analysis of data also favored the social learning theory (Krohn et al., 1985).

The *"elderly drinking project"* exhibited the 4 years longitudinal study about the frequency of use of alcohol and drinking issue among a huge number of mature people in 4 communities of New Jersey and Florida (Akers & Jensen, 2006). The results were the same and in favor of the social learning variables depicted in past two projects where more than 50% of the explained variance was accounted for social learning variables.

"Rape and sexual coercion study project" included two college men samples (Boeringer, Shehan & Akers, 1991). Interestingly, the results again mirrored the results collected in the previous three projects where the social learning variables were the prime factors which instigate moderate to strong effects on the respondents. In addition, Akers also worked with his associates in a few other projects to validate the strength of its social learning theory (Hawang & Akers, 2003; Akers & Jensen, 2006; Akers & Silverman, 2004).

Overview of Conflict Theory

The basic premise of *"Conflict Theory"* can easily be described in a way that basically society is an amalgamation of different competing interest groups who always try hard to gain strength and knowledge about which side of the bread is buttered. One can say that the society is basically divided into different groups (2 or more) with competing values and ideas. This is what makes the social structure of a society and this is what defines and instigate criminality and deviance in a society as well (Akers, 2011). The reason being, the powerful groups control the society as they make the laws and *most of the time, they play a weak hand to fit the laws to their advantage despite if they are low in numbers* (Quinney, 1970). *Quinney even said that the crime which tries to muck up the system wasn't necessarily a 'real' thing since it has been socially created*. The flip side of the coin shows the larger society i.e. those groups that are large in numbers but they lack the formal power to rule and make the laws. This unequal distribution of power and resources create a point of tension within a society where the criminal justice system also shows the unequal power distribution as well (Walker, Spohn & DeLone, 2012).

In the wake of conflict theory, many theorists furrowed their brows in argument that the powerful groups try to control law and pass only those laws that are favorable to maintain their power, and the comparative advantages and disadvantages are based upon the attributes like sexual orientation, gender, class, and race (Taylor, 2003).

The backdrop of 1960's and 1970's eras were those which voiced huge concerns about the escalation of different types of conflict within a society that's why the conflict theory concept received much attention in that time and space. It became more tangible when Thorsten Sellin (1938) floated the idea of conflict theory in 1930's and the criminological approach. Later, George Vold (1958) also highlighted the importance of groups' conflict with regards to criminology.

Consensus and Functionalist Theories of Criminal Justice

To gain insight on Conflict theory, it's very necessary to draw a line between conflict and *consensus theory's* perspective. The consensus theory emphasizes that in a society, the common interests are not put on a back burner because laws are enacted according to the general agreement in a society. In other words, society is organized and potent enough to enact those laws which exhibit the interest of the society from a holistic approach thus laws are designed to enhance the common good of the people. The consensus is the glue that bonds a society together exactly opposite to the conflict theory where the balance of opposing group interests and efforts hold the society together (Vold, 1958). The imprint of consensus theory provides a rational way to investigate the cultural diversities across continental boundaries as well as in social movements (Caulkins & Hayatt, 1999).

The *Functionalist Theory*" borrowed its existence from the consensus theory since it is like the consensus theory with an exception that it exhibits that how the system (e.g. law) is working and acting in a society in a bid to resolve disputes among members. The functionalist approach took its first breath through the works of Durkheim who critical observed the issue of functioning of the various institutions in a society and analyzed their structures to understand their power and contribution in its development (Pope, 1975; Turner & Maryanski, 1979). The functionalist theory places its eyes on how the law is serving everybody, and not just those who are in power.

Conflict Theories of Crime and Criminal Justice

The dominant versions of conflict theories into the criminology field have been represented in the works conducted by Austin Turks, William Chambliss, and Richard Quinney in 1960's. As explained earlier, conflict theory tries to figure out the prospects of crime by analyzing uneven distribution of power within a society. This surely explains the marriage of conflict theory with crime; for example, one might read the conflict theory in between these lines: "*people who live in the gap between their dreams and the hard realities of economics are susceptible to commit crime.*" In this regard, any unequal distribution would incline the affected people to commit crime.

There was much social turmoil during late 1960's to early 1970's, for instance; gay rights movements, power of black people, feminist rights movements, and the like. The field of criminology was also influenced with the induced changes which were prominently seen within the domain of criminology as well. The current understanding of crime and delinquency needed an obvious air of alternative rehabilitation approach away from the contemporary dominant liberal response. Herman and Julia step forwarded by publishing their first article with regards to the concerns about the scope of criminology and its limited approach towards understanding crime and delinquent behavior at large (Herman & Schwendinger, 1972, 1974, 1977, 1982, 1985). *This new idea wasn't born out of the ashes of the previous theories; in fact, it was established on the shoulders of solid foundation erected by the never-ending criticism, making it need of the hour.* Despite its solid existence, many theorists graded it underwater for the reason that research funding, in those old times, was habitual in funding radical criminologists rather than this new crybaby.

The conflict theory encapsulates two facets of criminology at large; it looks to explicate the behavior of law, and it analyzes crime as a secondary product of the conflict between group and culture. *Law* is generally enacted and exercised to maintain the social control through sanctions that are defined and exercised by the state. This seems okay; *yet the conflict theory marks a red line which states that the criminal justice system and the behavior of law can be truly expressed from the conflict between the exercise of power and the groups.* The definitions of deviance and normalcy would be created by those who are powerful, and they would define it keeping in view which side of the bread is buttered (Quinney, 1970). They won't enact laws in a bid to shape the common interest of the society, but the interests and values of their own interests. *Its best example can be given in the recent context of Pakistani Politics where NAB (National Accountability Bureau) gave a clear chit to Mushtaq Ahmed Raisani (Former Finance Secretary of Baluchistan govt.) after plea bargaining of 200 crores in Pakistani rupees and freeing him from the charges worth 4000 crores in Pakistani Rupees* ("Bureaucrat facing corruption charges 'cleared'", 2017).

The crime thus exhibits the conflict between political, economic, and social interest groups in general. Both group conflict and culture conflict can result in criminal behavior. The *culture conflict* takes its breath when people of certain group, conflict with the standards and norms of a dominant group who are in power and they define the laws. Hence crime alongside the justice system can discharge its effects in favor of the powerful groups. *That power group, if witness the deviating behavior of the less powerful group, will perceive them as delinquent in their very own society. Hence, a conflict criminologist might perceive crime as a mere competition of group competition.* For example, the less powerful group might try to steal recourses that they are deprived off, by hook or crook. They might burst out in shape of political action intended to the sole intention of uplifting their own group. According to Thorsten Sellin (1938), conflicting conduct exhibits a knee jerk reaction in shape of crime. If a society is having fewer shared norms between groups, the propensity of crime in that society will be higher in return.

As stated by Quinney (1970), crime *has been socially created*, this social reality of the entity 'crime' leads to following conclusions:

In a politically organized society, crime is nothing short of a human conduct instigated by authoritative agents.

Criminal definitions are nothing short of the conflicting behaviors of less powerful groups with those groups that are in power.

Criminal definitions are the creations and implementations of those who are powerful in the society.

Behavior patterns can be predicted because they've been structured with respect to criminal definitions.

Simply put, the definition of crime and the relative imposition by the justice system is in the hands of the power groups who toy with it favorable to their own interests. Turks (1969) furrowed his brows by arguing that when the legal authorities enforce the law as the law has been written, without realizing about the social norms which has not been written, despite that conflict group can explain their tendency of crime due to their own social norms, crime takes place. Chambliss and Seidman (1971) investigated the same using an organizational approach to the criminal justice system in an effort to figure out whether the state exercises its powers to resolve the conflict peacefully OR the power of the state is itself a gift for the most powerful groups in the society. They came to the same conclusion and hardly were the first critics to comment and won't be the last either.

Empirical Testing and Validity of Conflict Theory

When it comes to empirically testing crime with respect to the conflict theory, Brunk and Wilson (1991) found a relationship between the types of interest groups and crime. The conflict theory has had been constantly lending a helping hand in figuring out the crime patterns of minority groups, patterns of arrest and sentencing, and for exploring the ins and outs of white collar and organized crimes in societies. The said theory has also been helpful in finding out the relationship between perceived minority threat and the police expenditures (Holmes et al., 2008; Ruddell & Thomas, 2010). It has also been tested by theorists against police brutality and racial profiling (Holmes & Smith, 2006). Jacob and Kent (2007) investigated the execution data and drew upon a conclusion that the public support for the process of executions is affected in the wake of perceived threat from minorities.

2.   Summary

The social learning theory borrowed its initial breath from the works of Burgess and Akers (1966) differential association reinforcement theory which was a fine effort to combine the sociological approach of Sutherland's (1947) *differential association theory* alongside the principles of behavioral psychology within the differential association theory. Burgess and Akers (1966) postulated that there is an information fog in the said theory that's why it doesn't suffice a substantial empirical support thus needs modification in a bid to make it more visible, fill the void of information fog and its empirical validity against the criticisms and shortcomings. *Differential association* remains a very important factor in describing Akers social learning theory. "*Definitions*" are like rolling the dice on one's own attitudes and compass reading towards a certain behavior. "*Differential Reinforcement*" resembles the differential association but it creates another point of tension i.e. the imbalance or disproportion of attitudes, value, and norms toward engaging in a criminal act enhances the likelihood that the individual would indulge in such behavior. *Imitation* is the simplest rule which expresses the same explanation as the name "Imitation" i.e. when an individual simply copies another individual (models, film stars, politicians etc.) by viewing and observing them directly or indirectly. "*Differential social organization*" is nothing short of structural associations of crime in the society which put an impact on the rate of criminality. "*Differential location in the social structure*" points toward the socio-demographic attributes of social groups and individuals which reflect their position / role inside a bigger social structure. "*Theoretically defined structural variables*" commands attention of theorists toward the theoretical concepts which had been induced in the old and new literature to pinpoint the criminogenic conditions of groups, communities, and societies at large. "*Differential social location*" reflects the membership of an individual with regards to his association with the primary groups, secondary groups, and the reference groups. The basic premise of "*Conflict Theory*" can easily be described in a way that the society is basically divided into different groups (2 or more) with competing values and ideas. The *consensus theory* emphasizes that in a society, the common interests are not put on a back burner because laws are enacted according to the general agreement in a society. The *Functionalist Theory*" borrowed its existence from the consensus theory since it is like the consensus theory with an exception that it exhibits that how the system (e.g. law) is working and acting in a society in a bid to resolve disputes among members.

3.   References

Akers, R. L. (1973). Deviant behavior: A social learning approach (Belmont, CA: Wadsworth, 1977). *An upper level text written from a cultural transmission perspective. Evaluates major theories of deviance and examines a wide variety of deviant activities.*

Akers, R. L. (1977). Deviant behavior: A social learning approach.

Akers, R. L., Krohn, M. D., Lanza-Kaduce, L., & Radosevich, M. (1979). Social learning and deviant behavior: A specific test of a general theory. *American Sociological Review*, 636-655.

Akers Ronald, L. (1985). Deviant behavior: A social learning approach. *Belmont, CA: Wadsworth.*

Akers, R. L., & Jensen, G. F. (2006). The empirical status of social learning theory of crime and deviance: The past, present, and future. *Taking stock: The status of criminological theory*, *15*, 37-76.

Akers, R. L. (1990). Rational choice, deterrence, and social learning theory in criminology: The path not taken. *The Journal of Criminal Law and Criminology (1973-)*, *81*(3), 653-676.

Akers, R. L. (1998). *Social learning and social structure: A general theory of crime and deviance*. Transaction Publishers.

Akers, R. L., & Sellers, C. S. (2004). Criminological theories. 4. *Aufl. Los Angeles/CA.*

Akers, R. L., & Silverman, A. (2004). Toward a social learning model of violence and terrorism. *Violence: From theory to research*, 19-30.

Akers, R. L. (2011). *Social learning and social structure: A general theory of crime and deviance.* Transaction Publishers.

Akers, R. L. (2013). *Criminological theories: Introduction and evaluation.* Routledge.

Bandura, A., Ross, D., & Ross, S. A. (1961). Transmission of aggression through imitation of aggressive models. *The Journal of Abnormal and Social Psychology*, *63*(3), 575-582.

Bandura, A., Grusec, J. E., & Menlove, F. L. (1966). Observational learning as a function of symbolization and incentive set. *Child Development*, 499-506.

Bandura, A., & Jeffrey, R. W. (1973). Role of symbolic coding and rehearsal processes in observational learning. *Journal of personality and social psychology*, *26*(1), 122.

Bandura, A., & Walters, R. H. (1977). Social learning theory.

Bandura, A. (1990). Mechanisms of moral disengagement in terrorism. *Origins of terrorism: Psychologies, ideologies, states of mind*, 161-191.

Brunk, G. G., & WILSON, L. A. (1991). Interest groups and criminal behavior. *Journal of Research in Crime and Delinquency*, *28*(2), 157-173.

Bureaucrat facing corruption charges 'cleared'. (2017). *DAWN.COM.* Retrieved 11 January 2017, from http://www.dawn.com/news/1303806

Burgess, R. L., & Akers, R. L. (1966). A differential association-reinforcement theory of criminal behavior. *Social problems, 14*(2), 128-147.

Calhoun, J. F. (1974). Attitudes toward the sale and use of drugs—A cross-sectional analysis of those who used drugs. *Journal of youth and adolescence, 3*(1), 31-47.

Caulkins, D., & Hyatt, S. B. (1999). Using consensus analysis to measure cultural diversity in organizations and social movements. *Field Methods, 11*(1), 5-26.

Chambliss, W. J., & Seidman, R. B. (1971). *Law, order, and power* (p. 3). Reading, MA: Addison-Wesley.

Cressey, D. R. (1953). Other people's money; a study of the social psychology of embezzlement.

Cressey, D. R. (1960). Epidemiology and individual conduct: A case from criminology. *The Pacific Sociological Review, 3*(2), 47-58.

Fejer, D., & Smart, R. G. (1973). The knowledge about drugs, attitudes towards them and drug use rates of high school students. *Journal of Drug Education, 3*(4), 377-388.

Hollinger, R. C., & Clark, J. P. (1983). Deterrence in the workplace: Perceived certainty, perceived severity, and employee theft. *Social forces, 62*(2), 398-418.

Holmes, M., & Smith, B. (2006, November). Race, threat, and police brutality: A social psychological perspective. In *annual meeting of the American Society of Criminology (ASC), Los Angeles*.

Holmes, M. D., Smith, B. W., Freng, A. B., & Muñoz, E. A. (2008). Minority threat, crime control, and police resource allocation in the Southwestern United States. *Crime & Delinquency, 54*(1), 128-152.

Hwang, S., & Akers, R. L. (2003). Substance use by Korean adolescents: A cross-cultural test of social learning, social bonding, and self-control theories. *Social learning theory and the explanation of crime, 11*, 39-63.

Jacobs, D., & Kent, S. L. (2007). The determinants of executions since 1951: How politics, protests, public opinion, and social divisions shape capital punishment. *Social Problems, 54*(3), 297-318.

Jessor, R., & Jessor, S. L. (1973). A social psychology of marijuana use: Longitudinal studies of high school and college youth. *Journal of Personality and Social Psychology, 26*(1), 1.

Johnston, L. (1973). *Drugs and American youth*. U. Michigan, Inst. for Social Resea.

Kendall, R. F. (1976). *The context and implications of drinking and drug use among high school and college students*.

Krohn, M. D., Skinner, W. F., Massey, J. L., & Akers, R. L. (1985). Social learning theory and adolescent cigarette smoking: A longitudinal study. *Social Problems, 32*(5), 455-473.

Lanza-Kaduce, L., Akers, R. L., Krohn, M. D., & Radosevich, M. (1984). Cessation of alcohol and drug use among adolescents: A social learning model. *Deviant Behavior, 5*(1-4), 79-96.

O'Donnell, J. A. (1976). Young men and drugs – a nationwide survey. National Institute on Drug Abuse Research Monograph Series 5.

Pearce, J., & Garrett, H. D. (1970). A comparison of the drinking behavior of delinquent youth versus non-delinquent youth in the states of Idaho and Utah. *Journal of School Health, 40*(3), 131-135.

Pope, W. (1975). Durkheim as a functionalist. *Sociological Quarterly*, 361-379.

Quinney, R. (1970). The social reality of crime. Boston: Little, Brown. 1974a. *Criminal Justice in America. Boston: Little, Brown. 1974b. Critique of Legal Order: Crime Control in Capitalist Society. Boston: Little*.

Ruddell, R., & Thomas, M. O. (2010). Minority threat and police strength: an examination of the Golden State. *Police Practice and Research: An International Journal, 11*(3), 256-273.

Sellin, T. (1938). Culture conflict and crime. *American Journal of sociology, 44*(1), 97-103.

Spear, S. F., & Akers, R. L. (1987). Social learning variables and the risk of habitual smoking among adolescents: the Muscatine study. *American journal of preventive medicine, 4*(6), 336-342.

Sutherland Edwin, H. (1937). The professional thief.

Sutherland, E. H. (1947). Principles of criminology: A sociological theory of criminal behavior.

Schwendinger, H., & Schwendinger, J. R. (1972). The continuing debate on the legalistic approach to the definition of crime. *Issues in Criminology, 7*(1), 71-81.

Schwendinger, J. R., & Schwendinger, H. (1974). Rape myths: In legal, theoretical, and everyday practice. *Crime and Social Justice*, (1), 18-26.

Schwendinger, H., & Schwendinger, J. (1977). Social class and the definition of crime. *Crime and Social Justice*, (7), 4-13.

Schwendinger, H., & Schwendinger, J. (1982). The paradigmatic crisis in delinquency theory [Corrected title: The Paradigm Crisis in Delinquency Theory.]. *Crime and Social Justice*, (18), 70-78.

Schwendinger, H., & Schwendinger, J. R. (1985). *Adolescent subcultures and delinquency* (p. 99). New York: Praeger.

Sykes, G. M., & Matza, D. (1957). Techniques of neutralization: A theory of delinquency. *American sociological review*, *22*(6), 664-670.

Taylor, P. N. (2003). *A national analysis of racial profiling and factors affecting the likelihood of traffic stops for African Americans* (Doctoral dissertation, Virginia Tech).

Turk, A. T. (1969). *Criminality and legal order*. Rand McNally.

Turner, J. H., & Maryanski, A. (1979). *Functionalism*. Benjamin-Cummings Publishing Company.

Vold, G. B. (1958). Theoretical criminology.

Walker, S., Spohn, C., & DeLone, M. (2012). *The color of justice: Race, ethnicity, and crime in America*. Cengage Learning.

Warr, M. (2002). *Companions in crime: The social aspects of criminal conduct*. Cambridge University Press.

Chapter 4
Psychological Theories and Social
Movement Theory

1. Psychoanalytic Theory (A New Image of The Man)

Criminology's early marriage with Psychoanalysis without any real buffers began with the works of Austrian neurologist Sigmund Freud (1856-1939). To rationalize the human delinquent behavior, Freud led the way to psychoanalytic approach which didn't lose its luster even today. This theory provides a burst of sunshine to the field of criminology by postulating that *"Crime is nothing but an outcome of some mental disturbance"* (Freud, 2003).

The Freudian explanation of delinquency focuses on the *"Unconscious"* part of the brain. The main objective of Freud's theory is to spot the unconscious, and then start dealing with the problems by using the *"Conscious Methods"*. He believes that the antisocial tendencies in a person are associated with the intangible unconscious memories, which branches back to a disturbed childhood (Freud, 2005). In a way, Freud created *"a new image of the man"* where the unconscious kingdom of mind follows its own laws without any apparent communication with the conscious contents of mind. Since man is unaware of his unconscious part and the unconscious part still intervenes with his conscious brain, the man doesn't seem to be a complete *"rational being"* (Silving, 1960).

Following table describes the three distinct parts of Freud's human behavior:

Id	associated with the unconscious desires, instincts and drives
Superego	associated with an individual's moral character, his learned Values, what's unacceptable and what's acceptable
Ego	associated with an individual's social identity, real behavior, and conscious activity.

The *Id* exhibits the desires, drives, and instincts of the unconscious part of brain. Simply put, Id is a kind of selfish entity that seeks pleasure without giving any regard to the morality, logic, or reason. Freud relates the first development of mind with the construction of Id, which starts working when the babies are born. Freud says that Id doesn't concern about any type of moral restrictions and it behaves like a totally spoiled, pleasure seeking child who doesn't bother about sweating the details of morality, logic, or reason whatsoever (Rennison, 2015). The superego draws a sketch line of the moral code or conscience and it tells a person which things or doings are acceptable and which are unacceptable. *In other words, superego tends to box-in the delinquency through societal norms and etiquettes.* The early moral training develops the superego (Post, 1972). There is a strong association between Id and Superego in the sense that Id shows exponential rise in desires without any moral code whilst Superego answers about what Id can have and what can't have. *In a way, superego analyses the gravity of desire and aligns it with a value system and responds through either* "*Yes*" or "*No*".

The last but certainly not the least part of the psychoanalytic system is the "*Ego*" that defines the social identification of an individual that is shown through the very foundation of his external behavior (Freud & Strachey, 1962). Simply put, "*the ego shows the actual realization of the argument between Id and Superego*". The aspect of ego is always a conscious thing and this is where psychoanalytic theory comes in handy since "*it tries to unearth the unconscious parts of Id and Superego and analyses the conscious part of ego to figure out the ground realities alongside the intangible realities behind a delinquent behavior.*"

2. Exploring Personality Theory of Crime

Personality is what represents us before others and what makes us visible before the society, clearly depicting what we are and what are the things which makes us distinguishable from others (Clark et al., 2007). Why does a person with a specific personality try to toy with the social norms? Without sliding a knife in old theories, Sheldon Glueck and Eleanor Glueck (1956) provided an early classification of the very personality and delinquency:

"Delinquents are more extroverted, vivacious, impulsive, less self-controlled ... are more hostile, resentful, defiant, suspicious, destructive ... and are less fearful of failure or defeat than the non-delinquents. They are less concerned about meeting conventional expectations and are more ambivalent toward or far less submissive to authority. They are, as a group, more socially assertive"

The above personality picture clearly shows that delinquents have different personality traits in many aspects when compared with non-delinquents. At the very least, if someone wants to dig deep into the few slices of delinquent personality, he must put his eyelids on the most prominent theory of *"Big Five Model of Personality"*:

The Big Five of Personality and Behavior

This model exhibits a well thought out structure into which personalities can be categorized. According to this very model, the following five factors either make or break a personality, thus accounts for making different personalities. The five factors are particularly tagged as Neuroticism, Extraversion, Openness, Agreeableness, and Conscientiousness (Clark et al., 2007).

Neuroticism: implies to emotional stability of a person. It defines a distinguishable trait at the apex of personality categorization. The individuals, who have a high degree of Neuroticism exhibits irrational ideas, frequently show anger and sadness alongside uncontrollable impulses. Eysenck & Eysenck (1985) argued that Neuroticism, as a trait of emotional personality, triggers the quick arousal of emotionality when stimulated, and this tendency slows down the emotions at a slow rate. Their opposite are the personalities tagged with relaxed, calm, and even-tempered behavior.

Extraversion: depicts a tendency of sociability, excitement, and stimulation. Individuals with this personality trait are normally optimistic about the future, assertive, talkative, and extremely active. Numerous theorists marked extraversion as a distinguishable trait of personality (Costa & McCrae, 1992; Goldberg, 1990). Their opposite is tagged as *"introverts"* who are believed to be shy and reserved, and they normally take more time in mixing up with people and get to know the new people at a slow rate (Tieger & Barron-Tieger, 1995).

Openness: is the third personality trait that is tagged with the imaginative qualities, they seek pleasure in beauty, and they seek variety in things since they are inquisitive and curious about things (COSTA, 1996). On the flip side, their opposites are tagged with similar behavior but in traditional manners and they also exhibit conservative point of view.

Agreeableness: people with this personality trait show skills relating to relationships or communication between people. High scoring people with this trait fall in the category of trusting, sympathetic, forgiving, soft hearted, altruistic, and warm (Kernberg & Caligor, 1996). Their opposites would fly in the face of aforementioned attributes like argumentative, impatient, intolerant, and hard hearted.

Conscientiousness: people who get a high score in Conscientiousness, if fall on hard times, would exhibit self-control since they are strong willed, determined, efficient, thorough, and organized at large. They are likely to touch the limits of high occupational and academic targets (Tomkins, 1962). People with low score come to a naught in these aspects since they are susceptible to laziness and carelessness and they put blame on others thus overlook the very foundation of their responsibilities (Healy, Bronner & Bowers, 1930).

A few slices of the discoveries with regards to personality traits give credence to the view that personalities are potent enough to masquerade in different forms. The characteristics of antisocial youth were investigated by Sheldon and Eleanor Glueck (Schmallenger, 2008). Hans Eysenck (2013) also did a great deal of work in identifying criminal's personality traits who postulated that the self-destructive behavior is strongly associated with neuroticism.

Psychopathic Personality: Descriptions, Types, and Behavior

Since the name *"Psychopathic"* speaks for itself, psychopathic people fly in the face of normal or acceptable personality people in a society. For being an obvious champion of destructive personality traits, they fall prey to antisocial behavior, sociopath, and psychopath (Blair, Mitchell & Blair, 2005). *To be very honest, the psychopaths are not rare as unicorns* since the society figures them out as a product of a destructive home environment or a product with abnormality within themselves. Psychopaths generally send shockwaves to the societal norms since they fall in line with cold heartedness, forcefulness, manipulativeness, egocentricity, risk taking, and inability to form stable relationships (Jacoby, Severance & Bruce, 2004).

This class of persons was first diagnosed by a Bristol physician Prichard who postulated that psychopathic personality is a *"moral insanity condition"* which is independent from intellectual disorder and this behavior is life-long and persistent (Prichard, 1837). Since then, numerous terms have been coined for this condition but as a matter of fact, the theory swept into power the very instance it came into existence. The modern writers like Partridge (1930) gave it a new luster with the name *"Sociopathic Personality"*. His school of thought states that this condition born out of the relationship between the society and the patient. On the other hand, Alexander (1930) coined the name *"Neurotic Character"* for the said condition.

For being a psychopathic patient, a longitudinal study of life history is very important and the physician has to uncover the life-long dust of the patient's persistent anti-social behavior. Delinquency of all kinds, right from persistent childhood behavior to the untruthfulness and unreliability would be visible. In terms of explaining the Psychopaths, David Henderson (1939) espoused the theory by providing valid reasons that they can be classified into three main types:

Who are principally aggressive towards themselves or others such as alcoholics or drug addicts.

Who are mainly passive and show mild aggressiveness frequently and they indulge in minor delinquencies such as swindling or petty thieving etc.

Who are predominantly creative and they leave deep signs of remembrance for the world through their special gifts.

There is no mistaking the fact that a normal behavior is tagged with a healthy, satisfying, and socially acceptable behavior (Lower, 1944). A person with neurosis shows unsatisfying behavior but acceptable to societal norms. On the contrary, *a psychopathic personality is satisfying to the person but unacceptable to societal norms*. Few mothers sidestep the complexities of life with children and exhibits ambivalent behavior toward their child in the early years, which can deeply affect the child mother relationship leaving deep scars on the children who become psychopaths later in the life. In fact, maternal rejection and deprivation acts as pouring fuel on fire and the disturbed parental relationships with children in early years serve as a catalyst in making a psychopathic child (Bowlby et al., 1956). In this regard, the feeling of rejection and guilt of unfair treatment translates into acts, apparently seems like irresponsible acts but deeply rooted in shape of a desire either to be noticed and punished or to obtain what is desired (Maslow & Mittelmann, 1941). With regards to physical factors in etiology, Knott et al. (1953) unearthed an interesting discovery that these patients as well as their parents exhibit abnormal E.E.G.s with an excess of slow rhythms for their age groups. When these factors were tested against fostered children with foster parents (by removing the real patients from the picture), the math failed. This clearly corroborates the fact that a parent with psychopathic tendencies is liable to transfer this tendency to the offspring through genetic means.

Curran & Mallinson (1944) observed an interesting difference between a permanent psychopathic personality and a personality with an episodic relationship with psychopathic condition due to some "*short-circuit*" type of reactions engendered at certain occasions without any history of psychopathy. With regards to psychopath personalities, the "*Royal Commission on Capital Punishment*" (1953) states that no doubt prevalence of crime undermines the very foundation of the justice system, "*and despite that a person is mentally abnormal, still this argument doesn't satisfy the insane murder. With all due consideration, when it comes to charging criminal with a death penalty, psychopathic abnormality is ought to be weighed as well.*"

Psychological Counseling in Delinquency

There is no longer any room for the illusion that despite presenting so many theories in a row, when it comes to committing a crime, all bets are off. For all the praise that numerous psychological theories received, it becomes inevitable to bridge the gap between a criminal delinquency and the deep-rooted diagnosis, and later on his psychological counseling in the best way possible. There is a strong need for a multi-pronged and a dynamic mental health system in place that extends beyond the boundaries of justice system (Regier et al., 2000). Numerous studies have indicated that the justice system, in the absence of mental therapies, might act with a lame duck approach. Additionally, the mental health disorders put an adverse impact on the emotional symptoms which further increase the risk of aggression in return (Stoddard-Dare et al., 2011; Grande et al., 2011). Considering the juveniles' involvement in criminal activities, around 40% to 80% imprisoned juveniles are affected with, at the very least, one mental disorder capable of being diagnosed (Collins et al., 2010).

Well... sitting on hands and doing nothing won't solve the problem that's why many theories are on the beat when it comes to psychological counseling of delinquent behaviors. Numerous theorists break the back of cognitive behavioral treatment over psychological treatments in delinquency (Blakely & Davidson, 1984). Michaelson (1987) postulated that a combination of social training skills alongside psychological problems solving skills and the cognitive behavioral approaches should be utilized in an effort to break the back of delinquent behavior. Kazdin (1987) showed another side of the coin which shows a burst of positivity in treatments which involved family and peer system.

*Lest one be tempted into thinking that there isn't a single psychological treatment for delinquency...*the hypothesis is right as well as wrong...right in the sense that a mentally affected criminal might need a combination of two or more than two techniques in a row...wrong in the sense that he might require only one for instance family therapy to strip off his tendency towards criminality. Some theorists strongly hold the opinion that family therapy treatment is best to enhance the effectivity of other psychological treatments in delinquency (Hazelrigg, Cooper & Borduin, 1987).

Prevention and Treatment

In a bid to take the largest 'bite' out of delinquency, the earlier the better (during childhood) would be the key theme in prevention and treatment of delinquency. At the same time, there is no single bullet to achieve this seemingly easy task since time and consistency both would be required to send shockwaves through a delinquent mind.

Cognitive Behavioral Interventions: might put a full stop or the very least disentangle the complexity of delinquent mind. The National Mental Health Association (2004) states that this approach is quite an effective approach especially for youth since its focus is on the causation of disruptive aggressive behavior. The said approach has been effectively utilized against several delinquent triggers like anger management, problem solving, and interpersonal problems. In this regard, *"Thinking for a Change Theory"* presented by Bush, Glick and Taymans (1997) is worth noting which sweeps into empowering the thinking of juvenile offenders by incorporating various cognitive approaches. Although a few theorists oppose this approach for juvenile offenders still it has not gathered dust due to its wide acceptance. For instance, Shelton (2005) argued that the model of this approach is not suited for juvenile offenders as compared to the adults.

Functional Family Therapy: with a few but effective slices of family centered approach have been successfully tested against a broad range of high risk youth offenders since it has been regarded as a burst of hope for the problems associated with adolescent behavior at large (Mendel, 2000; Sexton & Alexander, 1999). The youths that fall in the age domain 11-18, involved in delinquency acts like bad conduct, disruptive behavior, oppositional defiance, substance use, and violence can be subjected to FFT theory. FFT method, over a period of clinical studies and empirical evidences, brings a fall to recidivism more effectively than other psychological therapies in place (Alexander et al., 2000). The basic mode of FFT involves family as a key focus of intervention, and it keeps a strong check on multiple domains within which the family of the offender and the offender himself lives. Its flexibility extends to almost all family members across culturally diverse populations (Sexton & Alexander, 2003).

Family Integrative Transition: is an effective rigorous treatment intervention for juvenile offenders 2 months prior to their release from the prison till 4 to 6 months in a bid to strip off delinquency behavior from his mind (Aos, 2004). The reason being, reentry to the community is surely a crucial time for the offender and particularly for the offender who has been suffering from mental disorders. This psychological intervention program consists of empirically supported interventions alongside Family Integrative Transition primarily Dialectical Behavior Therapy, Relapse Prevention, Motivational Enhancement Therapy, and Multisystemic Therapy. The main aim behind FIT is to make the offender realize and generalize the skills he learned during the course of imprisonment with those associated within their community and their daily lives (Trupin et al., 2011). The good news is, results and evaluations after an offender is subjected to this program, showed a considerable decrease in recidivism (27%) when compared with the earlier findings (Garfinkel, 2010).

Multisystemic Therapy: also exhibit much of its luster for juvenile offenders with mental disorders. It also falls in the line of family based approach which focuses on identifying the casual triggers and then making a relationship with substance use and delinquency. The findings of Timmons Mitchell et al., (2006) with regards to improvement in 4 areas of functioning based on the Child and Adolescent Functional Assessment scale is worth noting. The findings espoused that community based treatment suffices the best requirements for delinquent youths affected with mental health abnormalities.

3. The Concept of Social Movement Theory

"Change is the only thing which is constant in the world"; The same factor *'change'* gave birth to a new theory in 1960's that is based on the collective action of individuals forming networks. Simply put, *"Social Movement Theories"* describe all forms of collective action which initiates and mark its inevitable presence in response to situations of cultural, economic, or political demands OR securing a reason against situations of oppression and inequality at large. Theorists argue that these situations across continental boundaries gave birth to organized set of components seeking a collective political outline of *'change'* over time in shape of social movements (Batliwala, 2012). In other words, Social Movements imply a unique social process that is formed through complex mechanisms on the shoulders of which a collective action is performed by the actors (Diani, 1992; Diani & Bison, 2004).

Someone said that *"facts are stubborn things"* since they never change and they remain in their original shape the very moment they start breathing. In this scenario, the emergence of social movements is the hardest facts of this century that is born with the realization that:

Social movement actors are engaged in conflictual collective action designed to either oppose or promote the social change.

Social movements are properly linked through complex informal networks with clearly identified enemies

Social movements share a unique but collective individuality.

Why Social Movement Theories Emerge

Despite that social movements are the components of civil society systems; they work in a bid to search for alternative states of the society OR to drive a hard protest against the subsisting social structures of the society. They either give a call for change in a society OR exhibit their dissatisfaction for the norms currently prevailing in the society. It is vital to remember that the social movements are shaped by the circumstances and they mature or reduce in size in correspondence with the circumstantial factors that either grow or shrink those (Sogge & Dutting, 2010). Hence there is no mistaking the fact that they emerge based on their historical context and the impact of their presence, their choice of strategies, their politics, and their overall impact are deeply rooted in the historical facts. In a way, *"they define their own terms of existence AND they are what they say they are"* (Castells, 1997). Also note down that not all circumstances of inequality and injustice give birth to social movements (Mahmud, 2010). They are built in the sense that they gain consciousness out of a deliberate investment of resources and thought in perfect collaboration of the favorable external environment. It is also worth mentioning here that *"Time"* is a crucial factor in comprehending social movements since their time span might crosses generations or over a lifetime till such time they fulfill the objective of their ideology.

Social Movements Across Continental Boundaries

The emergence of new social movements in 1960's and 1970's argue that the social movements can be coupled with contemporary social movements if they face troubles of their belonging and identity. This is very much to the contrary of social movements before the 2nd world war, since all those theories were focused and meant against the type of structural discriminations such as inequalities among social classes seeking the reallocation of politics (Frazer, 1995; Benhabib, 1996).

As social movements roll the dice on clearly identified targets, the unavoidable factors of social discriminations in south, with regards to the colonization histories, led to the existence of structural marginalization social movements (Thompson & Tapscott, 2010). The social movements intend to provide an *actionable blue print of their line of action*; for instance, the world has already witnessed the target mobilization and active participation of women deeply rooted in the ethnic nationalism and neo-Nazism factors (Ferber, 2004).

Tools Utilization for Activism of Social Movements

Utilizing a range of tactics and tools and driving a hard bargain in the hope of much gain are parts and parcel of social movements. Social movements can be seen in shape of civil disobedience, protest marches, or even using an armed resistance if need be for example guerrilla or national liberation movements such as in South Africa where an armed wing of African National Congress was fighting in south Africa (Cock, 2001). Communication, being an active medium for disseminating information across the members of a movement, even across borders in a jiffy, it has been successfully used for building social movements. In the current era of 21ˢᵗ century where internet highway has transformed the world into a global village, communication has been revolutionized in shape of digital network society (Castells, 2010). The flip side of the coin shows that it's not the technology that makes or break a social movement at large. This has been clarified this in the following comments:

'While technology is increasingly becoming a critical tool for social mobilization, it is not an end by itself [...] While a majority of western media and cyber-utopians may call the Arab Spring a Twitter or Facebook revolution, the mere supposition is far from the truth. It takes courage, creativity faith, and great risk, a belief in freedom and human dignity that pushes these groups to harness the power of these tools.'
(Philip Thigo, BRIDGE e-discussion, October 2011)

What's More, the social communication platforms are owned by private entities which may or may not lend a hand to social movement agendas (Horn, 2013).

Major Trends in Social Movement Theory

Theories provide societies and legal justice systems, a laser like focus of the deep-rooted problems. In this regard, social movement theory is born with the realization that instigates humanity to deeply analyze the underlying causation for the formation of social movement. The major trends exhibited by social movement theory are as follows:

Mass behavior

Resource mobilization theory

Political opportunity processes

New social movements

Mass behavior or Collective Behavior represents a collective behavior or many individuals who are active with other individuals or being influenced by them spontaneously and comparatively unstructured. This collective behavior in social movements can grab everybody's' retina in shape of crowds, disaster behavior, riots and panics. When a large number of people gather on a certain place with an obvious air of short term or long-term purpose, it is nothing short of a social movement's crowd (Mass behavior) (Blumer, 1969). Collective behavior is also seen in shape of "*riots*" which is represented by a sudden outburst of violence by many individuals (Rubenstein, 1970). Rioting was somewhat a normal phenomenon in the initial many decades of 19th century and it was deemed as part and parcel of civilian life (Rosenfeld, 1997). The world has clearly witnessed a major riot of East St. Louis, Illinois in 1917 in which 48 Americans were deprived of their lives (Waskow, 1966). *Disaster behavior* is another form of mass behavior which focuses on "*How people behave during and after a disaster*" such as floods, hurricanes, earthquakes, plane crash etc. It's an open secret that the disaster behavior literally disrupt the normal lives of people (Miller, 2013). A very common type of belief argue that in that particular period of disaster, people strip off their very moral sense and engage in exploitive, individualistic, selfish and wild behavior (Goode, 1992). Be that as it may, the flip side of the coin shows the picture where the very much opposite of the fact is deemed true where people tend to absorb the shock with a calm behavior and follow an appropriate line of action accordingly in the best way possible (Goode, 1992).

Resource Mobilization Theory is also a famous name that has been underscored many times in place of social movements rolled in the 1970's (McCarthy and Zald, 1977; Tilly, 1978). Resource mobilization falls in line with the concept that the unsatisfactory conditions in a society give rise to a rational response in shape of social movement. An interesting point is *"these unsatisfactory circumstances always subsist in the society but people rarely take the formation of social movement"*; in this regard, it becomes almost inexplicable when and how leaders mobilize the resource primarily energy, time, and money and conduct the people to fill the vacuum of social movement. For instance, a cut in the spending of higher education resulted in a sudden burst of protests in California campuses alongside many other states in 2009 and 2010 (Rosenhall, 2010). A few critics also argue that the resource mobilization theory lacks the element of emotions, and social movement actors go with a calculated and cold flow of their mind without a single drop of emotion under their skin (Goodwin, Jasper & Polletta, 2004). At the same time, there are numerous arguments afoot against this concept as well.

"Political Opportunity Theory", an idea so compelling, states that social movements are born or succeed in the wake of potential political opportunities. Simply put, *"social movements stalk through the loopholes of political opportunities"*. Political opportunity scenarios could be like when a government is seemingly sinking due to foreign or economic crises, it is likely to open a gateway for a social movement (Snow & Soule, 2010). In the presence of such loopholes, the discontented people perceive a successful political action perfectly favorable to fill the void of social movement. This is the reason behind less social movements under the shadow of authoritarian governments rather than democratic environments because people feel the fear repressive responses, beatings, and arbitrary arrests.

The *"New Social Movement Theory"* takes theorists out of the woods by explaining *'why'* rather than *'how'* a social movement emerges. It emphasizes that *the changes in a society alongside the structural circumstances both takes the baby out from the embryo of social movements* (Horkheimer & Adorno, 2010). An interesting thing about NSM theory is that it cannot be explicitly explained on the structural changes if it doesn't touch the non-class issues like neighborhood, age, ethnicity, and gender. The new social movement theorists identify the group- interests by constructing collective identities exactly opposite of assuming them as structurally determined (Klandersman, 1994).

4.   Summary

The Freudian explanation of delinquency focuses on the "*Unconscious*" part of the brain. The Id exhibits the desires, drives, and instincts of the unconscious part of brain. The superego draws a sketch line of the moral code or conscience and it tells a person which things or doings are acceptable and which are unacceptable. The last but certainly not the least part of the psychoanalytic system is the "*Ego*" that defines the social identification of an individual that is shown through the very foundation of his external behavior. The five-factor model of personality exhibits a well thought out structure into which personalities can be categorized. This class of persons was first diagnosed by a Bristol physician Prichard who postulated that psychopathic personality is a "*moral insanity condition*" which is independent from intellectual disorder and this behavior is life-long and persistent. In a bid to take the largest 'bite' out of delinquency, the earlier the better (during childhood) would be the key theme in prevention and treatment of delinquency. "*Social Movement Theories*" describe all forms of collective action which initiates and mark its inevitable presence in response to situations of cultural, economical, or political demands OR securing a reason against situations of oppression and inequality at large. Communication, being an active medium for disseminating information across the members of a movement, even across borders in a jiffy, it has been successfully used for building social movements. *Mass behavior or Collective Behavior* represents a collective behavior or many individuals who are active with other individuals or being influenced by them spontaneously and comparatively unstructured. Resource mobilization falls in line with the concept that the unsatisfactory conditions in a society give rise to a rational response in shape of social movement. "*Political Opportunity Theory*", an idea so compelling states that social movements are born or succeed in the wake of potential political opportunities. The "*New Social Movement Theory*" takes theorists out of the woods by explaining '*why*' rather than '*how*' a social movement emerges.

5. References

Alexander, J. F., Pugh, C., Parsons, B. V., & Sexton, T. L. (2000). Functional family therapy. In DS Elliott (Series Ed.), Blueprints for violence prevention (Book 3). *Boulder, CO: Center for the Study and Prevention of Violence, Institute of Behavioral Science, University of Colorado.*

Aos, S. (2004). Washington state's family integrated transitions program for juvenile offenders: Outcome evaluation and benefit-cost analysis. *Olympia, WA: Washington State Institute for Public Policy*, 105-114.

Batliwala, S. (2012). Changing their world. *Concepts and practices of women's.*

Benhabib, S. (Ed.). (1996). *Democracy and difference: Contesting the boundaries of the political* (Vol. 31). Princeton, NJ: Princeton University Press.

Blair, J., Mitchell, D., & Blair, K. (2005). *The Psychopath: emotion and the brain*. Blackwell Publishing.

Blakely, C. H., & Davidson, W. S. (1984). Behavioral approaches to delinquency: A review. *Advances in Child Behavioral Analysis & Therapy.*

Blumer, H. (1969). Social movements. *Studies in social movements: A social psychological perspective*, 8-29.

Bowlby, J., Ainsworth, M., Boston, M., & Rosenbluth, D. (1956). The effects of mother-child separation: a follow-up study. *British Journal of Medical Psychology*, *29*(3-4), 211-247.

Bush, J., Glick, B., & Taymans, J. M. (1997). *Thinking for a change: Integrated cognitive behavior change program*. US Department of Justice, National Institute of Corrections.

Castells, M. (1997). The power of identity (Vol. 2). *Malden (MA, USA) and Oxford (UK): Blackwell*.

Castells, M. (2010). The culture of real virtuality: The integration of electronic communication, the end of the mass audience, and the rise of interactive networks. *The Rise of the Network Society: With a New Preface, Volume I, Second edition with a new preface*, 355-406.

Clark, J., Boccaccini, M. T., Caillouet, B., & Chaplin, W. F. (2007). Five factor model personality traits, jury selection, and case outcomes in criminal and civil cases. *Criminal Justice and Behavior, 34*(5), 641-660.

Cock, J. (1992). Colonels and cadres: War and gender in South Africa.

Colins, O., Vermeiren, R., Vreugdenhil, C., van den Brink, W., Doreleijers, T., & Broekaert, E. (2010). Psychiatric disorders in detained male adolescents: a systematic literature review. *The Canadian Journal of Psychiatry, 55*(4), 255-263.

Costa, P. T., & McCrae, R. R. (1992). Four ways five factors are basic. *Personality and individual differences, 13*(6), 653-665.

COSTA JR, P. T. (1996). Of personality theories: Theoretical contexts for the five-factor model. *The five-factor model of personality: Theoretical perspectives*, 51.

Curran, D., & Mallinson, P. (1944). Recent progress in psychiatry. *J. ment. Sci, 90*, 266.

Diani, M. (1992). Analysing social movement networks. *Studying Collective Action*, 107-135.

Diani, M., & Bison, I. (2004). Organizations, coalitions, and movements. *Theory and Society, 33*(3-4), 281-309.

Eysenck, H. J., & Eysenck, M. W. (1985). Personality and individual differences: A natural science perspective.

Eysenck, H. J. (2013). *Crime and Personality (Psychology Revivals)*. Routledge.

Ferber, A. L. (2004). *Home-grown hate: Gender and organized racism*. Psychology Press.

Freud, S. (2003). *An outline of psychoanalysis* (Vol. 839). Penguin UK.

Freud, S. (2005). *The unconscious* (Vol. 8). Penguin UK.

Garfinkel, L. (2010). Improving family involvement for juvenile offenders with emotional/behavioral disorders and related disabilities. *Behavioral Disorders*, 52-60.

Glueck, S., & Glueck, E. (2013). *Family environment and delinquency* (Vol. 7). Routledge.

Goldberg, L. R. (1990). An alternative "description of personality": the big-five factor structure. *Journal of Personality and Social Psychology*, *59*(6), 1216.

Goode, E. (1992). *Collective behavior*. Saunders College Pub.

Goodwin, J., Jasper, J. M., & Polletta, F. (2004). *Emotional dimensions of social movements* (pp. 413-432). London: Blackwell Publishing.

Grande, T., Hallman, J., Caldwell, K., & Underwood, L. (2011). Using the BASC-2 to assess mental health needs of incarcerated juveniles: Implications for treatment and release. *Corrections Today*, 100-102.

Hazelrigg, M. D., Cooper, H. M., & Borduin, C. M. (1987). Evaluating the effectiveness of family therapies: An integrative review and analysis. *Psychological Bulletin*, *101*(3), 428.

Healy, W., Bronner, A. F., & Bowers, A. M. (1930). *The structure and meaning of psychoanalysis as related to personality and behavior* (No. 6). AA Knopf.

Henderson, D. K. (1939). Psychopathic states.

Horkheimer, M., & Adorno, T. W. (2010). *Dialektik der aufklärung: philosophische fragmente*. S. Fischer Verlag.

Horn, J. (2013). *Gender and social movements: overview report*. IDS.

Jacoby, J. E., Severance, T. A., & Bruce, A. S. (Eds.). (2004). *Classics of criminology*. Long Grove, IL: Waveland Press.

Kazdin, A. E., Bass, D., Siegel, T., & Thomas, C. (1989). Cognitive-behavioral therapy and relationship therapy in the treatment of children referred for antisocial behavior. *Journal of Consulting and Clinical Psychology*, *57*(4), 522.

Kernberg, O. F., & Caligor, E. (1996). A psychoanalytic theory of personality disorders. *Major theories of personality disorder*, 106-140.

Klandermans, B. (1994). Transient identities? Membership patterns in the Dutch peace movement. *New social movements: From ideology to identity*, 168-184.

Knott, J. R., Platt, E. B., Ashby, M. C., & Gottlieb, J. S. (1953). A familial evaluation of the electroencephalogram of patients with primary behavior disorder and psychopathic personality. *Electroencephalography and clinical neurophysiology*, *5*(3), 363-370.

Lowery, L. G. (1944). Delinquent and criminal personalities. *Hunt, J. McV., editor: Personality and the behavior disorders, New York*.

Mahmud, S. (2010). Why do garment workers in Bangladesh fail to mobilize? *Citizenship and social movements: Perspectives from the global south, London: Zed Books*.

Maslow, A. H., & Mittelmann, B. (1941). Principles of abnormal psychology.

McCarthy, J. D., & Zald, M. N. (1977). Resource mobilization and social movements: A partial theory. *American Journal of Sociology*, 1212-1241.

Mendel, R. A. (2000). *Less hype, more help: Reducing juvenile crime, what works – and what doesn't*. DIANE Publishing.

Michaelson, L. 1987, "Cognitive-behavioral strategies in the prevention and treatment of antisocial disorders in children and adolescents", in Prevention of Delinquent Behavior, eds J.D. Buchard & S.N. Burchard, Sage, Newbury Park.

Miller, D. L. (2013). *Introduction to collective behavior and collective action*. Waveland Press.

National Mental Health Association (NMHA). Mental health treatment for youth in the juvenile justice system: A compendium of promising practices; John, D., Catherine, T., Eds.; MacArthur Foundation: Chicago, IL, USA, 2004.

Partridge, G. E. (1930). Current conceptions of psychopathic personality. *American Journal of Psychiatry*, *87*(1), 53-99.

Post, S. C. (1972). Moral values and the superego concept in psychoanalysis.

Prichard, J. C. (1837). *A treatise on insanity: And other disorders affecting the mind* (Vol. 1837). Haswell, Barrington, and Haswell.

Regier, D. A., Narrow, W. E., Rupp, A., Rae, D. S., & Kaelber, C. T. (2000). The epidemiology of mental disorder treatment need: community estimates of medical necessity. *Unmet Need in Psychiatry (Eds G. Andrews, S. Henderson)*, 41-58.

Rennison, N. (2015). *Freud and psychoanalysis: Everything you need to know about id, ego, super-ego and more*. Oldcastle Books.

Rosenfeld, M. J. (1997). Celebration, politics, selective looting and riots: A micro level study of the Bulls Riot of 1992 in Chicago. *Social Problems*, *44*(4), 483-502.

Rosenhall, L. (2010). January 31, 'Class cuts wreak havoc at California universities'. *Sacramento Bee*, 1A.

Royal Commission on Capital Punishment 1949-1953: report: presented to Parliament by Command of Her Majesty, September 1953. HM Stationery Office, 1953.

Rubenstein, R. E. (1970). Rebels in Eden Mass Political Violence in the United States.

Schmalleger, F. (2008). Criminal justice: A brief introduction (7th ed.). Englewood Cliffs, NJ: Prentice Hall.

Sexton, T. L., & Alexander, J. F. (1999). Functional family therapy: Principles of clinical intervention, assessment, and implementation. *Henderson, NV: RCH Enterprises*.

Sexton, T. L., & Alexander, J. F. (2003). Functional family therapy: a mature clinical model for working with at-risk adolescents and their families.

Shelton, D. (2005). Patterns of treatment services and costs for young offenders with mental disorders. *Journal of Child and Adolescent Psychiatric Nursing*, *18*(3), 103-112.

Silving, H. (1960). Psychoanalysis and the criminal law. *The Journal of Criminal Law, Criminology, and Police Science*, *51*(1), 19-33.

Snow, D. A., & Soule, S. A. (2010). *A primer on social movements*. WW Norton.

Sogge, D., & Dütting, G. (2010). Moving targets: notes on social movements. *The Hague: HIVOS*.

Stoddard-Dare, P., Mallett, C. A., & Boitel, C. (2011). Association between mental health disorders and juveniles' detention for a personal crime. *Child and Adolescent Mental Health*, *16*(4), 208-213.

Thompson, L., & Tapscott, C. (2010). *Citizenship and social movements: perspectives from the global South.* Zed Books.

Tieger, P. D., & Barron-Tieger, B. (1995). Do what you are. Boston. *MA: Little, Brown and Company.*

Tilly, C. (1978). *From mobilization to revolution.* McGraw-Hill College.

Timmons-Mitchell, J., Bender, M. B., Kishna, M. A., & Mitchell, C. C. (2006). An independent effectiveness trial of multisystemic therapy with juvenile justice youth. *Journal of clinical child and adolescent psychology, 35*(2), 227-236.

Tomkins, S. S. (1962). Affect, imagery, consciousness: Vol. I. The positive effects.

Trupin, E. J., Kerns, S. E., Walker, S. C., DeRobertis, M. T., & Stewart, D. G. (2011). Family integrated transitions: A promising program for juvenile offenders with co-occurring disorders. *Journal of Child & Adolescent Substance Abuse, 20*(5), 421-436.

Waskow, A. I. (1966). From race riot to sit-in. *Garden City, New York.*

Chapter 5
Biological Theories of Crime

1. Overview of Biological Theories Within a 'Positivism' Paradigm

The "*Biological Theories*" are legendary theories which bear the burden of providing an insight of human behaviors that are in conflict with societal expectations, by examining individual's characteristics. The best pattern / model that explain these theories is renowned by the name '*Positivism*' (also called as determinism) which proposes that *the factors which determine delinquent behaviors in humans are largely beyond the reach of their control.*

Biological theories are literally at odds with '*classical theories*' which state that it is an individual who bears the burden of rationally deciding about committing a crime i.e. it is his logical decision making. Similarly, biological theories are also in-conflict with the '*Critical theories*' which claim that human's delinquent behaviors are the aftereffects of the factors like unequal distribution of wealth and power, social stratifications, and anomalies in law-making. Originally, biological criminology was discredited due to a general ignorance about the functioning of human brain and body, which doesn't suffice the methodological shortcomings of these theories (Glueck and Glueck, 1956; Hooten, 1939; Sheldon, 1949). The logical appearance of certain reports conducted at the end of 20th century rekindled the lifeline of biological theories (Moffitt and Henry, 1989; Hamparin et al., 1978). Theorists analyzed various reports in this regard and the biological theories were accepted in researchable context and people started arguing that these theories are not meant for going down the drain and it would be a mistake to write off these theories from consideration.

Biological theories are subdivided into following three types:

Which ground their arguments based on few inborn external bodily features ("*George Orwell in his book '1984' said that the worst thing in the world varies from individual to individual*", it is somewhat similar for the innate physical traits of criminals, which, according to biological theory, are different from the normal people).

Which attempt to argue that delinquent behavior is strongly connected with the hereditary or genetic characteristics of individuals.

Which attempt to postulate their arguments on the grounds of chemical, functional, or structural differences inside the body or particularly brain.

2.   The Positivist School of Thought

The classical theories of mid-1600's and late 1700's asserted that delinquent behavior is to be perceived because of rational choice rather than inherent attributes of criminals. The positivist school of thought disregarded the classical theories arguments and replaced it with "*Scientific Determinism*". It is basically focused on studying an individual rather than investigating other external or law-making factors. It is hard to provide an exact chronology of the positivist school of thought since it came to evolution simultaneously from different parts of the world. For instance, although the biological theories are tagged with positivism, the sole concept of positivism didn't develop until later than the development of early biological perception.

The biologist theories are considered as subtypes of positivist theory where positivism found its place during late 19th century exactly opposite of the guesswork and harshness of classical theories of early times. Positivist theory argued that classical theories are factually at odds when it comes to explaining the causes behind delinquent acts. One of the earliest positivist thinkers was Auguste Comte (1975), a French sociologist, who argued that social scientists should use the characteristics of positivism by emphasizing the various scientific techniques of observation and scientific experimentation to determine the delinquent behaviors of criminals. In the wake of positivism, people started seeing humans' behavior just like the organism in animal kingdom where behavior is influenced by biological antecedents alongside cultural and social norms. This also falls in line with one of the major goals of positivism i.e. uniting psychology with natural science (Graham, 2000).

The positive school of thought is literally incomplete without discussing Cesare Lombroso who had a strong opinion that people who fall prey to criminal activities are throwbacks and their delinquent behaviors need to be investigated by focusing on their inborn biological factors (Lombroso, 1876). His theory postulated that criminal bears the burden of criminality on the score that he is a born criminal (Gibson, 2002). It is the physical stigmata that defines a person a born criminal such as apelike long arms, flattened nose, long lower jaw, just to name a few (Horn, 2003). Lombroso identifies bodies as a propensity of delinquent behavior due to the inborn features of their interior states and external features. It is like interrogating the body to figure out the suspected delinquent behaviors associated with it. *Simply put, it provides us with a way to unfold the untold truths from the depth and the surface of the bodies*. Beneath the surface of continued criticism and controversies, instigated by even his most ardent advocates, didn't stop him for his continued investigation of biological positivism in a bid to find the differences between criminals and non-criminals.

The positivist Criminology is grounded on three primary elements:

The search for the possible triggers of delinquent behavior, whether sociological, psychological, or biological.

Applying scientific methods in a bid to put theories to test in contradiction with the observations of the world.

To base the treatment of the criminal on a medical rehabilitation model rather than punishing him on the grounds of law-violating or delinquent act.

3.   Physiognomy and Phrenology

Overview and Critical Analyses on Physiognomy

Physiognomy, an idea so compelling was born out of works of Pythagoras (Lambert, 1983), who was a scientist, mathematician, and philosopher during the time around 500 BCE. In matters of biological theories, Physiognomy formed a new stepping stone since the previous beliefs that an individual's behavior, character, and moral disposition can be determined by observing his physical features were believed to be very old.

Came from the Greek word '*physis*' which implies '*nature*' coupled with the word '*gnomon*' which means "*to interpret or to judge*". Theorists also subdivided it into three words i.e. '*physis* = nature, *Nomos* = Law and *Gnomon* = interpreter or judge, hence combined meaning is "*to know nature*" (Percival, 1999). It suffices the primary requirement of examining a person's outward appearance in a bid to evaluate his character or personality. Theorists also invoked the philosophical tradition of critical physiognomy which is a form of science that aims to provide us a scientific model in which the opinion about the inner mental states is determined by outer signs serving as evidence (Wack, 2014).

Physiognomy is an art that focuses on the face, making it a visible forefront against imposture and serving it as a visible signature of an individual. Lavater (1806) argued that physiognomy is a science of the correlation between the internal and external individual i.e. the reality of his inner side is visible superficially from his frontline face (Graham, 1961). The fundamentals of physiognomy reiterate that upon reading the countenance of an individual, his emotions and characteristics can be determined accordingly (Barasch and Bocchi, 1975). Medical practitioners particularly Sir Charles Bell (1774-1842) suggested that facial countenance of every individual are peculiar and his facial expressions reflect his emotions; this is the feature not shared by animals (Clue, 1993). The critical analysis of this concept demonstrates that mastication through jaws coupled with the adjacent musculature influence the structure of bones right at the junctions of muscle origin thus changing the overall facial structure in response.

An Italian scholar Giambattista della Porta published his book on Physiognomy in 1586 who gave a lifeline to this belief by investigating patients through medical practice and revealed a fact that the character of individuals and their appearance are strongly connected to each other. He classified humans on the grounds of their resemblance with animals in the sense that physical appearance of humans with certain animals fills the void of their characters like those animals. The persons who are similar to pigs will behave like pigs; similarly, those similar to donkeys will exhibit similar characteristics like stupidity and laziness we see in donkeys (Hoppe, 2008).

A legendary saying "*Face is the Index of mind*" also conforms the biological theory of physiognomy in the sense that an individual can hide his emotions and thoughts, he can try his best to hide his inner feelings, but he cannot hide his face which provides an ideal frontline platform to reveal his real inner self. Theorists also postulated that the amended inner-self of a person will reflect on his facial appearance as well (William, 1982). If an individual takes care of his inner self, the resultant appearance of the external will be modified accordingly (Graham, 1961). For instance, if a person changes his inner characteristics such as his temperament, attitude etc., then the change will also be reflected upon his face (Wells, 1982). This also instigates a critical thinking upon a hypothesis *"you can interpret a face based on his present but you cannot predict the future since he/she can change their inner self which is likely to replicate on their face"*.

Phrenology "Responsibility of Behavior Relocated to the Brain"

Before *'Phrenology'* was given birth by a German physiologist and neuroanatomist Franz Joseph Gall (1758 – 1828), the human emotions and behaviors were centered around and associated with various organs. For instance, the courage and love were associated with blood, bad temper and anger related to yellow bile in the gall bladder, sadness and depression were associated with black bile in the spleen, just to name a few (Gevaert, 2002).

Phrenology showed the opposite side of the picture *"localization of all the emotions and behavior to the central agency i.e. brain"* thus marking a major departure from earlier beliefs to the new downtown of brain. Came into existence from Greek words, *'phren i.e. mind'* and *'Logos i.e. knowledge'* phrenology relocated the responsibility for emotions and behavior from the bodily organs to the central repository of brain. In other words, the skull is the signature of character of a person alongside his mental faculties (Noel & Carlson, 1970). Previously, knowledge about the brain was scanty and all the brain related experiments were in their initial stages. Due to the least technology available at hand, science about the brain was in the middle of almost nowhere. At that bleak time of around 200 years ago, Joseph Gall gave birth to the idea of '*Phrenology*' which was surely a major breakthrough for making brain culpable for all the emotions and behavior (Zola-Morgan, 1995).

Despite that there have been various contradictions associated with the localization of the brain, Science cannot turn its back to Franz Joseph Galls work *"The Anatomy and Physiology of the Nervous System in General, and of the Brain in Particular"* since its historical importance remained there which literally filled the void of unknown (Gall & Spurzheim, 1796). It threw a great attention to the fact that all human behavior, including his faculties, sentiments, and propensities are in a particular shape due to the specific organization and manifestation of the brain. All these propositions were not specifically based on guesswork or assumptions, because Gall made numerous experimental measures on the skulls of his pupils, friends, and relatives in an effort to correlate various behavioral characteristics with the depressions and bumps on the surface of the skull (Gall, 1835). That's how he could unfold the practicability of his theory with comprehensive topological maps before the world.

4. Lombroso and Atavism

Lombroso's Theory of Crime with Respect to Atavism

Born in Venice, Italy (1835), philosopher of psychiatry and medicine and a renowned professor of criminal anthropology, Caesare Lombroso turned the study of criminology into a science which pulls its targets from the clinical case studies and empirical data (Gibson, 2002). Filling the void of a vast backlog in the field of crime and science, Lombroso's renowned publications with regards to theory of criminology marked an epoch in the field of criminological science making the reader gain an accurate and concise view of biological explanation based on which the criminals are predestined by their physical characteristics. (Kurella & Paul, 1911). His early interest in the field of psychiatry became an open secret with the advent of his "*Dissertation on Cretinism*" which was a widespread mental disorder in the areas of Italy which were on the breadline (Westwood, 2007).

As a young military doctor in the era of war-wretched country, Lombroso closely observed the bodies of soldiers coupled with psychological interviews, applied his own empirical methods in a bid to study the criminal rather than the crime itself (Horn, 2003). Apparently, it seemed like an imperfect theory against a perfect era in which science, specifically biology, was in its ascendancy. But later on, it turned out as his intellectual trajectory shattered the old patterns of investigating crime and created a new validity of criminal investigation. Even the current era of genetic revolution takes frequent help from Lombroso theory of crime from time to time (Cheema & Virk, 2012).

His early publication "*The Criminal Man*" conforms to the Charles Darwin's idea that primitive ancestry is the predestined force which makes criminal, a "*born criminal*" (Darwin, 1977). He was the one who portrayed that delinquent behavior, despite being a potent instrument of crime, is predestined to the criminal who is deprived of any kind of freewill. He also presented an idea that a criminal should be culpable on the grounds of his physical makeup, and not by the nature of the crime itself (Rajadhyaksha, 2006). He made the same point by observing 832 living prison inmates and measured / compared their body parts minutely (Frank, 2004). From this research, he unearthed the concept of '*Atavism*' which proposes a reversion to an earlier ancestral characteristic OR reappearance of features in someone after absence of numerous generations that is described later in this section. Lombroso believed that delinquent behavior is nothing short of an attack on legal system but crime results due to the biological differences between the criminals and non-criminals. In this regard, he referred atavism as '*throwback*' based on his investigations, and he hypothesized that females have a much stronger propensity of committing crime "*by passion*" (Lombroso, 2003). Although he based his theory on the concept that "*crime is nothing born criminals live without due to the inherited atavistic throwbacks*", still he proposed that one cannot ignore the environmental influence on the perspective of crime at large. For instance, a criminal is likely to commit crime due to illiteracy, climatic effect, or alcoholism.

'*Atavism*' took root in the soil of Lombroso's theory of criminology which reiterates that a criminal is likely to be a hereditary receptor in his evolutionary chain (Williams, 2012). Based on atavism, Lombroso performed legendary physical measurements of bodies such as bushy eyebrows, prominent eyebrows, dark skin, enlarged jaws, upturned and flattened nose, failure to blush, abnormal shape and size of head, premature skin wrinkling, excessive cheek bones, plenty of facial hair in women, just to name a few (Curran & Renzetti, 2001; Winslow & Zhang, 2008). According to Lombroso's atavism theory, a criminal is said to be a born criminal if he shows 5 or more than 5 times the proposed atavisms (Williams, 2012). It is worth mentioning here that under the shadow of activism, Lombroso published his first book "*The Criminal Man*" in 1876 where he propounded the fact that all criminals are actually "*born criminals*" and after 20 long years when he published his last book '*Crime*' alongside the 5th edition of "*The Criminal Man*", he fixed his theory by weighing up that environmental factors also hold the accountability for committing crime (Vold, 2002).

Critical Overview on Lombroso Activism Theory

After a strong hail and appreciation of Lombroso theory of activism from all corners, its adversaries gained strength from across the globe who almost rejected his postulations alongside unscientific methods and continually changing formations (Manheim, 1955). Based on the findings conducted by Adolf Baer and Charles Goring's "*The English Convict*" in 1913, the new theorists almost disapproved the postulations placed by Lombroso (Manheim, 1955). The scientific activism theory got its biggest refutation in the year 1942 when US Supreme Court negated the idea that certain criminal attributes were inheritable (Oklahoma, 1942). Despite this disapproval, science continued to take leverage from Lombroso's atavism, particularly in 1968 when USA scientists figured out the inherited abnormality of XYY chromosomes in criminals (Briken et al., 2006; Baker et al., 1970). Again, the scientific validity of chromosome related abnormality was discredited by the law due to undependable scientific dependence, still Lombroso theory of activism left its deep effects on further evaluation of atavism in future (Denno, 1988).

In the presence of latest technology today and the allergic lines stated by Hans Gross *'we may say that it is finished', and 'the dream of the "Born Criminal", "the natural delinquent" as a special human type has been dreamed to a finish"*, it seems like writing on Lombroso's theory of atavism might be nothing short of wasting lines, still it paves the way for testing this theory on a broader scale using latest technological tools. The ideas of Lombroso do not seem to be dead because of the heated discussions and disputes still in the air. After all the criticisms in place, the Lombroso theory might be requiring a little tethering of the latest technology to rekindle the systematic linking of body traits with the delinquent behavior of criminals.

5.   Body Type Theories

The search for the born criminal wasn't surrendered when William Sheldon (1949) went to the extra mile in linking crime with the physical physique of the criminals, a legendary idea commonly known as '*Somatotype theory*'. Sheldon, while investigating *more of the same approach* (since Lombroso linked the facial characteristics of criminals), drew upon three types of bodies at large:

Ectomorphs: who are very sensitive in nature, like their privacy, and fall in the category of introverts.

Mesomorphs: who have a strong desire for power, they are aggressive and active.

Endomorphs: who are extrovert, comfortable, and relaxed in their activities.

In a bid to grant considerable latitude for being a born criminal, Sheldon tested his theory on 4000 male college students and 200 imprisoned juvenile offenders. He drew upon a conclusion that most of the delinquent behavior criminals were Mesomorphs and a very few falls in the category of Ectomorphs. On the flip side, Endomorphs showed no considerable differences (Sheldon, 1949). Furthering this research, Sheldon Glueck and Eleanor Glueck analyzed 500 delinquent bodies with 500 non-delinquents and corroborated the same i.e. the delinquents had a strong attraction towards Mesomorphs at large (Glueck & Glueck, 1956). Similar findings were concluded by Juan Cortes and

Florence Gatti (1972) when they conducted the experiments on 100 high school students and 100 delinquents. Without leaving any yawning gaps between William Sheldon's theory and his contemporary theories, Sean Maddan et al. (2008) gave a further boost by comparing the delinquency behavior with regards to the "*Body Mass Index*" BMI. The research landed on the same grounds where Mesomorphs were more likely to be involved in delinquent behaviors at large.

Despite that the body type theories don't fill the void of uncanny prescient, yet they point towards a strong relationship between '*temperament*' and the "*body type*". The experiments conducted by Adrian Rain, David Farrington et al. (1998) on 1130 children revealed the facts that the large body size at the age of 3 increases the propensity of aggressive behavior at the age 11.

Critical Review on Body Type Theories

There seems to be no yawning gaps between the results conducted in the perspective of body type theories, still the on-ground realities might present logical evidences to the contrary. For instance, Mesomorphs, due to their fit body, might be more effective in draining out their desires and frustrations as compared to the other children. Perhaps, they are more muscular than others; that's why delinquent gangs encourage them to be part of their criminal activities OR maybe Mesomorphs assume themselves fit and muscular enough to be part of their community. Perhaps the physical fitness persuades them to fill the void of a tough guy in an area and they presume themselves as toughest guy in their particular area. A recent research also made the same point that male street offenders show criminal behavior like substance abuse and offending etc. to show others their '*manhood*' and they presume that the incapacity to commit crime is a sure sign of weakness tagged with the weak people (Copes & Hochstetler, 2003).

6. Genetic Theories

At the face of it, crime marks a whammy for a society; on the positive note, it either fixes old theories or gives birth to a new one. In this regard, biological theories lost much of their grounds in 1960's on the score that people started deeming that the theories were being misused and cast a shadow over the issues of discrimination and prejudice at large. A new lifeline was bestowed to them by the new advances in genetics which took science beyond the reach of human retina thus providing more linkage between hereditary factors and delinquent behavior (Rajadhyaksha, 2006). Despite giving a make-shift breakthrough to biological theories in shape of genetic explanation, people are still hesitant to investigate delinquent behavior through genetics ways and means (Lappe, 1994).

Genetic inheritance studies emphasize on two important aspects of studying delinquent behavior as follows:

Analyzing the behavior of twins in this regard *"Twin Studies"*

Analyzing the behavior of adopted offspring with regards to their biological blueprint.

Twin Studies and Adoption Studies

Numerous studies on twins argue that genetics provide a potent relation to crime in the sense that MZ (*identical twins*) portray more similarity in behavior as compared to the DZ (*twins born out of two separate eggs by separate sperm*) (Lange, 1929). 30 pairs of twins were put under observation and the propensity of criminality was much more in MZ twins. Furthering this observation, an extensive research was conducted by Karl O. Christiansen in 1974, who conducted a broad research on 3586 twin pairs in Denmark who were born between 1881 and 1910. He drew upon that the propensity of an individual MZ twin to be engaged in criminal behavior considering his other pair is already a criminal was found to be 50% when compared to the DZ twins. Later research conducted by David C. Rowe (1983) and his associates also supported the same alongside an addition that more delinquent peers were associated with MZ twins as compared to the DZ twins.

Adoption studies brought in a second method of investigation in which a twin is adopted by some party other than their biological parents. This theory proposes that any similarity between an adopted child and his real biological parents depicts a sure sign of genetic similarity. A study conducted by Mednick, Gabrielli and Hutchins (1984) on 14427 Danish children who were adopted between the periods of 1924-1947 depicted that their propensity towards antisocial behavior was due to their biological patterns. Walters and White (1989) while highlighting the methodological and theoretical hindrances associated with the approach of adoption studies, reiterates the fact that genetics and environment both shake hands to shape up the criminal behavior. All these facts and figures clear indicate that "*Crime takes the most cautious genetic path which makes the genetic predisposition to criminal behavior, a hard, but a true reality in every sense of the word.*"

7. Contemporary Genetic Theories

The genetic explanations of crime provide us with proofs that there are valid reasons to be vigilant for all types of theories which partly or fully explain delinquent behavior under certain circumstances. Since humanity is still in the thick of investigating delinquent behavior in every way possible, it's worth mentioning the internal factors which continue to create new investigative avenues for the old criminal behaviors such as:

Heart rate

Brain activity

Effect of diet and hormones

The criminal behavior is frequently associated with a delinquency "*autonomic hypoactivity*" that shows a resting heart rate generally found in males and proven by various samples collected from USA, New Zealand, Mauritius, Germany, England, and Canada (Raine, 2002). Low resting heart rate also bore the burden of strongest and consistent criminal behavior when David Farrington (1997) minutely analyzed 48 biological, psychological, and sociological independent variables.

The type of brain activity the brain is holding inside also marks a line between a delinquent and normal behavior i.e. how the brain is processing the information inside its structured boundary. For instance, literature confirms that some brains either produce fewer or more chemicals under certain conditions than the particular person actually require. Those with violent anger and aggression are susceptible to be lacking the desired production of '*serotonin*' (Fishbein, 1990; Moffitt et al., 1998). Latest research also revealed the fact that the people with "*behavioral inhibition dysfunction abnormality*" are tagged with reduced brain activity in certain areas of the brain like bilateral temporal region, posterior cingulated gyrus, and left dorsolateral prefrontal cortex (Rubia et al., 2008). In 1848, a railroad worker Phineas Gage underwent a freakish explosive accident in which 3 feet long and 13 pounds weight tamping iron pierced across his anterior frontal cortex of head through his cheekbone. Magically, he survived the crucial accident with a dramatic shift in his behavior. Before the accident, he was a friendly man, well-disciplined and responsible but after the accident, he was nothing but the contrary i.e. irresponsible, indiscipline, and impulsive (Macmillan, 2002).

Hormones and delinquent behavior are closely related and their relation has been underscored many times in the literature. The types of hormones that are generally responsible for aggression are reproductive hormones (Shah & Roth, 1974). Numerous studies second the correlation of *Androgen* (male sex hormone found in testosterone) with aggressive behavior (Booth & Osgood, 1993; Kreuz & Rose, 1972). Also note down that the level of testosterone varies with social factors, exercise, and diet (Katz & Chambliss, 1991; Nassi & Abramowitz, 1976). There have been numerous arguments afoot in compliance with hormonal changes and aggressive behavior which also supports the fact that aggressive behavior also raises the levels of testosterone (Harris, 1999).

The contemporary genetic theories as described above provide new avenues of investigating delinquent behavior of criminals. What's more! The male sex offenders were put under treatment to control their male sexual urges through inserting female hormones. This has been an effective treatment for a few types of sex offences; still much investigation is needed in genetic theories to curb other types of delinquent behaviors and crimes at large.

8.   Recent Biological Theories

The latest century tagged with the new technology is characterized by a great boom in biological theories across the globe. The new biological streams are stretching out resulting in the formation of new explanatory areas of already studied theories. In an effort to touch new areas of crime and delinquent behavior, the new biological investigations are providing us enriched view by collaborating with other theories and factors. *This collaboration doesn't reflect their retreatment from their defined positions; the collaboration is helping us creating a grouped net of propositions in a more systematic way.* No doubt that these theories don't fill the void of various other problems because the interdisciplinary communications and integrations are not always easy and compatible as it seems (Schlieifer, 2000).

According to Moffitt (1993), a person develops in terms of maturing and learning throughout his life cycle i.e. Maturing is purely internal bodily situation whilst learning is attributed to the external environment. In this regard, Moffitt argues that criminal behavior is amalgamation of a person's intrinsic genetics aftereffects coupled with the reflection of his/her external environment alike. The biological theories also confirmed that the occurrence of neurological deficits in children can trigger *"Life-course-persistent antisocial behavior (LCP)"* (Moffitt & Caspi, 2001). The children affected with this syndrome generally don't adhere to the social etiquettes and norms and the ailment, in adulthood, attacks them with chronic and severe aggressiveness (Moffit, 1993).

Adolescent is the period when a juvenile act in a revolting behavior against the society, his elders, in a bid to search for his own identity and ideals and to test his limits against the odds (Macek, 2003). The period of adolescence is linked with an antisocial behavior called *Adolescence limited antisocial behavior (ADL)*. Numerous theories have accepted the need of connecting biological theories with social elements so that the possibilities of treatment and prevention of crime can be increased (Walsh & Beaver, 2009). Hence the advancement in biological theories on the shoulders of latest technological tools will surely pave the way to further investigate the ins and outs of criminal behavior.

9.   Summary

The "*Biological Theories*" are legendary theories which bear the burden of providing an insight of human behaviors that conflict with societal expectations by examining individual's characteristics. The biologist theories are considered as subtypes of positivist theory where positivism found its place during late 19th century exactly opposite of the guesswork and harshness of classical theories of early times. The positive school of thought is literally incomplete without discussing Cesare Lombroso who had a strong opinion that people who fall prey to criminal activities are throwbacks. Physiognomy is an art that focuses on the face, making it a visible forefront against imposture and serving it as a visible signature of an individual. Phrenology showed the opposite side of the picture "*localization of all the emotions and behavior to the central agency i.e. brain*". Lombroso theory of atavism states that Criminals are atavist throwbacks. '*Atavism*' took root in the soil of Lombroso's theory of criminology which reiterates that a criminal is likely to be a hereditary receptor in his evolutionary chain. A new lifeline was bestowed to biological theories by the new advances in genetics which took science beyond the reach of human retina thus providing more linkage between hereditary factors and delinquent behavior.

10.   References

Baker, D., Telfer, M. A., Richardson, C. E., & Clark, G. R. (1970). Chromosome errors in men with antisocial behavior: Comparison of selected men with Klinefelter's syndrome and XYY chromosome pattern. *JAMA*, *214*(5), 869-878.

Barasch, M. (1975). Character and Physiognomy: Bocchi on Donatello's St. George: A renaissance text on expression in art. *Journal of the History of Ideas*, *36*(3), 413-430.

Booth, A., & Osgood, D. W. (1993). The influence of testosterone on deviance in adulthood: Assessing and explaining the relationship. *Criminology*, *31*(1), 93-117.

Briken, P., Habermann, N., Berner, W., & Hill, A. (2006). XYY chromosome abnormality in sexual homicide perpetrators. *American Journal of Medical Genetics Part B: Neuropsychiatric Genetics*, *141*(2), 198-200.

Cheema, A. A., & Virk, A. (2012). Reinventing Lombroso in the era of genetic revolution: Whether criminal justice system actually imparts justice or is based on 'convenience of assumption'? *International Journal of Criminology and Sociological Theory*, *5*(2).

Christiansen, K. O. (1974). *Seriousness of criminality and concordance among Danish twins*. na.

Comte, A. (1975). *Auguste Comte and positivism: The essential writings*. Transaction Publishers.

Copes, H., & Hochstetler, A. (2003). Situational construction of masculinity among male street thieves. *Journal of Contemporary Ethnography*, *32*(3), 279-304.

Cortes, J. B., & Gatti, F. M. (1972). Delinquency and crime: A biopsychosocial approach. Seminar press.

Cule, J. (1993). The enigma of facial expression: Medical interest in metoposcopy. *Journal of the history of medicine and allied sciences*, *48*(3), 302-319.

Curran, D. J., & Renzetti, C. M. (2001). *Theories of crime*. Pearson College Division.

Darwin, C. (1977). The collected papers of Charles Darwin.

Denno, D. W. (1988). Human biology and criminal responsibility: Free will or free ride? *University of Pennsylvania Law Review*, *137*(2), 615-671.

Farrington, D. P. (1997). The relationship between low resting heart rate and violence. In *Biosocial Bases of Violence* (pp. 89-105). Springer US.

Fishbein, D. H. (1990). Biological perspectives in criminology. *Criminology*.

Frank, S. (2004). Criminology Today – An Integrative Introduction.

Gall, F. J. (1835). *On the functions of the brain and of each of its parts: with observations on the possibility of determining the instincts, propensities, and talents, or the moral and intellectual dispositions of men and animals, by the configuration of the brain and head* (Vol. 1). Marsh, Capen & Lyon.

Gall, F. J., & Spurzheim, G. (1796). The anatomy and physiology of the nervous system in general, and of the brain in particular.

Gevaert, C. (2002). The evolution of the lexical and conceptual field of ANGER in Old and Middle English. *Costerus*, *141*, 275-299.

Gibson, M. (2002). *Born to crime: Cesare Lombroso and the origins of biological criminology* (p. 22). Westport, CT: Praeger.

Glueck, S., & Glueck, E. (1956). Physique and delinquency.

Graham, J. (1961). "Lavater's Physiognomy": A checklist. *The Papers of the Bibliographical Society of America*, *55*(4), 297-308.

Graham, G. (2000). Behaviorism.

Hamparian, D. M., Schuster, R., Dinitz, S., & Conrad, J. P. (1978). The violent few: a study of dangerous juvenile offenders. *Lexington, MA, DC Heath*.

Harris, J. A. (1999). Review and methodological considerations in research on testosterone and aggression. *Aggression and violent behavior*, *4*(3), 273-291.

Hooton, E. A. (1939). *Crime and the Man*. Cambridge, Mass., Harvard U.

Hoppe, B. (2008). Physiognomy in science and art: Properties of a Natural Body Inferred from Its Appearance. In *Science Matters: Humanities as Complex Systems* (pp. 52-73). World Scientific.

Horn, D. G. (2003). *The criminal body: Lombroso and the anatomy of deviance*. Psychology Press.

Katz, J., & Chambliss, W. J. (1991). Biology and Crime (From Criminology, P 245-271, 1991, Joseph F Sheley, ed.).

Kreuz, L. E., & Rose, R. M. (1972). Assessment of aggressive behavior and plasma testosterone in a young criminal population. *Psychosomatic Medicine*, *34*(4), 321-332.

Kurella, H., & Paul, E. (1911). *Cesare Lombroso: A modern man of science*. Rebman limited.

Lambert, E. Z., & Tytler, G. (1983). Physiognomy in the European Novel: Faces and Fortunes.

Lange, J. (1929). Leistungen der Zwillingpathologie für die Psychiatrie [The importance of twin pathology for psychiatry]. *Allgemeine Zeitschrift für Psychiatrie und psychisch-gerichtliche Medicin, 90*, 122-142.

Lappé, M. (1994). *Justice and the human genome project*. University of California Press.

Lombroso, C. (1911). Criminal Man. [1876]. *New York: GP Putnam*.

Lombroso, C., & Ferrero, G. (2003). *Criminal woman, the prostitute, and the normal woman*. Duke University Press.

MACEK, P. (2003). Adolescence. 2. vyd. Praha. *Portál, 2*.

Macmillan, M. (2002). *An odd kind of fame: Stories of Phineas Gage*. MIT Press.

Maddan, S., Walker, J. T., & Miller, J. M. (2008). Does size really matter? A reexamination of sheldon's somatotypes and criminal behavior. *The Social Science Journal, 45*(2), 330-344.

Manheim, H. (1955). Group Problems in Crime and Punishment and Other Studies in Criminology and Criminal Law.

Mednick, S. A., Gabrielli, W. F., & Hutchings, B. (1984). Genetic influences in criminal convictions: Evidence from an adoption cohort. *Science, 224*(4651), 891-894.

Moffitt, T. E., & Henry, B. (1989). Neuropsychological assessment of executive functions in self-reported delinquents. *Development and Psychopathology, 1*(02), 105-118.

Moffitt, T. E., Brammer, G. L., Caspi, A., Fawcett, J. P., Raleigh, M., Yuwiler, A., & Silva, P. (1998). Whole blood serotonin relates to violence in an epidemiological study. *Biological psychiatry*, *43*(6), 446-457.

Moffitt, T. E. (1993). Adolescence-limited and life-course-persistent antisocial behavior: a developmental taxonomy. *Psychological review*, *100*(4), 674.

Moffitt, T. E., & Caspi, A. (2001). Childhood predictors differentiate life-course persistent and adolescence-limited antisocial pathways among males and females. *Development and psychopathology*, *13*(02), 355-375.

Nassi, A. J., & Abramowitz, S. I. (1976). From phrenology to psychosurgery and back again: biological studies of criminality. *American journal of orthopsychiatry*.

Noel, P. S., & Carlson, E. T. (1970). Origins of the Word" Phrenology". *American Journal of Psychiatry*, *127*(5), 694-697.

Percival, M. (1999). *The appearance of character: physiognomy and facial expression in eighteenth-century France* (Vol. 47). MHRA.

Raine, A., Reynolds, C., Venables, P. H., Mednick, S. A., & Farrington, D. P. (1998). Fearlessness, stimulation-seeking, and large body size at age 3 years as early predispositions to childhood aggression at age 11 years. *Archives of general psychiatry*, *55*(8), 745-751.

Raine, A. (2002). Annotation: The role of prefrontal deficits, low autonomic arousal, and early health factors in the development of antisocial and aggressive behavior in children. *Journal of Child Psychology and Psychiatry*, *43*(4), 417-434.

Rajadhyaksha, M. (2006). Condemned by Birth: The implications of Genetics for the Theories of Crime and Punishment. *Socio-Legal Rev.*, *2*, 85.

Rowe, D. C. (1983). Biometrical genetic models of self-reported delinquent behavior: A twin study. *Behavior Genetics, 13*(5), 473-489.

Rubia, K., Halari, R., Smith, A. B., Mohammed, M., Scott, S., Giampietro, V., ... & Brammer, M. J. (2008). Dissociated functional brain abnormalities of inhibition in boys with pure conduct disorder and in boys with pure attention deficit hyperactivity disorder. *American Journal of Psychiatry.*

Schleifer, R. (2000). The difficulties of interdisciplinarity: Cognitive science, rhetoric, and time-bound knowledge.

Shah, S. A., & Roth, L. H. (1974). Biological and psychophysiological factors in criminality. *Handbook of criminology.*

Sheldon, W. H. (1949). Varieties of delinquent youth: an introduction to constitutional psychiatry.

v Oklahoma, S. 316 US 535 (1942). *Griswold v Connecticut, 381.*

Vold, B. Snipes (2002). Theoretical Criminology.

Wack, D. K. (2014). Wittgenstein's critical physiognomy.

Walsh, A., & Beaver, K. M. (2009). Biosocial criminology. In *Handbook on crime and deviance* (pp. 79-101). Springer New York.

Walters, G. D., & White, T. W. (1989). Heredity and crime: Bad genes or bad research? *Criminology, 27*(3), 455-485.

Wells, R.D.B. Faces we meet and how to read them. Vickers, London, p 14 (1870).

Westwood, L. (2007). Criminal Man. *Social History of Medicine, 20*(2), 420-422.

William, M. An introduction to study of physiognomy In : The mind in the face, Fowler, London (1882).

Williams, K. S. (2012). *Textbook on criminology*. Oxford University Press, USA.

Winslow, R. W., & Zhang, S. (2008). *Criminology: A global perspective*. Pearson Prentice Hall.

Zola-Morgan, S. (1995). Localization of brain function: The legacy of Franz Joseph Gall (1758-1828). *Annual Review of Neuroscience, 18*(1), 359-383.

Chapter 6
Deterrence and Rational Choice Theories

1. Steep Difference Between Deterrence Doctrine and Rational Choice Theory

It is so easy to describe "*deterrence*" whilst it is extremely hard to break the thread of criminal behavior despite the worthiness of its existence in the criminal justice system. The notion of deterrence doctrine is quite simple---Deterrence reflects the exclusion of a criminal behavior on the score of the fear of punishment or sanctions (Andenaes, 1974). The *deterrence theory* assumes that people act on the grounds of their rational decisions i.e. an act of committing crime is based on the information about the possible consequences of that crime. In other words, when a person tries to size an opportunity of crime at a particular place and time, the deterrence theory pokes its tongue out, makes him calculate the pain of legal punishment thus cancelling out the motivation for the crime in response.

The "*Rational Choice Theory*", on the other hand, presents man, as a calculating (same as deterrence theory) creature who will manage to commit crime on the grounds of minimizing pain and maximizing pleasure. The rational choice theory gives a reflection to his choice during committing crime i.e. before he sets out and decides to commit crime against the law, he is likely to calculate the options which minimize costs and maximize payoff.

Deterrence and Rational Choice Theory share a great deal of common things, where RCT being a much wider theory when compared to deterrence. One can say, they both are almost the same thing, where RCT being the subtype of the deterrence theory (Miller, 2009).

2.   Deterrence Doctrine: Classical Philosophies

The deterrence theory has been extensively complemented in the early works of classical philosophers primarily Thomas Hobbes England (1588-1679), Cesare Beccaria Italy (1738-1794), and Jeremy Bentham England (1748-1832). In a bid to protest against the classical theories of punishment, which according to them were a gross inconvenience to the legal systems that had been ruling the Europeans for over 100 decades, they posited a new foundation of deterrence theory thus ruling out classical spiritual rationalization of crime on which the old theories were based (Beccaria, 2009; Norrie, 1984).

Thomas Hobbes presents man as a creation who is neither bad, nor good. According to him, there is but too much reason to see man as a creature that pursues his own self-interest at large, and doesn't bother to harm others in the process of gaining his own personal safety, material benefits, and social reputation (Hobbes, 2006). He also argued that the punishment for committing a crime must be bigger than the advantages one might procure upon committing a crime. Deterrence is what decreases the probability of committing crime in a society. Hobbes sees deterrence as a vantage point where criminality is decreased through the idea of "*Social Contract*" i.e. social contract is of paramount importance in the sense that it squeezes down your liberty and other people's liberty to save everybody from similar victimization in the overall benefit of the society. For example, nobody is allowed to snatch your car by hook or crook; similarly, you are not allowed to snatch some other person's car with all your might and main. Hence this social contract saves you from the same victimization and everybody else in a bid to trade-off everybody's little freedom (for not snatching by force) for the potential gain of the whole society (Miller et al., 2011).

Put this down to partisanship, Cesare Beccaria also uprooted the old stereotype notions by following the legacy of Hobbes and challenged the rights of states in the perspective of punishing the criminals. He found no cause to do otherwise than rejecting the states right on the score that *"Punishments are unjust when their severity exceeds what is necessary to achieve deterrence"* (Beccaria, 1963). According to him, it is the sole responsibility of the state to increase the cost of committing crimes over the benefits of indulging in criminal activities. His contemporary Jeremy Bentham argued that every person on this planet is administered by two independent masters i.e. pleasure and pain. He had a strong opinion about happiness and he believed that state is responsible to promote the happiness in a society, by sticking to the rule of punishment and reward (Bentham, 1879). He held a strong opinion against severe punishment to deter criminal behavior; simply put, it is the state's responsibility to broaden the happiness in a society by lessening the pain and increasing the pleasure of community.

The classical criminology deterrence doctrine, through the unflagging energy and unshaken struggle of criminologists of those times, positively stamp out crime from the religion. At that time, religion was indeed, flirting with Crime to a considerable extent. Dealing Crime as an entity of religion beyond the control and comprehension of human senses wasn't far-fetched. Consistent decline in the formation of comprehensible criminal justice system put the societies '*underwater*'. The legal systems were worth less than accusations on them. There was no guarantee that the legal system's downward spiral wouldn't continue if those three criminologists won't had contributed their share. *The starkest of these was a fall in understanding crime as a myth which is beyond human control.*

It wasn't considerably repaired till the onset of these three criminologists because people were wrongly fostering the notion that Crime theories can accomplish almost nothing. After they contributed their share, Crime literally divorced all types of myths and superstitions of the religion that put everything beyond the reach of human comprehension. What's more! People started seeing crime as an act of freewill. This implies that "Crime took the form of freewill in terms of deciding about committing a crime thus they found a way to express crime because of rational choice (Cornish and Clarke, 1987). The facts and figures about crime proposed by classical criminologists paved the way for the later legal reformers to refine rational choice theory keeping deterrence as one of its major goals (Paternoster and Brame, 1997).

3. Types of Punishment in Deterrence Theory

The three water marks of theory of deterrence (*certainty, severity, and celerity*) were based on the works of Hobbes, Baccaria, and Bentham. As their names indicate, the three components of deterrence speak for themselves:

'C*ertainty*' is about making sure whenever a criminal falls prey to a delinquent act, punishment must take place

'Severity' implies that the punishment should be severe enough to ensure the criminal fall short of the perception of gaining benefits over the punishment upon committing a crime.

'Celerity' reflects the swiftness of the application of punishment in a bid to deter crime.

Beneath the surface of controversy over the results gained by deterrence theory and its components, theorists do have faith in believing that if a punishment is tagged with certainty, severity, and celerity, a rational criminal will measure the costs of crime, and likely to refrain from committing such act if the potential losses are greater than the expected gains (McCarthy, 2002; Piliavin et al., 1986). This is exactly what Gibbs underscored in 1986 as:

"In a legal context, the term 'deterrence' refers to any instance in which an individual contemplates a criminal act but refrains entirely from or curtails the commission of such

an act because he or she perceives some risk of legal punishment and fears the consequence."

4. Importance of Perception in Deterrence

According to Deterrence theory, the actual chance of punishment seems plausible, but leaving crime onto the mercies of actual punishment won't give a huge blow to the criminal psychology unless it is coupled with the "*perception of punishment*" (Apel and Pogarsky, 2009). People are likely to do away with crime in the present if they foresee punishment in the future (Nagin and Pogarsky, 2001). On the contrary, if the criminals perceive that they have a very little probability of being caught and penalized, the actual punishments and imprisonments in place would have almost negligible effect on crime rate (Bursik, Grasmick and Chamlin, 1990).

An empirical research conducted by Canadian Criminologists Jean-Luc Bacher and Etinne Blais (2007) revealed a tangible association between perception and deterrence. They sent a written threat to a random sample of insured people in a bid to inform them that any type of insurance fraud would leave deep scars on their lifelines in shape of punishments. Afterwards, they made a comparison of insurance claims with those people to whom they didn't send any threatening letter. A clear sign of deterred illegal activity was seen where perception acted as a bulwark against the entity of fraud (crime).

5.   Certainty of Punishment and Deterrence

Based on the deterrence theory, if the arrest and conviction falls in line with the criminal act without any runaround, even the most notorious criminal may refrain from committing crime since he would perceive an act of crime similarly to pouring fuel on fires as the risks of crime go beyond its rewards (Daniels et al., 1999). Prevalence of certainty of punishment will ensure that only the most irrational criminal mindset will seek pleasure in committing crime (Nagin and Pogarsky, 2001). In this scenario, the state should grapple with the issue by rolling into minds of the rational people, convincing them to avoid the risk of crime always. "*Project Safe Neighborhoods*" initiated by US President George W. Bush is worth mentioning here where the US government ought to convince the citizens by streaming into media campaigns that holding handgun was a serious crime that can subject to prosecution, severe punishment, and prison sentences. The outcome of those media campaign was encouraging in shape of sudden decline in gun crimes (O'Shea, 2007).

The flip side of the coin shows that certainty of punishment looks good on the paper but the criticism is set to get even worse, not better in the coming years due to significant variation in its implementation. The bleak picture shows that almost 80% of the serious offenses do not result in apprehension. Even police don't bother to arrest suspects who lead to violence in their private disputes (Klinger, 1995). Deterrence theory has no lifeline if it doesn't fall in line with the certainty of punishment and it amounts to sow a strong belief in offenders that whatever they do against the social norms, they won't be severely punished.

6. Severity of Punishment and Deterrence

It stands to reason that severity of punishment will surely deter the criminal activities. Apparently, it looks good and rational because severity in punishment is likely to show great potential of blowback against the crime; as a matter of fact, a bulk of research on severity punishment regarding deterrence effects unfolds '*severity*' as halting and unreliable (Doob and Webster, 2003). Let's consider a severity of imposing longer periods of imprisonment. The roots of the mistrust in this theory can be traced back to a detailed study conducted in 1999 by theorists Gendreau, Cullen and Goggin (1999) who conducted a Meta-analysis on 336052 offenders and found out that the rate of recidivism gained a 3% in longer prison sentences. It accounted an increase of 7% in case when the imprisonment was applied by a community based sanction. Theorists have a high opinion that certainty of punishment is much more beneficial in deterring crime as compared to severity of punishment (Nagin, 1998).

7. Celerity of Punishment and Deterrence

The 3rd leg of deterrence theory talks about the positive contribution of speed of punishment; faster application of punishment after a criminal act will deter the criminal mindset and the crime rate (Clark, 1988). Otherwise, the criminal mindset would perceive crime as an instant pleasure whilst punishment as an entity far away. Same is the mindset of young criminals with long history of criminality (Pogarsky, Kim and Paternoster, 2005). The deterrence law is likely to go on a chopping block if there is a considerable lag between the arrest and punishment. For instance, in USA justice system, the time period between an arrest of a murderer and his execution is normally 10 years, let alone talking about the bargaining time the prisoners seek in plea negotiations for life sentence in a bid to avoid death penalty which also negates the celerity of punishment (Keckler, Econ & Poly, 2006). In a bid to strip crime of its power, in nearly every arena to strengthen the entity of deterrence, the significant lag between crime and punishment should be decreased to deeply affect the criminal mindset (Listoken, Crim & Rev, 2007).

8. Deterrence Theory and Criminal Justice System

In the presence of metastasizing properties of crime all around the globe, the deterrence theory remains a key foundation for criminal justice systems. The continuous rise and acceptance of deterrence theory has passed policies like construction of sufficient prisons, sentencing severities, beyond doubt certainty of conviction and sentencing, and a rise in law enforcing force. An earnest and empirically based deterrence research began in 1968 when theorists tested this theory and concluded that both certainty and severity of punishment might deter the metastasizing homicide. Before that, the theorists were only focusing on the deterrence philosophy, and its implications for punishment. Charles Tittle (1969) supported this theory with a condition that severity would only be effective if it is befitted with certainty as well (Tittle, 1969). The later studies in 1970's counteracted the empirical findings but the process gave a good start to the modern deterrence theory. Ross (1984) argued that severity enhancing policies instigate an effect that reduces the certainty of punishment. The modern deterrence theory, in terms of the empirical findings on severity of punishment, concludes that severity of punishment like the death penalty doesn't act as a catalyst to deter murder.

9.   Research and Findings in Deterrence Theory

Research and findings in deterrence theory would continue to be waged in criminological research because criminals fall prey to their brain's justifications behind their delinquent desires but this doesn't let go off the perception of punishment nor it makes punishment a relative term; the fact of the punishment is still there but its temporarily broken into false calculations during the course of committing crime. Up to 1990's, the studies on deterrence have been grouped in 3 parts primarily the experimental and quasi experimental, aggregate, and perceptual deterrence studies (Nagin, 1998). Different researches and studies on deterrence with regards to empirical observations and the ground realities have long been marching in different directions; despite that various laws being enacted throughout the recent decades, there is a little credible evidence that severity of punishment plays a pivotal role in deterring crime rates (Tonry, 2008). Criminologists argue that crime cannot be strip of its power with the aid of severe capital punishment as compared to the other types of less-severe penalties (Blumstein, Cohen and Nagin, 1978).

10. The Effects of Severe Sanctions

It's an open secret that sanctions and enforcement of laws can deter crime and the behavior of delinquency to some extent such as over-speeding, compliance to tax laws, parking laws, and the relevant offending circumstances, still there is plausible evidence against the severity of punishment vs. certainty and promptness (Klepper and Nagin, 1989). A very few theorists have attempted to formulate the effects of severe sanctions on would-be offenders despite that they did conclude to a vantage point emphasizing the fact that every single execution saves around 18 lives (Dezhabakhsh, Rubin and Shepherd, 2003). The theory was hypothesized to deter the would-be offenders. But the roots of mistrust in this theory can be traced by the disapproval of some other theorists such as Fagan, Zimring and Geller (2005), Wolfers and Donohue (2006). Even a few theorists have a strong opinion that sever capital punishment paves the ways of increasing brutalization effect on criminals thus increasing the numbers of would-be offenders in response (Katz, Levitt and Shustorovich, 2003).

One can infer that whether the research has not been able to gather enough evidence to provide this theory with a valid proof OR severe punishment has zero deterrent effect on would-be offenders. Investigators during 1970's and 80's made considerable research in a bid to investigate whether the increase in penalties reduce crime rates such as punishment of 5 years for carrying a gun during robbery etc. The thing is, increase in penalties only made short-term effects and nothing else (Tonry, 1996). Two later studies also corroborated the same pattern of findings (McCoy and McManimon, 2004; Merritt, Fain, and Turner, 2006). One reason might be because the would-be offenders are mostly unaware about the real severity of the criminal acts since they don't study law and justice system at large (Roberts et al., 2002), let alone talking about the implementation as per announced. Cook (1980) also argued that *"there exist feasible actions on the part of the criminal justice system that may be effective in deterring [certain] crimes .... [But the] studies do not demonstrate that all types of crimes are potentially deterrable, and certainly they provide little help in predicting the effects of any specific governmental action"*. Von Hirsh (1999) also endorsed the same by concluding that firm evidence has yet to be found by the theorists with regards to the linkage between increasing penalties and the enhancement of deterrence in crime rates. Even by applying the *null hypothesis approach*, Doob and Webster (2003) concluded the absence of a plausible body of evidence in this regard.

No doubt that no criminal justice system in the world would consider doing away with the penalties altogether, however, research would continue furthering and exploring it. The induction of new technology in the system on a broad range of deterrence subjects is likely to broaden its horizon in the coming years; maybe we get enough evidence with regards to the linkage between criminal sanctions and deterrence in general.

11. Deterrence and Perception

There have already been so many arguments afoot regarding *'Perception''*, still we don't know how perceptions are engendered at a place and time. The good news with regards to deterrence theory is, perceptions do not stick to their original formation; they modify themselves through experiences of the person himself and the experiences of others alike. In fact, the perception of the risk of punishment is inversely proportional to the process of committing crime and getting away with it accordingly. For instance, if an offender commits crime and get away without any hassle, his perception of risk of punishment will be modified downward or vice versa. In literature, this effect is called by the name *"experiential effect"* (Saltzman et al., 1982). Paternoster et al. (1982) concluded that the newbie's or novice offenders possess elevated sanction risk perceptions as compared to the experienced criminals. It is worth mentioning the study conducted by Lochner (2001) in both the datasets of NLSY97 and NYS where he figured out that non-arrested offenders showed lower perceptions with regards to punishment certainty. An interesting fact was echoed as "this relationship was good enough in cases of serious crimes but it didn't have a considerable impact on minor offenses." Another study was conducted by Anwar and Loughran (2011) where high risk youth offenders were included who were prosecuted for a serious felony offence. They too figured out the same phenomenon i.e. the risk perceptions increase after an arrest but the magnitude of increased perception was only 5% though. What's more! The perceptions effect was only specific to the crime for which the offender got arrested i.e. if the offender was caught for a violent crime then his risk perceptions for committing a property offence would not be altered.

12. Revival of Deterrence Theory

In the absence of deterrence, the society is going to be up a creek that's why deterrence theory has had its group of supporters every step of the way. Numerous researches being done in this field have kept deterrence theory alive with all its attributes visible to the readers' retina. The justice system should be coupled with a well-oiled deterrence which must be echoed in a bid to make everyone aware of the possible consequences if they act delinquently. The deterrence theory got a new lifeline and interest from its friends and foes in 1968 when an economist Gary Becker and a sociologist Gibbs published their articles in the wake of empirical testing of a few propositions of deterrence theory. In the wake of continuous empirical research on deterrence theory to date, justice systems and societies have issued praise after praise. Up till now, the deterrence theory is continuing its revival and didn't face an ax under the shadow of its non-believers. Since the theory has been successfully echoed across the globe, it has a strong propensity to reach criminals' brain cells with a clear water mark "*Think before you decide*".

13. Rational Choice Theory

When it comes to explaining Rational Choice Theory, it is best seen as a family of theories OR a framework that serves its purpose by logically guiding the theory's construction, connecting theoretical statements, and categorizing findings (Hechter and Kanazawa, 1997). The rational choice theory calls off the environmental, psychological, and biological behaviors, which might put a criminal under influence during the course of committing crime (Cornish and Clarke, 2014). This theory states that the criminals willfully and voluntarily go with the idea of committing crime in the same way as they get along with doing other things such as going to the market or using recreational drugs etc. Hence the theory takes a harder line with peoples' choices that are behind their criminal acts (Nagin, 2007). The choices are literally made considering the costs and benefits (McCarthy, 2002).

Rational choice theory believes that Crime is a product of peoples' own choices to commit crime (Nagin, 2007). If this is true then why do people not commit crime always? Why do they only commit crime at certain circumstances? Simply put, what are the grounds on which they make choice to commit crime? The right answer is, while deciding to commit a crime, people use and guided by their brain cells and they calculate the cost and benefits of criminal behavior as well as the cost and benefits of non-criminal behavior alike. Rational choice theory provides an upshot that before committing a crime, people do consider the costs and benefits of non-crime just like they consider the costs and benefits of committing a crime (McCarthy, 2002)

14. Critical Analysis on Rational Choice Theory

The rational choice theory presumes that people consider two types of costs and benefits while deciding to commit a crime i.e. the cost and benefits of crime as well as non-crime. For instance, if someone needs some money for his personal needs, he might consider two choices. Firstly, make some security breach in a bank, take cash, and run. Secondly, get a job in a factory and earn money. Before deciding which way to choose, the person will consider various costs and benefits of both criminal and non-criminal scenarios. In this regard, RCT is a broader type of theory when compared with deterrence theory in the sense that deterrence theory hypothesizes that delinquent behavior is affected by the cost of the crime (potential punishments associated with it) while RCT presumes that criminal act is affected by the cost and benefits of non-crime activity as well as the potential rewards of the criminal activity (Miller, 2009).

At the same time, the rational choice theory doesn't hypothesize that the decision-making ability by the people is 100% perfect or rational. The reason being, people fall prey to shortcuts, they are susceptible to be misinformed about the facts, and they are vulnerable to make wrong analyses about the costs and benefits of the crime thus underestimate the actual costs and benefits with regards to rewards and punishments at large. In this scenario, the costs and benefits turned as subjective rather than objective on the score that they are being perceived by the criminal based on his understanding or comprehension which might be limited or even with minimal rationality that vary from person to person (Paternoster et al., 1983). This is the reason that RCT is considered as a *"subjective expected utility theory"* of criminality (Clarke and Cornish, 1985). It is based on the calculation of the would-be offender how he weighs the costs and benefits. For instance, if a would-be criminal tries to analyze the costs associated with bank robbery, he might consider that there are chances he might get caught on the spot and get arrested by the law enforcement agencies. This is just common sense and anybody can perceive this risk and the terror of the legal punishments associated with it. On the flip side, a criminal with a very low IQ might think that for the past 6 months, nobody was caught and arrested in bank robbery at a particular area, hence the ratio of getting caught and arrested is 0 percent thus he can safely take the risk of bank robbery in that particular area. In this case, his hypothesis would be based upon his own understanding and objectively speaking, according to the statistics, there is very low risk of getting caught in bank robbery in that particular area. But the chances are, he might not know how many bank robberies were taken place in that particular area for the past 6 months. Maybe there was not a single attempt of bank robbery, maybe the law enforcement agencies have upgraded and reinforced more force for the security of banks in that specific area. Hence, in the current circumstances, the risk factor would not be 0% as perceived by the criminal. In that case, the rational choice theory would not let him stop from the committing the bank robbery crime but his rational choice for committing that crime would be on wrong grounds.

As mentioned above, RCT is considered as a *"subjective expected utility theory"*, where utility is the cumulative outcome of the costs and benefits of alternative paths of action OR one can say it is the expected profit involved in both crime and the alternate non-crime. More the utility, much is the chance that the person would decide to commit the crime. As a result, a rational person will rationalize the utility gains and would select the behavior with greatest utility for him. Again, this will be according to one's own assumption and understanding of utility.

Criminal Act if: Utility of criminal act is greater than the utility of non-criminal act.

15. Analyzing Rational Choice Theory in a Particular Scenario (Marijuana Use)

As proposed by *"Strain Theory"* people use marijuana due to different reasons; for example, they use marijuana if they feel great strain or stress due to a certain stressful event in their lives such as breaking up with a partner, failing an exam test and the like. This overwhelming stress persuades a person to use marijuana in response (Agnew, 1992). On the other hand, *"Differential Association Theory"* explains marijuana use in the sense that people, in company of the groups which use marijuana, are prone to marijuana use just like etiquette or a tolerable norm (Matsueda, 1988).

When it comes to explaining the above scenario of marijuana use with respect to Rational Choice Theory, the offender is likely to analyze the following costs and benefits in particular

Costs of Crime:

He would consider *certainty of formal sanctions* i.e. what are the chances that police or other legal authorities would catch me? Is there any way that I would minimize this risk of getting caught?

He would consider the *severity of formal sanctions* i.e. if the police catch me, would I be put under severe punishment, would I be sent to jail and prosecuted?

He would analyze *informal certainty of punishment* i.e. what would be the result if I'm caught by my teacher or employer? What would be the level of disappointment of that particular person?

He would analyze *informal severity of punishment* i.e. in the wake of catching me by that person, would something extremely bad would occur to me?

He would analyze *Guilt and Shame* i.e. after I get caught by someone, would I consider myself down in my own eyes.

Benefits of Crime:

What would be the level of pleasure in using marijuana?

Would my friends consider me a person of high class when they see me using marijuana?

Would using marijuana increase my self-esteem in my own eyes and in the eyes of my friends?

Costs of Non- Crime:

Would my friends grade me a timid person when they see my going away without using marijuana?

Not using marijuana would make my life boring enough?

Benefits of Non- Crime:

Would I be able to do my daily tasks at work as well as at home?

Would I feel better in my own eyes when I take a rain check from marijuana?

Would I be able to save much money which I would have spent on marijuana?

The offender is likely to determine the utility of using marijuana according to rational choice theory before he decides on using marijuana.

16. Interactional Theories and Routine Activities Theory

In the wake of growth of modern criminology in the 21st century, many legitimate theories born out of the curiosity that how seasons, climate, or weather affects our daily social interactions. Upon testing a variety of complex methodologies, theorists panned out with two primary models

Interactional theories based on stress

Routine activities theory

Interactional theories focus on the social background in which individual lives. This model is based on the entity '*stress*' i.e. an individual must constantly fit himself to the varying conditions and put up with others in social interaction (Thornberry et al., 1994). Our culture provides us with the norms, which we need to care about while reacting and responding to people working in the same milieu. Under the shadow of these adaptations, an individual can easily manage his normal levels of stress. When it comes to handling this stress level in extreme weather conditions, an individual is likely to be worse off to adapt to those conditions, producing an upshot that he starts breaking down his social reactions. An individual might be dead set against any type of delinquent behavior but the increased stress level triggered by extreme weather conditions might offset their mental stableness to a considerable extent. For instance, in extreme hot conditions, men can take the liberty to put off their shirts but women are not allowed to do the same. Similarly, the economically sound parties can enjoy in their air-conditioned homes whilst the labor class cannot do the same due to their poor economic conditions. *Despite its eye glazing name, for them, air condition is anything but affordability.* Hence adaptability to increased stress depends on everything from gender to economic outlook. This increased stress can further escalate to delinquent or criminal behavior. Quetelet's thermic law of delinquency also argued that there is a strong connection between violent behavior and heat, yet this theory has many proponents and opponents' due to various conflicting empirical findings across the globe.

Routine activities theory is an authentic model that is broadly used to explain the connection of season, climate, and weather with the entity 'crime' (Cohen and Felson, 1979). According to this theory crime is an upshot of the junction of time and space of the criminals, appropriate targets, and the non-provision of capable protectors. Statistics unfolded by FBI conforms to this theory that crime takes place more regularly in the deep winter months like Christmas (Falk, 1952). The reason being, everybody walks around for Christmas shopping with sufficient cash and robbers easily predict that people are walking around with cash and valuables. Secondly, the security personnel are also overwhelmed in Christmas season due to mass of shoppers everywhere from parking lots to shopping malls, leaving appropriate targets without sufficient security protectors. In this scenario, McCleary and Chew (2002) investigated the relationship of murder of children under 5 years of age by their young mothers during the winter season. They figured out that increased demand for food and clothing by the children during the deep winter season instigated this homicide victimization resulting in higher murder rates of those infants during deep winter season.

Crime is and should be the scary thing even for the seasoned criminal in the world; and most of the time, crime pans out badly because perception of the criminal doesn't come to fruition at large. The routine activities theory reiterates that crime counts on the two models. Firstly, the model proposing that our interactional stress increases when weather increases, and this pushes our adaptation level to a boiling point. Secondly, the likelihood of crime changes with a change in weather, which further changes our patterns of social interaction and routine activities alike. For instance, LeBeau (2002) investigated the impact of weather (Hugo Hurricane in this case) on burglary and found out an increase in defensive guns in the public due to the onslaught of burglars throughout the area after the hurricane was passed. They also figured out that the motivated offenders didn't attack the homes during the course of hurricane passing through, not because they didn't want to, but because the burglars were not able to walk on the streets. After the incident, burglars spread out throughout the area resulting in intense calls to police from homes.

17. Empirical Validity of Routine Activities Theory

Despite various theories in the favor of crime and climatic linkage, DeFronzo (1984) considered this anything but a weak idea. He was dead set for only the association of population's demographics, urbanization, and economic conditions behind the overall crime rate in a particular area. The fact of the matter is, the empirical validity of routine activities theory, despite its eye glazing name, doesn't display consistent results when it's tested without sidestepping various complexities. The theorists need significant leverage from the latest technology in a bid to find more consistent empirical evidence. Now, theorists propose legitimate and heartfelt difference of opinion about the said theory. Only temperature seems to be related but the findings with regards to wind, barometric pressure, weather fronts, fog, snow, and rain provide inconsistent results (Miller, 2009).

18. Summary

The deterrence theory assumes that people act on the grounds of their rational decisions i.e. an act of committing crime is based on the information about the possible consequences of that crime. The Rational Choice Theory, on the other hand, presents man, as a calculating (same as deterrence theory) creature who will manage to commit crime on the grounds of minimizing pain and maximizing pleasure. The deterrence theory has been extensively complemented in the early works of classical philosophers primarily Thomas Hobbes England (1588-1679), Cesare Beccaria Italy (1738-1794), and Jeremy Bentham England (1748-1832). The three water marks of theory of deterrence (*certainty, severity, and celerity*) were based on the works of Hobbes, Baccaria, and Bentham. Leaving crime onto the mercies of actual punishment won't give a huge blow to the criminal psychology unless it is coupled with the "*perception of punishment*". An earnest and empirically based deterrence research began in 1968 when theorists tested this theory and concluded that both certainty and severity of punishment might deter the metastasizing homicide. Perceptions do not stick to their original formation; they modify themselves through experiences of the person himself and the experiences of others alike. Interactional theories focus on the social background in which individual lives. *Routine activities theory* is an authentic model that is broadly used to explain the connection of season, climate, and weather with the entity 'crime'.

19. References

Agnew, R. (1992). Foundation for a general strain theory of crime and delinquency. *Criminology*, *30*(1), 47-88.

Andenaes, J. (1974). *Punishment and deterrence* (pp. 9-10). Ann Arbor: University of Michigan Press.

Anwar, S., & Loughran, T. A. (2011). Testing a Bayesian learning theory of deterrence among serious juvenile offenders. *Criminology*, *49*(3), 667-698.

Apel, R., Pogarsky, G., & Bates, L. (2009). The sanctions-perceptions link in a model of school-based deterrence. *Journal of Quantitative Criminology*, *25*(2), 201-226.

Assembly of Behavioral and Social Sciences (US). Panel on Research on Deterrent and Incapacitative Effects, Blumstein, A., Cohen, J., & Nagin, D. (1978). *Deterrence and incapacitation: Estimating the effects of criminal sanctions on crime rates* (p. 431). Washington, DC: National Academy of Sciences.

Beccaria, C. (1963). On crimes and punishments. Translated with an introduction by Henry Paolucci.

Beccaria, C. (2009). *On crimes and punishments and other writings*. University of Toronto Press.

Becker, G. S. (1968). Crime and punishment: An economic approach. In *The Economic Dimensions of Crime* (pp. 13-68). Palgrave Macmillan UK.

Bentham, J. (1879). *An introduction to the principles of morals and legislation*. Clarendon Press.

Blais, E., & Bacher, J. L. (2007). Situational deterrence and claim padding: results from a randomized field experiment. *Journal of Experimental Criminology*, *3*(4), 337-352.

Candace McCoy, J. D., & McManimon Jr, P. New Jersey's" No Early Release Act": Its Impact On Prosecution, Sentencing, Corrections, And Victim Satisfaction.

Clarke, R. V., & Cornish, D. B. (1985). Modeling offenders' decisions: A framework for research and policy. *Crime and justice*, 147-185.

Cohen, L. E., & Felson, M. (1979). Social change and crime rate trends: A routine activity approach. *American sociological review*, 588-608.

Cook, P. J. (1980). Research in criminal deterrence: Laying the groundwork for the second decade. *Crime and Justice*, 211-268.

Cornish, D. B., & Clarke, R. V. (Eds.). (2014). *The reasoning criminal: Rational choice perspectives on offending*. Transaction Publishers.

Cornish, D. B., & Clarke, R. V. (1987). Understanding crime displacement: An application of rational choice theory. *Criminology*, *25*(4), 933-948.

DeFronzo, J. (1984). Climate and crime tests of an FBI assumption. *Environment and Behavior*, *16*(2), 185-210.

Daniels, R. S., Baumhover, L. A., Formby, W. A., & Clark-Daniels, C. L. (1999). Police discretion and elder mistreatment: A nested model of observation, reporting, and satisfaction. *Journal of Criminal Justice*, *27*(3), 209-225.

Dezhbakhsh, H., Rubin, P. H., & Shepherd, J. M. (2003). Does capital punishment have a deterrent effect? New evidence from postmoratorium panel data. *American Law and Economics Review*, *5*(2), 344-376.

Donohue III, J. J., & Wolfers, J. (2006). *Uses and abuses of empirical evidence in the death penalty debate* (No. w11982). National Bureau of Economic Research.

Doob, A. N., & Webster, C. M. (2003). Sentence severity and crime: Accepting the null hypothesis. *Crime and justice*, 143-195.

Fagan, J., Zimring, F. E., & Geller, A. (2005). Capital punishment and capital murder: Market share and the deterrent effects of the death penalty. *Tex. L. Rev., 84*, 1803.

Falk, G. J. (1952). The influence of the seasons on the crime rate. *The Journal of Criminal Law, Criminology, and Police Science, 43*(2), 199-213.

Gendreau, P., Cullen, F. T., & Goggin, C. (1999). *The effects of prison sentences on recidivism*. Ottawa: Solicitor General Canada.

Gibbs, J. P. (1968). Crime, punishment, and deterrence. *The Southwestern Social Science Quarterly*, 515-530.

Gibbs, J. (1986). Punishment and deterrence: Theory, research, and penal policy. *Law and the Social Sciences. New York: Russell Sage Foundation.*

Hechter, M., & Kanazawa, S. (1997). Sociological rational choice theory. *Annual review of sociology*, 191-214.

Hobbes, T. (2006). *Leviathan*. A&C Black.

Katz, L., Levitt, S. D., & Shustorovich, E. (2003). Prison conditions, capital punishment, and deterrence. *American Law and Economics Review, 5*(2), 318-343.

Keckler, C. N. (2006). Life v. death: Who should capital punishment marginally deter. *JL Econ. & Pol'y, 2*, 51.

Klepper, S., & Nagin, D. (1989). Tax compliance and perceptions of the risks of detection and criminal prosecution. *Law and society review*, 209-240.

Klinger, D. A. (1995). Policing spousal assault. *Journal of Research in Crime and Delinquency, 32*(3), 308-324.

LeBeau, J. L. (2002). The impact of a hurricane on routine activities and on calls for police service: Charlotte, North Carolina, and Hurricane Hugo. *Crime Prevention & Community Safety*, *4*(1), 53-64.

Listokin, Y. (2007). Crime and (with a lag) punishment: the implications of discounting for equitable sentencing. *Am. Crim. L. Rev.*, *44*, 115.

Lochner, L. (2001). A theoretical and empirical study of individual perceptions of the criminal justice system. *Available at SSRN 273598*.

Matsueda, R. L. (1988). The current state of differential association theory. *Crime & Delinquency*, *34*(3), 277-306.

McCarthy, B. (2002). New economics of sociological criminology. *Annual Review of Sociology*.

Merritt, N., Fain, T., & Turner, S. (2006). Oregon's get tough sentencing reform: A lesson in justice system adaptation. *Criminology & public policy*, *5*(1), 5-36.

McCleary, R., & Chew, K. S. (2002). Winter is the infanticide season seasonal risk for child homicide. *Homicide Studies*, *6*(3), 228-239.

Miller, J. M. (Ed.). (2009). *21st century criminology: a reference handbook* (Vol. 1). SAGE publications.

Miller, J. M., Schreck, C. J., & Tewksbury, R. (2011). *Criminological theory: A brief introduction*. Pearson Higher Ed.

Nagin, D. S. (1998). Criminal deterrence research at the outset of the twenty-first century. *Crime and justice*, 1-42.

Nagin, D. S., & Pogarsky, G. (2001). Integrating celerity, impulsivity, and extralegal sanction threats into a model of general deterrence: Theory and evidence. *Criminology*, *39*(4), 865-892.

Nagin, D. S. (2007). Moving choice to center stage in criminological research and theory: the American Society of

Criminology 2006 Sutherland address. *Criminology*, *45*(2), 259-272.

Nagin and Pogarsky, "Integrating Celerity, Impulsivity, and Extralegal Sanction Threats into a Model of General Deterrence."

Norrie, A. (1984). Thomas Hobbes and the philosophy of punishment. *Law and Philosophy*, *3*(2), 299-320.

O'Shea, T. C. (2007). Getting the deterrence message out: The project safe neighborhoods public–private partnership. *Police Quarterly*, *10*(3), 288-307.

Paternoster, R., Saltzman, L. E., Chiricos, T. G., & Waldo, G. P. (1982). Perceived risk and deterrence: Methodological artifacts in perceptual deterrence research. *J. Crim. L. & Criminology*, *73*, 1238.

Paternoster, R., Saltzman, L. E., Waldo, G. P., & Chiricos, T. G. (1983). Perceived risk and social control: Do sanctions really deter? *Law and Society Review*, 457-479.

Paternoster, R., & Brame, R. (1997). Multiple routes to delinquency? A test of developmental and general theories of crime. *Criminology*, *35*(1), 49-84.

Piliavin, I., Gartner, R., Thornton, C., & Matsueda, R. L. (1986). Crime, deterrence, and rational choice. *American Sociological Review*, 101-119.

Pogarsky, G., Kim, K., & Paternoster, R. (2005). Perceptual change in the national youth survey: lessons for deterrence theory and offender decision-making. *Justice Quarterly*, *22*(1), 1-29.

Roberts, J. V., Stalans, L. J., Indermaur, D., & Hough, M. (2002). *Penal populism and public opinion: Lessons from five countries*. Oxford University Press.

Robert Bursik, Harold Grasmick, and Mitchell Chamlin, "The effect of longitudinal arrest patterns on the development of robbery trends at the neighborhood level," Criminology 28

(1990): 431–450; Theodore Chiricos and Gordon Waldo, "Punishment and crime: An examination of some empirical evidence," Social Problems 18 (1970): 200–217

Ross, H. L. (1984). *Deterring the drinking driver: Legal policy and social control* (Vol. 1982). Lexington, MA: Lexington Books.

Saltzman, L., Paternoster, R., Waldo, G. P., & Chiricos, T. G. (1982). Deterrent and experiential effects: The problem of causal order in perceptual deterrence research. *Journal of Research in Crime and Delinquency, 19*(2), 172-189.

Thornberry, T. P., Lizotte, A. J., Krohn, M. D., Farnworth, M., & Jang, S. J. (1994). Delinquent peers, beliefs, and delinquent behavior: A longitudinal test of interactional theory. *Criminology, 32*(1), 47-83.

Tittle, C. R. (1969). Crime rates and legal sanctions. *Social problems, 16*(4), 409-423.

Tonry, M. (1996). *Sentencing matters*. Oxford University Press.

Tonry, M. (2008). Learning from the limitations of deterrence research. *Crime and Justice, 37*(1), 279-311.

Von Hirsch, A., Bottoms, A. E., Burney, E., & Wikstrom, P. O. (1999). *Criminal deterrence and sentence severity: An analysis of recent research* (p. 63). Oxford: Hart.

Chapter 7
Labelling and Reintegrating Shaming Theory

1. Introduction

Criminology is one of the more popular topics for research in the social studies field of literature. The focus of studies in this field is mostly on identifying the reasons that influence people to commit crime while other people opt to live a life as a law abiding citizen, even if the life scenarios are similar. Over the years, many researchers have proposed many differential theories that provide insights on the social structures and various factors that contribute to criminal behavior or delinquency. Some of the most popular theories that have come forward as explanation of the criminology theory include social bonding and social control theories (Walklate, 2007). These theories attempt to explain the criminal behavior among people for the community as a whole. Along with these commonly used theories of criminology, there are some additional theories as well that attempt to explain the act of delinquency in a more specific and scenario based manner.

This chapter performs a detailed analysis of the labelling theory and the reintegrating shaming theory. Both theories have gained positive reception in criminology and have specific purpose analysis of delinquency behavior. Both theories are discussed and analyzed in this chapter for the definitive characteristics of criminology and validation through empirical research evidences.

2.   Labelling Theory and Criminal Behavior

The labelling theory is known with this name because it has a high emphasis on the commonly used approach of stigmatization in formal or informal application. It is not an uncommon occurrence in our society to stigmatize people into groups and put a deviant label on people. In the labelling theory of criminology, the presence of label is defined as both independent variables (causes) as well as dependent variables (effects). According to this theory, the labels function in form of dependent variables in cases where the label is used to explain social acceptance or violation of certain behavior activities for purpose of stigmatization. On the other hand, these labels are considered as independent variables or causes when used for hypothesizing that certain labels result in continuation of delinquent behavior.

One of the most commonly used examination of the labelling approach used for labelling theory is given by Bernburg and Krohn (2003), and it is argued that all social groups and communities develop deviance by creating some rules and any infraction of the rules is considered deviance. In later stages of society, the same rules are then used on specific groups to label them as outsiders for the social rules. In this approach, it is considered that deviance is not something that is given to a person on basis of the crimes committed rather it is the consequence of applying the label of 'offender' on certain people of group of people. Deviant is a person in this process to whom the label of deviance applies successfully and a label applied on a person increases the probability of that person committing crime.

It is proposed by the believers of labelling theory that the criminal behavior of a person who has been labelled as criminal is of secondary importance in the grand scheme of things. The most important that needs to be considered is in what conditions the label of deviant should be assigned, to whom such a label is assigned and what influence does it have? It is further important to understand what constitutes the labelling of deviant behavior and what are the determining characteristics of the way stigmatization is performed? A common belief in the labelling theory of criminology is that the deviant labels in a community are applied by powerful people in the community and are used as a way of imposing power on the less powerful people within the community. Management of deviant labels in the society is perfumed by the elite and powerful people and they get to decide what behavior is acceptable or what kind of behavior should be banned. In addition to this, one of the most damaging parts of the labelling approach is that in many cases, people are not stigmatized as criminals based on any criminal activity that they have committed and such a label is assigned even if the person has no prior history of criminal behavior. Furthermore, for a same level of violation of law, a less powerful person in the community is more likely to get assigned the label of delinquent than someone who has more power and influence in the community. In this manner, assigning labels to people and deeming them as criminals is depending a lot on who these people are and less on the activities that they have taken part in.

One of the most notable concepts that represent the social interactionism of the labelling theory is the 'looking-glass self' concept (Wellford, 1975). This concept makes use of natural human behavior for explaining activities performed by us in assigning labels. According to this concept, a person starts to see own self-concepts in the manner that is reflected by others. This theory states that a person becomes what is considered by that person as other's belief for that person. Therefore, if a significant number of people will interact with a person in a specific certain way then it is likely for that person to simply accept that behavior as reality and started behaving in the manner that others expect. For example- if majority of people are treating a person as a criminal then it is likely for that person to accept own-image as a criminal and engage in criminal activities. The proposal made in the labelling theory is that the whole process of labelling is type of symbolic interaction and it also links well with delinquent behavior.

3. Crime and Deviance: Stigmatizing by the society

At the very core of the labelling theory is the inherent symbolic interactionist proposition that a person forms identity for self on basis of reflection presented by other people for him or her (Bernburg, 2006). The argument given by this theory is that the people who are stigmatized as deviant by the society or powerful groups within the society are far more likely to engage in the activity of delinquency than others and the likelihood is dramatically high. This theory further proposes that the arguments holds true even in cases where the person assigned label of a delinquent has not been involved in any criminal activities before. This promotes the idea that these people may have been less deviant had there been no label assigned on them. The process of labelling is generally promoted as a way of preventing criminal behavior or in most cases, as a reaction to occurrence of delinquent behavior. The primary conceptual objective of labelling is to discourage and prevent delinquency and not to promote it. It is an ironic situation that in many of the real-life cases, the implementation of labelling process takes place in such an environment that ends up assigning the label to a person who does not have a delinquency history and ends up encouraging that person to engage in criminal activities.

The theorists who study the labelling theory suggest that the whole approach of assigning labels to a person for their criminality is a one-way determination approach and once such an identity is assigned, it remains fixed permanently. Theorists believe that assigning a label to a person does not remain limited to just the society's view of that person and it also influences changes in the self-concept of a person assigned the label. According to this theory, every person engages in the process of role-playing, self-reflexing and negotiation for the portrayal of own image among others and having a known assigned label from the society impacts this decision-making process for self-identify of that person. It is a natural human process for many people manage and maintain a good perception among other people as well as ensuring that other people communicate positively about him or her. Arguments that are made against the labelling theory's benefits indicate that this theory is not a simple and one-way approach and assigning a label to someone also gives back some reaction from the labelled person as well. While labelling a person as deviant may not ensure that the person will inevitably behave in a deviant manner, but it certainly becomes one of the influencing components in the behavior of that person.

It is reasonable to make the interpretation of the labelling theory that this theory is designed to propose and establish lawful and right decisions in the society according to the most powerful people in the community, including- courts, police and governments. When a label of delinquency is assigned to a person from the highly powerful people or social bodies than the person has very little power to resist the labelling process and therefore, the probability of that person accepting and identifying with the label increases. While the supporters of the labelling theory suggest that labelling of deviant behavior is quite effective when performed in a formal manner by a legally accepted criminal justice system, the same cannot be said about the informal way of assigning labels on people by the members in the community. In the systematic analysis of the process of labelling theory and the stress caused by the labelling process focus on the impact that it has on the social control aspects. Such an analysis results in suggesting that the social controls are reduced upon assignment of deviant label to a person and this increases the occurrence of criminal behavior. This analysis approach has been on the forefront of the labelling theory of criminology and tries to explain delinquent behavior using this approach.

4. Acceptance and Reception of Labelling Theory in Criminology

For the most part, the labelling theory of criminology has received a widespread level of acceptance and positive reception in the criminology field, from the practitioners and academics alike. However, there do exist some other elements in the society which are very critical of the theory of labelling from the very beginning. According to Andrews et al. (1990), the very first objection with the theory is that the labelling theory entirely disregards the aspect of actual real-life behavior of an individual deemed deviant and puts all the focus on the image of that person getting influential in making that person commit crimes and engage in criminal activities. This criticism argues that even the most powerless people do not necessarily accept their own identity based on the label of deviant that they have received and do not end up adopting it as a real part of their life. At the very least, such a shift would not happen immediately and the label will not be the only part that contributes to the decision-making process of a person assigned label of deviant. According to the authors of this critic, it is far more likely that the people wrongly assigned deviant label would fight back, protest and deny the labelling of their actions and after that negotiate with own identity. Additional criticism is given based on the structure of labelling theory as it is not the label that creates the criminal behavior rather the criminal behavior that demands labelling.

Critics of the labelling theory of criminology argue that there are other notable factors that influence initiation of deviant behavior in a person and presence of the same factors is also likely to be the cause of continuous criminal behavior for the person. It is suggested that the labelling theory may have slight impact on the individual's perception of self or the judgement on self-concept, but even that plays very limited role in initiation or continuation of criminal behavior. It is very common for people to commit crime or violate some kind of law intentionally and in most cases, it has nothing to do with the label of deviance on them as such a label may not even apply to them and they still commit a crime. The criticism indicates that criminal behavior is influenced by a large number of different factors and what the labelling theory does is largely ignore presence of other factors and the continuing influence that such other factors might have on an individual and focuses solely on the deviant label approach of explaining criminal intention. The criticism of labelling theory that suggests ignorance of other contributing factors comes from the high emphasis of labelling theory on the powerful people of the society singling out other offenders in the community for invoking a specific deviancy label and the very little power that the powerless in the community must resist such labelling.

The argument given by Akers (1985) regarding this approach of labelling theory suggests that making the basic assumptions of labelling theory is incorrect and in accurate. Applying labelling theory does not happen in an arbitrary process and it functions in an unrelated manner from the actual behavioral characteristics of the people getting labelled as deviant. It is true that many times in the process labelling, errors occur and people who are not deserving a deviant label gets the label applied to them and the criteria of labelling the people with deviant behavior does not include only the people who are deviant. However, it is also wrong to simply make the argument that the society applies the label of deviant on a person in a complete vacuum. Like the way police offers do not arrest people just out of their intention and must have a probable cause to do so, criminal justice system also does not stigmatize people with labels and punishments without evidence. Majority of big criminal labels such as mentally ill, murders, criminal, pedophile and drug addict are applied to a person based on actual behavior and evidence of such behavior. In this manner, the actual deviant behavior takes place prior to getting assigned label and functions as the basic level of information to develop and stigmatize a label.

5. Labelling Process and Delinquent Behavior

The labelling theory of criminology is practiced as one of the most popular and useful theoretical approaches in understanding and explaining deviant behavior among people. According to this theory, if a person is labelled as deviant by the society then that person automatically becomes likely to commit crime and engage in criminal behavior activities by adopting the deviant label in his own perception of self-concept. In most cases, labels are assigned by the most powerful people and social bodies in the society such as politicians, police and criminal justice system. The labelling process assigns labels to both individual and groups, however, its primary objectives remains on separating the non-deviants from the deviants in context of social formations and defining a framework of criminal activity interpretation. A theory relating to the delinquency behavior by Akers (2009) indicates that there is no such thing as a deviancy activity by nature and it all depends on what is perceived as deviant by either most members of the community or by some prominent powerful members of the community who have influence over other people.

The purpose of labelling theory is to understand why only some members of our society get assigned a label of deviant while others are relatively away from getting such a label. In explaining the real-life practice of deviant labels, this theory suggests that society assigns labels in an inaccurate manner and it purposefully targets the less powerful people in the community. For example- for the same crime and intensity of crime, it is far more likely for a powerless person to get labelled as deviant in comparison to the deviancy labelling of a prominent figure. The underlying argument of the labelling theory of criminology is that once people are defined by the deviant label, they automatically become likely to engage in activities that are criminal in nature as they develop a self-concept and perception of themselves based on what other people expect from them.

Once an individual receives a deviancy label from the society then it becomes immensely difficult to remove that label. A person having the deviant label is stigmatized by the society a lot as a criminal and delinquent. Furthermore, that person is generally treated by the society as an untrustworthy individual and it likely becomes difficult for that person to continue education, engage in social activities and get a decent job opportunity. Presence of such factors can certainly create an environment for a deviant labelled person to engage in criminal activities as they are not able to gain acceptance in the society easily. These ideas of the labelling theory provide a way for making applications of the labelling theory arguments.

One of the most prominent applications of the labelling theory is in juvenile correctional system and juvenile diversion system. This system identifies that juvenile crimes are largely non-intentional and take place in an encouraging environment and that such a crime is in not indicative of the behavior of the juvenile in many cases. The juvenile diversion program understands that putting a juvenile person in the juvenile justice system would likely put a deviant label on them and that can easily disrupt their future by limiting their abilities to join social groups and get a decent job. This program offers an alternative program to the first-time juvenile offenders in order to avoid the juvenile justice system entirely. The purpose of this system is to keep the juveniles protected against deviancy label, which has the potential of changing perception of the society for that juvenile. Having a deviant label at that young age without any prior history of criminal activity can be very unjust according to the labelling theory and may as well lead the juvenile towards criminal activities. The existence of whole juvenile diversion program functions as an application of the labelling theory and avoids such actions.

6. Braithwaite's Re-Integrative Shaming Theory

Shame is a concept of self-conscious emotion for most people and in practice, it functions as a way of forcing the people towards engaging in activities that are of social cohesion and conformity in nature. In is considered in the shaming theory that if an individual is either anticipating shame or is trying to avoid shame then it acts as a motivator to accept the duties and role in the society and welfare of the society. In the literature of criminology, shaming is a reference to all types of social gestures that represent disapproval or disappointment in a person that are designed to invoke the sense of remorse in that person towards any violation of legal or social laws. Shaming is a way of the society to condemn acts that do not conform to the society (Murphy, 2008). Shaming in criminology can be perceived in two different manners: shaming in a manner that functions as a way of stigmatizing a delinquent person making that person excluded from the other non-deviant people in the community, and shaming a way of shaming that also brings forgiveness of the crime and attempts to re-integrate the offender in the society.

Braithwaite presented the theory of re-integrative shaming and suggested that most effectiveness can be achieved with the theory of shaming in cases where the shaming is not performed by all members of the community rather takes place in micro-groups of people who are inter-dependent (HAY, 2001). This theory argues that implementation of the re-integrative shaming would help in reducing the rate of crime by providing a way of showing disapproval of the offender without explicitly rejecting the person from social interactions with the disapprovers and by creating fear of further disapproval from the same people. Engaging in excessive shaming and by rejecting the people from social interactions would develop stigmatization that leads to formation of a sub-group of criminals who are all rejected from the society and this sub-group then proceeds to reject the rejecters.

One of the more powerful and impacting way of stigmatization is to assigned labels of deviant on people offending laws and according to the labelling theory, once a person is labelled as deviant by the society, it inevitably becomes a part of that person's identity and changes the behavior of other people for the deviant person negatively. Stigmatization has the potential of making the deviant person accept deviancy as a natural part of own behavior and further engage in criminal activities as this is what is expected from him or her by the society. Due to this reason, if a person is given the label of a deviant behavior without taking part in an activity that is primarily deviant then it is possible for that individual to perceive the label as an inherent part of own identity and take part in further activities that affirm to this new identity.

The importance of shame is quite high in developing a deterrence based approach of reducing crime and encouraging people to leave and avoid criminal activities entirely. Shaming can actively function as a way of preventing the criminal behavior as well as motivating such a behavior. However, the approach taken with shaming makes it a distinguished experience to function as either motivator for crime or a prevention of criminal activities. The most optimum approach is to engage in re-integrative shaming process as it allows for more optimized process of helping the individuals in understanding that their criminal activity does not end their way back to normal non-deviant life while the gesture of disapproval indeed causes remorse among them, as a discouragement of committing crimes any further (Ahmed & Braithwaite, 2005). Furthermore, re-integrative approach of shaming prevents formation of sub-culture of all rejected deviants, which is a very positive factor for the society.

7. The Process of Restorative Justice and Faith-Based Programs

The re-integrative theory of shaming makes use of shaming as a way of deterring people from committing crime by showing a visible disapproval to the person. According to this theory, the disapproval of the crime and criminal is an important part of the justice system, however, doing it in excess and implementing disapproval in such a manner that is completely separates the criminal from the society is a harmful approach. Using this approach of excessive shaming creates a sub-culture of people who have been rejected by the society through shaming and this sub-culture rejects the rejecters and despises others who do not accept them as an integral part of the society (Coricelli, Rusconi, & Villeval, 2014). The re-integrative process makes use of the shaming approach for representation of disapproval for the crime, however, it also focuses on reintegration of the person in the community and encourages forgiveness of the crime after showing disapproval. Furthermore, it argues that most effective outcomes from shaming approach is achieved when shaming or disapproval is shown by some limited inter-dependent people of the criminal and not from all people in the society.

The process of 'restorative justice' refers to a program that is coined to describe a specific approach of justice that puts a high emphasis on restitution rather than putting focus on retribution. The approach of restorative justice is a very broad field of philosophy and does not point to any one specific program of application of criminal justice as it serves as an important conceptual approach to criminal justice that can be implemented in various situations of criminal justice system. The objective of the restorative justice is to remain present as a guideline philosophy and not as a specific approach as its implementation may differ from one situation to another. In most situations of criminal justice, the framework offers a punishment for violation of a law or social policy. These punishments are designed to function on a retribution based model of justice and any approach of restitution of the criminal is a secondary goal of this process or is non-existent in the punishment process. The whole idea of restorative justice is to keep the restitution of individuals in society as the primary goal and keeping punishment the secondary process in the philosophy.

Faith based programs are mostly community run and these are designed to invoke a sense of faith and spirituality among the deviants. Like the approach of re-integrative theory and restorative justice theory, the faith based programs are also designed to motivate the deviants to seek forgiveness and adopt to a lifestyle that is non-deviant. Such programs require participation from the community and many times, these programs are designed as a way of prisoner re-entry in the society. A criminal who has been declared deviant by the criminal justice system is labelled as deviant by the community as well and it becomes difficult for that person to live a normal life as a non-deviant person due to lack of acceptance for these people from the society. The faith based programs are designed to achieve just this objective by developing a framework of prisoner re-entry in the society in a way that is most suitable to them and grants them acceptance in the community.

There is a similarity in the underlying concept of each of these three approaches to deal with criminal behavior as the primary focus of each theory is to facilitate and make it convenient for criminals to gain acceptance in the community towards a normal non-deviant life. None of these theories reject the notion for punishment for crime rather the emphasis on forgiveness for the crime and re-integrating the deviants in the community instead of rejecting them.

8. Why Restorative Justice and Its Effectiveness

The approach of restorative justice is on developing a framework that has most emphasis on re-integrating the criminals back in society and not to reject them outright for their crimes. This approach helps in developing a process that has its aim in restitution of criminals back in the society rather than making them separate from the community, which only contributes to development of a sub-culture that includes all criminals and deviants (Morrison & Vaandering, 2012). There are many different applications of the restorative justice and some of the most prominent examples include the following:

Victim-offender mediation: this is one prime approach of applying the restorative justice approach. In this process, the victim of the crime and the offender is put in the mediation process and the activity is managed by one or more mediators. In some cases, the offender and victim may meet in face-to-face scenarios and in later stages, the meetings may take place in absence of the mediators. During the face-to-face mediation process, family and friends are many times present to provide moral and emotional support to both parties. The primary objective of this process is to help both parties involved in having a greater understanding of why the said crime took place and how it has impacted the lives for both parties as well as identifying ways of achieving restitution from the crime (Harris, Walgrave, & Braithwaite, 2004). This approach of restorative justice is not used in every criminal context or in every type of jurisdiction, however, many of these programs have a good historical record of successful restitution for both parties based on decades of implementation.

Conferencing: a group based conference allows for broadened reach and range for the restorative process. The name of group conference approach changes heavily in its name and the style used for implementation purposes. In most commonly used process of a conference meeting for restorative justice, it includes a combination of different types of attendees such as offenders, victims and families of the victims and offenders and some representatives of social bodies. A conference discussion is led by someone representing a neutral side and decides the order of speaking for the individuals (Trenczek, 2015). The objective of this process is to listen to arguments and thoughts of all individuals, providing them a platform to represent their thoughts. In the final stage of the process, a common consensus is reached among all members about what actions should be taken by offenders and the best ways of re-entry for the offenders.

Circles: circles function in very much the same way as a group conference meeting in terms of the number of people involved and the type of individuals involved in the process. However, in case of a circle, the number of people involved can be increased to further include other individuals from the community to give their input and opinion about the situation. This process is given the name of a 'circle' because of the way the framework works by putting all members in a circle ad given each member equal opportunities and priorities in the process. The process is led by the community leader and he or she is responsible for the task of managing the discussion. In many cases, circles do not focus on specific cases that involve the victims or offenders rather the emphasis is on specific talking points that are more general in nature and have a widespread meaning attached to the process (Cullen, Wright, & Blevins, 2006). Circle is a process that takes input from the community and is largely as a community-driven program.

The process of mediation, conferences and circles allow for great deal flexibility in the framework and can be implemented in different ways depending on the context and circumstances.

The theory of restorative justice approach has its roots in the labelling theory as well. The labelling theory suggests that by assigning a deviant label to a person, society actively separates that person from the society and further promotes deviant behavior as it slowly becomes a part of that person's identity in his or her own perception of self. The restorative justice theory takes the similar explanation approach and attempts to avoid the focus on punishing criminals just for the sake of punishing them and emphasizes on ways of restitution for these people throughout the process.

The complete concept of the restorative justice is not a specific theory rather a basic criminology philosophy. According to this theory, a person who is deemed as a criminal by the criminal justice system once, becomes separated from the society and loses trustworthiness from other members of the community (Smith, 2005). This further helps create a separation between the society and the criminal, making it increasingly difficult for the deviant person to gain acceptance back in the community and restitution of normal non-deviant life. The most effective approach of making the deviant members of the community more likely to join the community is to open a line of dialogue between the offenders and other members of the society. This philosophy attempts to develop programs where offenders can interact with other members in the community in order to help the community have a better understanding of them. This approach significantly helps in making the society more understanding of the deviant personnel as well as having more likelihood of accepting the deviant person in the community. Existence of an open dialogue between different members of the community and the offenders is a very helpful step in bridging the gap created by the deviant act of the offender (Wilson, 2006). Furthermore, by taking part in a community meeting where the victims and their families are present, an offender is highly likely to understand the true scope of consequences resulting from their crime and have a true sense of remorse. This makes it more likely for the deviant to regret own criminal actions as well as have more reluctance in engaging in similar activities again.

In practice, restorative justice programs have been quite popular and successful in many jurisdictions and context. Such programs are not suitable for each type of crime, but can be implemented in a wide variety of commonly and regularly occurring crimes and delinquent acts. For example- a person driving under influence of alcohol is more likely to resist drunk driving upon meeting a victim who was involved in an accident caused by someone driving while under influence (Mathieson, 2005). The success of restorative justice has even influenced government sanctioned programs to facilitate prisoner re-entry.

9. Implications of Labelling Theory

Labelling theory has been around for a very long time and in this meantime, this theory has gained widespread acceptance from the practitioners and academics alike. In the past, the applications of labelling theory have remained mostly in theoretical approaches and framework, not allowing for real life implementation of such a process that is based on the labelling theory of criminology. The existing model of labelling theory of criminology also gains some criticism about the outcomes of the theory as well as the assumptions that are made by this theory. Based on the growing popularity of this theory and more empirical evidences supporting this theory, it is likely that this theory will remain relevant in near future as well.

Some of the criticisms that are made about the theory of labelling is quite valid and does indeed question the accuracy of assumptions made by this theory. However, the most important part to note in this is that the theory does indeed provides realistic outputs for the concept of wrong people getting labelled as deviant and this having an impact on their perception of self-concept (Farrington, 2014). Inherently, the labelling theory suggests that by simply labelling some people as deviant, our society is separating them from non-deviant people and as an unintended consequence of this process, such people become more likely to engage in criminal behavior.

It is anticipated that the in future, applications of labelling theory will allow for more careful implementation of labelling people deviant. In such a scenario, informal labelling of people would be discouraged and the focus would be on development of programs that are community-driven and allow the deviant labelled people to earn their spot back in the normal life as a way of showing that they are resisting the label of deviant and have every intention of restitution. A community driven approach that is based labelling theory would not be very different from the restorative justice theory applications as both are based on the similar concepts of preventing formal or informal separation of people who are deviant and offering them some way of gaining acceptance in the mainstream community rather than getting rejected by a major part of the community.

Labelling theory has gained its acceptance in the criminology theory and many other criminology and social justice theories make a reference to the labelling theory. This provides strength to the assumptions and arguments made by the theory of labelling. As more theories adopt the labelling theory concepts, highly refined and more specific ways of implementing solutions to social justice problems would come forward (Abelius, 2011). A major example of this is seen in the restorative justice approach and in re-integrative shaming theory that avoids permanently assigning the label of deviant on a person to increase the chances of social restitution for the deviant individual.

10.   Summary

The study of criminology is one of the most popular fields of study in the social studies segment of literature. Over the years, many popular theories of criminologist have attempted to explain presence of deviant behavior among people as well as understanding various factors that influence people towards committing crime. Emphasis of these criminology theories is also on identifying why some people tend to have higher tendency of committing crime while other do not, despite living in practically similar scenarios.

This book chapter has covered and analyzed the labelling theory of criminology as well as the re-integrative shaming theory. The theory of labelling suggests that assigning labels to people for deviance acts as a way of separating these people from the non-deviant people and can severely damage the potential deviants from becoming a productive member of the society again. A similar approach is present in the theory of re-integrative shaming theory as excessive shaming can be very harmful and lead to rejection of deviants from the society. According to both theories, the focus of the criminal justice system should be on re-integration and restitution of criminals and not on merely punishment for violation of crime.

11. References

Abelius, V. (2011). Crime, disorder, and justice – The Labelling theory as a way of explaining social reactions to deviant behavior (1st ed.). GRIN Verlag.

Ahmed, E. & Braithwaite, J. (2005). Forgiveness, shaming, shame and bullying. Australian & New Zealand Journal of Criminology, 38(3), 298-323. http://dx.doi.org/10.1375/acri.38.3.298

Akers, R. (2009). Social learning and social structure (1st ed., pp. 38-44). New Brunswick [N.J.]: Transaction Publishers.

Akers, R. (2013). Criminological theories: Introduction and evaluation (2nd ed., pp. 208-210). Routledge.

Andrews, D., Zinger, I., Hoge, R., Bonta, J., Gendreau, P., & Cullen, F. (1990). Does correctional treatment work? A clinically relevant and psychologically informed meta-analysis*. Criminology, 28(3), 369-404. http://dx.doi.org/10.1111/j.1745-9125.1990.tb01330.x

Bernburg, J. (2006). Official labeling, criminal embeddedness, and subsequent delinquency: A longitudinal test of labeling theory. Journal of Research in Crime and Delinquency, 43(1), 67-88. http://dx.doi.org/10.1177/0022427805280068

Bernburg, J. & Krohn, M. (2003). Labeling, life chances, and adult crime: The direct and indirect effects of official intervention in adolescence on crime in early adulthood*.

Criminology, 41(4), 1287-1318. Http://Dx.Doi.Org/10.1111/J.1745-9125.2003.Tb01020.X

Coricelli, G., Rusconi, E., & Villeval, M. (2014). Tax evasion and emotions: An empirical test of re-integrative shaming theory. Journal of Economic Psychology, 40, 49-61. http://dx.doi.org/10.1016/j.joep.2012.12.002

Cullen, F., Wright, J., & Blevins, K. (2006). Taking stock (1st ed., pp. 397-399). New Brunswick, N.J.: Transaction Publishers.

Farrington, D. (2014). Labeling theory: empirical tests (1st ed., pp. 170-173). Transaction Publishers.

Harris, N., Walgrave, L., & Braithwaite, J. (2004). Emotional dynamics in restorative conferences. Theoretical Criminology, 8(2), 191-210. http://dx.doi.org/10.1177/1362480604042243

HAY, C. (2001). An exploratory test of Braithwaite's reintegrative shaming theory. Journal of Research in Crime and Delinquency, 38(2), 132-153. http://dx.doi.org/10.1177/0022427801038002002

Mathieson, D. (2005). Book review: Juvenile justice reform and restorative justice: Building theory and policy from practice. Probation Journal, 52(3), 310-311. http://dx.doi.org/10.1177/026455050505200315

Morrison, B. & Vaandering, D. (2012). Restorative justice: Pedagogy, praxis, and discipline. Journal of School Violence, 11(2), 138-155. http://dx.doi.org/10.1080/15388220.2011.653322

Murphy, K. (2008). Enforcing tax compliance: To Punish or persuade? Economic Analysis and Policy, 38(1), 113-135. http://dx.doi.org/10.1016/s0313-5926(08)50009-9

Smith, D. (2005). Book review: Juvenile justice reform and restorative justice: Building theory and policy from practice. Youth Justice, 5(2), 139-140. http://dx.doi.org/10.1177/147322540500500207

Trenczek, T. (2015). Restorative justice: New paradigm, sensitizing theory or even practice? Restorative Justice, 3(3), 453-459. http://dx.doi.org/10.1080/20504721.2015.1109368

Walklate, S. (2007). Understanding criminology (1st ed., pp. 27-31). Maidenhead: McGraw-Hill/Open University Press.

Wellford, C. (1975). Labelling theory and criminology: An assessment. Social Problems, 22(3), 332-345. http://dx.doi.org/10.2307/799814

Wilson, F. (2006). Book review: juvenile justice reform and restorative justice: Building theory and policy from practice. Youth Violence and Juvenile Justice, 4(2), 213-214. http://dx.doi.org/10.1177/1541204006286321

Chapter 8
Feminist Theories

1.   Introduction

The concept of feminism is very popular yet it is not defined by a single definition as different feminist see themselves fitting into different branches of feminism. While some of the feminist theories are helping the concept of feminism move forward, there are certainly some additional conflicts in the feminist movement that comes from contradictions within different feminism theories. The basic idea behind feminism movement is that men and women are equal parts of the society and should receive equal treatment from the society, more specifically in economical manner, political manner and in social value. The approaches taken by different feminism theories are different, however, the goal of the theories remain similar.

In this chapter, the theory of feminism is evaluated and different theories are compared for their justification of feminism and the approaches taken to achieve the goal. The primary goal of this chapter is to identify the feminist theories in different fields of society, such as the feminist theories in criminal justice and the empirical validity of such theories. Ultimately, this chapter will present a comprehensive analysis of present day feminist theories and feminism movement in our society.

1.1 Feminism

In its most basic definition, feminism refers to the theory of idea that women are equal to their male counterpart in all parts of the community, be it political, economic or social. All of the different feminism theories and movement function this very core element of feminism. This idea of feminism is the core principle that remains active in all the feminism theories as the primary goal. One thing to point out with the idea of feminism is that the core concept only deems women as equal to men without describing the similarities or differences between them. This core concept does not demand treatment of women higher than men in any way. This is an important distinction to make because the idea of feminism does not require only furthering of women and not of men, but many of the different feminist theories and branches do just that.

1.2 Feminist

Any person who agrees or believes that in our society, men and women should receive equal rights and equal treatment from aspects like economic, political and social factors.

2.   Feminism and Major Feminism Theories

While the core concept of feminism has remained true to gaining equality for women in all aspects of society, the way different theories are developed for feminism and the different feminist movements have all followed different approaches and values as objective. This situation has resulted in several different types of feminist theories to come forward. Following are some of the most renowned and major theories of feminism that are followed in modern society:

2.1 Cultural Feminism

This theory of feminism is based on the idea that there are some certain differences that exist between men and women regarding their natural personality and assumes that the inherent differences that are present in women are more special and should be celebrated by the society. According to the feminists who believe in this feminism theory, the biological and personality differences between men and women are supported and celebrated. For example- argument is made that females are inherently kinder and gentler than male. These kinds of feminists believe that women should rule the governments as they are more reasonable, considerate, merciful and kinder.

2.2 Eco-Feminism

The eco-feminism theory of feminism believes in the core concept that the male-controlled policies and practices of modern world are harmful for the women that are part of the society. This theory establishes some parallels between the way society treats animals and environment to the way women are treated in our society. Feminists who believe in this theory of feminism consider that by protesting the male-dominance in our society, they are not just protecting rights of women, but that they are also protecting the environment from the destructive nature of male behavior. Most eco-feminists believe that the male-dominated social structure has developed in last 5,000 years and it is not the natural form of society as the original social form belongs to female-dominance.

2.3 Libertarian Feminism

This feminist theory is also known as individualist feminism theory. The basis of this feminist theory is on the ideologies of libertarian concepts that promote more rights to individual members of the society and very minimal use of government. The priority of this feminist movement is on giving individual members of the society higher level of autonomy, freedom and rights to pursue their interests. The libertarian feminists focus on many aspects of our society and target a lot of challenges and social barriers that are not exclusive to women only as men also face the same barriers from governments.

2.4 Material Feminism

Material feminist movement is a relatively new feminist movement and it only began in the late 19th century. The main principle of this theory of women empowerment is that the women will feel more liberated in the society and will take higher advantage of opportunities by improvement in their material condition. Feminists that are part of this movement focus on getting rid of the traditional burden off women that includes their role in household tasks and domestic jobs and promoting the idea among men and women that women are capable and well-equipped to do other jobs that are traditionally associated with men only.

2.5 Moderate Feminism

This branch of feminist movement is highly populated with young females or women who believe that they have not faced any kind of gender based discrimination directly in the society. This group of feminists believe that the core principles and objectives of the feminist movement are not viable anymore and it is completely based on last century ideologies of society. To some extent, moderate feminists raise questions about making any further efforts for the cause of feminism. A major part of the moderate feminist movement does not want the tag of feminist while still desiring for complete equality and rights for women in society.

3.   Feminist Theories in Criminology

3.1 Feminist Theories in Crime

Adler (1975) coined the idea that the liberation of women politically and socially in the 1970s era led to development of more economic opportunities for women in the business and social world and also allowed women to become as crime-prone as men. While there have been many feminist leaders demanding equal opportunities in legitimate areas of society such as legislation and businesses, a similar growth in number of women entering major crime scenarios as well such as white-collar crime and murder. The theory suggested by Adler is that by climbing the ladder of business and career success, women are also able to use this increased liberation to make their way into white-collar crime. Consistent positive trend of feminism has also ensured that there is also high visibility of female crime through policing and reporting in news as well as harder sentencing by the criminal justice system. Despite the increased visibility, the statistical portion of crime committed by women remains small in comparison to men. The theory coined by Adler has received both support and criticism in the field of feminism as some have called it a part of old criminology theory and not a new factor of feminism theory.

3.2 Feminist Theories in Criminal Justice

Feminism has become a major topic of debate in recent years and as such on global scale and because of it, more studies are getting conducted on the criminology aspect of feminism theories. One aspect of criminal justice system is the way women offenders are handled in the processing of criminal justice operations. In this regard, there are two major hypotheses that are commonly referred to by the scholars and researchers in the field. The first perspective is of the chivalry hypothesis or the paternalism concept which considers women inmates as the victims of inequality and suggests that in the complete process of criminal justice, women are treated in a relaxed manner that provides them more leniently than the male counterpart as the criminal justice system is dominated by male and they show mercy on the supposedly 'weaker' counterpart (Crew, 1991). The other popular hypothesis or theory is the "evil women" theory and it suggests that women receive more tough punishment and treatment from the criminal justice system as a way of male officers taking their offences as not just violation of the legal restrictions, but also of the social norm of women staying away from crime, that anti-feminist associate with women commonly (Baines, Barak-Erez, & Kahana, 2012).

3.3 Empirical Research on Feminist Theories in Criminal Justice

A common opinion presented in the scholarly literature is that as feminism continues to gain more support in the mainstream media and legal proceedings are designed to take this into account, the legal system will increasingly treat both men and women equally. For proving either of the liberation theories right based on evidence, the empirical evidence present provides support and contradictions for both theories. Some researchers even suggest that there does not exist much empirical data to support the theories of feminism in criminal justice system (Chesney-Lind & Pasko 2013). Differences in sentencing in criminal justice system based on gender allows different interpretations to be made and there are some groups of feminists who do not want the court system to adopt complete equality in the system for women (Chesney-Lind, 1986). The argument given by such feminist groups is that women are not taking part in the major crime and legal offences like band robberies, stock frauds, etc.

Based on some empirical evidence, Farrington and Morris (1983) did reach to the conclusion that women do tend to obtain less severe sentencing for their crimes in comparison to their male counterpart. However, they also found that the less severe nature of their punishment has multiple reasons and gender based argument can only be one of these reasons. Some of the most notable reasons for the less severity of the punishment for women include the fact that most women were the first-time offenders for any crime and it is usually the case that women committed less serious nature of the crime. The seriousness of the crime and any prior history of offenses play a very important part of the sentencing for the women as it is a fundamental part of the criminal justice system. Based on accounting of these factors into the equation of women receiving less severe punishment by criminal justice system, it can be argued that women are not treated differently in the criminal justice system than male. One point of difference and leniently among women was also found in this empirical research as the researchers found that a married female having a caring role of a mother is very likely to get less severe punishment.

4. Women Liberation Theory

The theory of women liberation addresses the involvement of women in crime from a feminism perspective and asserts the idea that as the existing gender inequality between men and women continues to fade away, involvement and seriousness of women in crime will continue to increase and reach the same extent as men. According to this theory, women will commit more crime like men as they receive equal participation opportunities in the society, which in turns provides women with more opportunities to commit crime. This theory indicates and promotes the idea that the lesser involvement of women in crime is heavily linked with the lesser social participation of women, resulting from the present inequality in society. There do exist some relevant case studies and evidences that indicate that women who belong to equally placed positions in the society, resemble a similar level of participation in crime as men (Cossman & Fudge, 2002). However, there is very little empirical evidence to support this theory in favor of the liberation theory of women crimes.

In the modern society, the mere concept of feminism seems like the root cause of majority of social issues. Naffine (1995) has promoted the suggestion that the way 'liberation theory of women' has received attention in our society, it is forcing women in our society to face increased level of hostility targeting the women's feminism movements.

According to Islam, Banarjee and Khatun (2016), in the 1970s era, there was a second major wave of feminism movement and afterwards, there was a very noticeable growth in the number of crimes committed by women.

The theory of women liberation has received a lot of criticism as well in the feminism circles. According to Bisi (2002), the theory of liberation is an embarrassment to the feminism concept and provides argument that the liberation of women has not contributed to higher number of crimes committed by women rather it has increased the level of reporting and public attention on the existing number of crimes committed by women. It is claimed in the same article that the theory of liberation of women does not take into account the concept of feminism at all and is entirely based on the traditional theory of criminology. This argument disputes the validity of women liberation theory and provides the lack of supporting evidences for the theory as a major indication of falsehood in the theory (Simpson, 1989). The argument against the women liberation theory suggests that the increment in crimes committed by women are not as high as made by the liberation theory believers and the most notable change has happened in the way women committed crimes are now getting reported, policed and tried in the court of law.

The claims made by the women liberation theory also do not address the aspects of internal factors such as ethnicity, race, class and age. According to many of the feminist theorists, there factors are very important to address for any theory to explain the concept of criminology associated with feminism theory. This is important to add factors like these because such factors may very well describe the reason for women committing a crime. For example- in many cases, a hike in number of arrests made against women has increased due to lowered stability of the economy and it may also come from sudden rise in cases of shoplifting. Inclusion of factors like this could very well support that the theory of relationship between the crime and employment is more effective than the claims made by the women liberation theory (Callanan & Teasdale, 2009). According to the economic theory of relationship between crime and employment, in good economic times, the rate of crime committed by women stabilize rather than increase in number. A troubling economic scenario means a certain lack of opportunity in the society for the women to earn their fair share and that may easily lead to increased number of crimes done by women. This theory also contradicts with the theory of women liberation that indicates that women would also commit similar level of crime to similar extent if equality in the society is promoted further.

It is commonly understood that a feminist activity is the person who supports and fight for the liberation and freedom of women towards equal rights in the society. Feminism is pro-equality and not necessarily pro-woman; however, a feminist movement may take any direction. Many of the existing feminist movements do not follow the simple goal of equality rather demands higher rights for the women and restrictions on the rights of men. Majority of the feminist groups also compare the condition of women in our society to animals and environment and suggest that the male dominated society does not treat them in the way others deserve to get treated.

The concept of feminism is quite a moral one at its root as the idea of women in the society who is bound by the social expectations and traditional men imposed rules for their behavior. It seems quite repugnant and hypocritical of the society to think that women do have equal rights if there is a thought that women belong to the stereotypical roles in the society such as staying at home, taking care of the children and following the orders of men. If not in one part of society, the inequality in our society certain exists against women to varying extent in different parts of world (Daly & Chesney-Lind, 1988). It is very important to give attention to the concept of feminism and true to feminism movements, however, there are some feminist movements that have varying degree of objectives with their efforts and perceive the inequality in our society in different mannerisms.

4.1 Female Crime Masculinity Hypothesis

The theory of masculinity linking to the criminal intent and behavior has existed for a long time now. On the topic of feminism and its relations to crime, the issue of masculinity has been discussed heavily in past as well as in present from the criminological thought perspective. One of the very first attempts to identifying link of crime with masculinity came from Stewart (2014) and it was found in this research that masculinity created a more aggressive nature among male participants and because of it, men are more likely to take part in a delinquent or irresponsible behavior in comparison to women. Similar study was also conducted by Lilly, Cullen and Ball 2007) and it was found that the element of masculinity has become an inherent part of our society and boys are taught to remain 'rough and tough' and the society, making it a lot more likely for the men to participate in criminal activity than women due to the very structure of our society. The theory of differential of opportunity is also worth a discussion with the concept of feminism crime and masculinity association. The proposal from Van Gundy and Kappeler (2014) about the theory of differences in opportunity is that young male learn about both good and bad manners and behavior tactics from their elders and their role models that are male, which creates a cycle of more aggression and criminal behavior among men due to the previous generation having this dynamic in criminal behavior. This idea promotes the social norm that young males learn that the basic traits of being tough and masculine is important for the male from their elders and keeping up with the norm, younger boys also take part in some illegitimate behavior in order to prove their masculinity to others as a way of showing dominance.

Johnsen (2006) performed a more thorough examination of the way masculinity impacts the increased criminal behavior among men and may also be the reason for lesser criminal activities among women. This research concluded that there are many factors that contribute to the male masculinity resulting in higher degree of irresponsible and illegitimate behavior from male and many of these factors are unique to men in our current social structure. The factors pointed out by the researcher included- influence of military, social norms, depiction of men in entertainment media, peer pressure and socialization. In a research that focused more on interaction between men and women, it was detected that the men having higher degree of masculinity orientation according to social norms were also more likely to engage in violent behavior than others. Additional research in this area also reveals that a significant part of masculinity perception and contribution to criminal behavior also comes from the way episodes of violence are depicted in media as well as in sporting events to showcase masculinity of actors or sportsmen. Many studies have focused on the contribution and influence of masculinity in criminal behavior, however, only a handful of research studies have actually attempted to define the characteristic of masculinity (Anderson, Daly, & Rapp, 2009). From the empirical research studies and evidence, it becomes clear that there is some link that associates criminal behavior with masculinity and a larger research is required to understand if the concept of masculinity used in these research studies is only linked to men or it is a socially awarded characteristic that may also exist among women if there is equality in the society.

A significant share of studies and examinations that evaluate presence of criminal behavior intent with masculinity most commonly consider the behavior study of adolescent boys living in inner city. A study conducted by Smart (2002) analyzed the empirical studies and suggested that it is also possible to explain the higher degree of criminal behavior in this sample population on the compulsive masculinity requirements among the adolescent boys as a kind of peer-pressure committed act. However, the studies that focused on this approach of explanation of masculinity and its link to crime did not operationalize masculinity and rather used aspects like lack of father figure to identify the level of masculinity. Many studies have pointed out masculinity as one of the major factors that are concerning for the modern society and have also raised concerns over the contradiction of the masculinity concept with feminist movement. In majority of the studies, masculinity is defined as a completely male characteristic and describes as the aggressive nature of male that is expressed physically. The actual study to link masculinity with criminal behavior and violent acts has not been performed on the extent that empirical evidences can get collected to identify its impact on criminology theories.

From the research studies and various theories of feminism criminal behavior associated with masculinity, masculinity is a factor that does contribute to high probability of potential criminal behavior. However, there can be multiple different definitions of the masculinity characteristics, it is either a characteristic that is specific to male or is the characteristics that are found among male due to current social structure of our society that expects men to behave in this certain stereotype manner. In both cases, it is evident that women do not share the same characteristic of masculinity as men and as a result, it is very likely that the level of violent behavior and criminal behavior from women would remain low even in scenarios where women do get equal opportunities in the society as well as equality across the society (Bernstein, 2012). The female crime masculinity hypothesis does not much empirical evidences to support either claims but the research studies do indicate that women are not in similar peer-pressure scenario and not constrained by the same expectation as men to behave irresponsibly to showcase their masculinity. This aspect of analysis indicates that equality for women in our society would not result in higher crime rate of crimes done by women because of inherent masculinity issues among women and a more responsible and law-abiding behavior is expected from women even after obtaining complete equality in rights and opportunities in society.

4.2 Female Crime Opportunity Hypothesis

Lagrange & Silverman (1999) based their research on the long-term debate over the relationship that exists between criminal behavior of a person and the role of gender in it. According to them, the whole argument about the crime and gender relationship relies on two prime factors of consideration: why is it seen that women are more likely to commit less offenses of criminal degree than men? And if the reasons of committing are same as men when women do commit crime? The basic theory of criminology indicates that a crime takes place because a combination of two different factors- the specifics of the situation that initiate crime scenario and the inclination of offender to commit a crime.

The hypothesis of female crime opportunity offers an answer to both questions based on the general criminology theory. It is possible to attribute the existing low number of crimes committed by women to the lesser extent of opportunities offered to men in our society and to the lesser inclination of women to commit a crime (Morgan, Reiner, & Maguire, 2012). It is found in this research that upon equating both factors, it is commonly assumed that women would also engage in crimes for the same reasons as men.

A research study by Nicolson and Bibbings (2013) suggests that reaching any conclusion in this regard would require a lot of future studies that are thorough and combines a very large sample population for research. This is warranted because of the sheer number of different personality factors that can influence the result of a study, such as the level of self-control, risk taking capabilities and role models based on social structure. One of the most notable factor that can explain the differences in criminal behavior activities of men and women is the willingness to seek risks as men tend to take more risks in their usual life to maintain their aggressive image among their peers while women tend to stay away from trouble keeping up with their traditional social expectation approach. Majority of differences between men and women are easy to explain based on factors like impulsiveness levels as well as risk seeking nature. These are the factors that closely link to the delinquency behavior in an individual and both factors are found inherently lowered among women when compared to men. This approach provides a good explanation of the lesser number of criminal activities committed by women and suggests that women are also less inclined to get involved in a criminal activity.

The theory of female crime opportunity makes the claim that in a situation where men and women are given same opportunities and same risks associated with a crime, the probability of committing the crime will also be same. This theory assumes to find same results with women as men because equal opportunities should appeal to both in the same way. Many of the feminism opposing groups take this approach as a way of promoting the idea that upon receiving equality in the society, women would also engage in crimes and delinquencies (Rader & Haynes, 2011). These kinds of efforts are made to minimize the force of feminist movements attempting to gain equal rights for women in society. Research studies have found that the female crime opportunity theory assumes women and men to be the same in behavior by nature and that is why this theory claims that both would make same decisions provided same level of opportunity. However, there are some obvious known differences in behavioral characteristics of men and women which makes this theory debatable at best. It becomes clear that women are less inclined to criminal behavior as there is no peer-pressure among women to commit such an activity, and women also tend to have lesser intentions of seeking risks.

4.3 Economic Marginalization Hypothesis Power-Control Theory

The theory of economic marginalization refers to the belief that in the liberalization trend of women across the globe, women are consistently feeling more pressured to economically support themselves and children on their own. In this manner, stepping back from the support of men on all financial fronts is a heavy burden on women and because of it, the economic pressure pushes a lot of women towards a life of crime and many criminal activities (BOX & HALE, 1984). According to this theory, liberation of women would lead to more and more women feeling pressured to earn economic independence for themselves and their children, leading to a social situation where women are forced into committing crimes for financial gains. This hypothesis is an anti-feminism theory as it suggests that to remain less prone to criminal behavior, women should remain less independent on financial fronts and accept the stereotypical social structure in which men is responsible to provide financial support for the family. Among all the feminism and anti-feminism theories of women criminology, the economic marginalization theory has very little evidence to support its claim of women economic independence leading to higher participation of women in crime (Burgess-Proctor, 2006). However, the power-control theory certainly has some reasonable claims to it as it relies heavily on the opportunity theory as well. According to this theory of women criminology, with constantly growth in the trend of equality for women, women would soon gain equal rights and opportunities in the society as men. In such a situation, women would also have to fight and struggle to gain and retain power in businesses, financial aspects and in society. Such a struggle to retain power and essentially control is a basic cause for many crimes. By getting exposed to more opportunities of power and control, women would also become more likely to engage in crimes that they are not usually in scenario of committing.

It is very important for these theories to gain huge support from empirical data and evidences to prove the point of research. All the women crime theories are based on ideologies and have very little scenario of ideal sample population to use for empirical research. The need for future research studies is quite apparent to examine and evaluate the case of women criminology linked with feminism.

5. Patriarchal Society and Crime Masculinities

In wake of consistent efforts of feminist movements to grant women equality in the society, popularity of patriarchal or male-dominated society has decreased significantly in recent years. The concept of patriarchal society has certainly become a lot less acceptable than ever before in modern society. In terms of criminology, removal of patriarchal society would help women gain more participation in the criminal justice system and in gaining fair treatment as criminals without having to worry about gender based inequality, favorable or unfavorable (Parker & Reckdenwald, 2008). The context of gender is highly disputed in many of these scenarios as some feminists claim that upon violation of law, women receive bad treatment from the criminal justice system through the entire process as the male-dominated society intends to punish women for not just violation of law, but also for violating the social expectations for a woman. The critics of feminism also claim that in current system, women get an unjustified and favorable treatment from the criminal justice system, which should get changed in a completely equal scenario of our society (Garland, Phillips, & Vollum, 2016). In both cases, having gender based equality is a positive change for the criminal justice system as it ensures that all alleged and convicted prisoners get fair treatment that is legally and morally justified.

Masculinity in Crime

Masculinity is a trait that is highly closely linked with the man and with the inclination of man with crime. Empirical evidence suggests that among men committing crime, masculinity is a major factor that leads to men having higher inclination towards crime and irresponsible behavior (Messerschmitt, 1993). Masculinity for men is presented in our society as a natural and essential characteristic for men that include factors like roughness, carelessness and high risk-taking ability. It is common for boys to feel pressured to behave in this manner to showcase their masculinity, making them more prone to behaving delinquently due to peer-pressure and the social expectations (Hagan, 2008). In case of women in our society, masculinity is not a characteristic that is associated with them in any way and this helps prevent them from feeling pressured to behave in an irresponsible manner.

There exists empirical evidence that shows that higher masculinity leads to more inclination towards crime which is a notable factor contributing to high rate of crimes among men. Lack of such a factor among women makes it possible for women to have lesser inclination towards committing crime. Overall, the factor of masculinity in crime does not hinder the idea of feminism as there is no link of masculinity crime to come forward among women as well.

6. Implications of Feminism on Involvement of Women in Crime

In recent years, the demand for equality for women has increased significantly as feminism has become a global scale movement. Many governments and societies have accepted this change and are developing legal proceedings in accordance to equality for women. On the issue of women equality, one of the most discussed factors is about the criminal behavior of women upon gaining equality in the society as men. There are different theories of women criminology that address the feminism aspect of movement. Most studies conducted so far assumes certain aspects and predict the scenario where women have equal rights based on evidence, which is gathered from very small sample population in present society structure (Brunsdon, 2013). In current situation, there is empirical data that can be used to both support and contradict the liberation theory and power-control theory of feminism criminology. In current structure of empirical evidences, following statements can be made about implications of feminism on involvement of women in crime:

The claim of women liberation theory is that with gain of equal rights and opportunity in our society, women would also gain equal opportunity to crimes that are traditionally considered male dominated crimes. The empirical evidence for such a claim do indicate that in some cases, women who were in similar job position and rights did commit similar level of crimes as men, however, it is also noteworthy that such empirical evidences do not consider other factors like seriousness of the crime, economic conditions and context.

On the issue of women criminology in criminal justice, it is well-supported idea that women are certainly less involved in criminal activities than men. However, the reason for this may vary from one situation to another. For example- the lesser number of convictions for women may indicate that women are treated more favorably by the criminal justice system as the weaker entity of the society or less capable of dealing with rough punishment (Carrington, 2014). However, some other feminists also claim that the empirical evidence shows growth in women criminal activities after the second wave of feminist movement in 1970s because of higher attention and coverage that women crimes have received.

7. Summary

Equality for all is one of the main principles of democracy in many of the independent countries today. However, social equality has not become ubiquitous across the globe in the social structure even if it exists from a legal standpoint. Feminism is the concept of having equal rights and opportunities for women in our society and in the modern society, there are many feminist movements going on that target the same objective. While the core principles of all the feminist movements remain the same, the direction of activities differs significantly.

In this chapter, different theories of gender inequality and feminism are examined considering criminology and criminal justice system. In all cases of criminology, it is likely that the gender inequality will come in the equation either for or against a woman who has committed a crime. The theory of women liberation suggests that because of feminist movements, women receive more opportunities in the society and therefore, there has been more cases of women criminals in areas that were previously heavily dominated by male. The opposing argument to this suggests that the increased number of women crime cases existed before as well, but are coming forward more due to stricter reporting, policing and justice system against women committed crimes now.

There is a definite lack of high volumes of empirical evidence to support any of the theories in a significant manner. It is important that more research studies are conducted to identify the complete nature of feminism and its effects on criminology.

References

Adler, F. (1975). Sisters in crime: The rise of the new female. Crime and Social Justice, 8, 74-79.

Anderson, T., Daly, K., & Rapp, L. (2009). Clubbing masculinities and crime: A qualitative study of Philadelphia nightclub scenes. Feminist Criminology, 4(4), 302-332. http://dx.doi.org/10.1177/1557085109343676

Baines, B., Barak-Erez, D., & Kahana, T. (2012). Feminist constitutionalism (1st ed., pp. 84-87). Cambridge: Cambridge University Press.

Bernstein, E. (2012). Carceral politics as gender justice? The "traffic in women" and neoliberal circuits of crime, sex, and rights. Theory and Society, 41(3), 233-259. http://dx.doi.org/10.1007/s11186-012-9165-9

Bisi, S. (2002). Female criminality and gender difference. International Review of Sociology, 12(1), 23-43. http://dx.doi.org/10.1080/03906700220135309

BOX, S. & HALE, C. (1984). Liberation/emancipation, economic marginalization, or less chivalry. The Relevance of Three Theoretical Arguments to Female Crime Patterns in England and Wales, 1951-1980. Criminology, 22(4), 473-497. http://dx.doi.org/10.1111/j.1745-9125.1984.tb00312.x

Brunsdon, C. (2013). Television crime series, women police, and fuddy-duddy feminism. Feminist Media Studies, 13(3), 375-394. http://dx.doi.org/10.1080/14680777.2011.652143

Burgess-Proctor, A. (2006). Intersections of race, class, gender, and crime: Future directions for feminist criminology. Feminist Criminology, 1(1), 27-47. http://dx.doi.org/10.1177/1557085105282899

Callanan, V. & Teasdale, B. (2009). An exploration of gender differences in measurement of fear of crime. Feminist Criminology, 4(4), 359-376. http://dx.doi.org/10.1177/1557085109345462

Carrington, K. (2014). Feminism and global justice (1st ed., pp. 7-11). Routledge.

Chesney-Lind, M. (1986). "Women and Crime": The Female Offender. Signs, 12(1), 78-96.

Chesney-Lind, M. & Pasko, L. (2013). The female offender (1st ed., pp. 12-17). Thousand Oaks: SAGE.

Cossman, B. & Fudge, J. (2002). Privatization, law, and the challenge to feminism (1st ed., pp. 355-357). Toronto: University of Toronto Press.

Crew, B. (1991). Sex differences in criminal sentencing: Chivalry or patriarchy? Justice Quarterly, 8(1), 59-83. http://dx.doi.org/10.1080/07418829100090911

Daly, K. & Chesney-Lind, M. (1988). Feminism and criminology. Justice Quarterly, 5(4), 497-538. http://dx.doi.org/10.1080/07418828800089871

Farrington, D. & Morris, A. (1983). Sex, sentencing and reconviction. The British Journal of Criminology, 23(3), 229-248.

Garland, T., Phillips, N., & Vollum, S. (2016). Gender politics and the walking dead: Gendered violence and the reestablishment of patriarchy. Feminist Criminology. http://dx.doi.org/10.1177/1557085116635269

Hagan, F. (2008). Introduction to criminology: Theories, methods, and criminal behavior (1st ed., pp. 184-188). SAGE.

Islam, M., Banarjee, S., & Khatun, N. (2016). Theories of female criminality: A criminological analysis. International Journal of Criminology and Sociological Theory, 7(1), 1-8.

Johnsen, R. (2006). Contemporary feminist historical crime fiction (1st ed., pp. 153-155). New York: Palgrave Macmillan.

Lagrange, T. & Silverman, R. (1999). Low self-control and opportunity: Testing the general theory of crime as an explanation for gender differences in delinquency*. Criminology, 37(1), 41-72. http://dx.doi.org/10.1111/j.1745-9125.1999.tb00479.x

Lilly, J., Cullen, F., & Ball, R. (2007). Criminological theory (1st ed., pp. 217-219). Thousand Oaks: SAGE Publications.

Messerschmidt, J. (1993). Masculinities and crime (1st ed., pp. 32-36). Lanham, Md.: Rowman & Littlefield.

Morgan, R., Reiner, R., & Maguire, M. (2012). The Oxford handbook of criminology (5th ed., pp. 21-22). Oxford: Oxford University Press.

Naffine, N. (1995). Gender, crime, and feminism (1st ed., pp. 18-21). Aldershot [England]: Dartmouth.

Nicolson, D. & Bibbings, L. (2013). Feminist perspectives on criminal law (3rd ed., pp. 25-26). London: Routledge.

Parker, K. & Reckdenwald, A. (2008). Women and crime in context: Examining the linkages between patriarchy and female offending across space. Feminist Criminology, 3(1), 5-24. http://dx.doi.org/10.1177/1557085107308456

Rader, N. & Haynes, S. (2011). Gendered fear of crime socialization: An extension of Akers's social learning theory. Feminist Criminology, 6(4), 291-307. http://dx.doi.org/10.1177/1557085111408278

Simpson, S. (1989). Feminist theory, crime, and justice*. Criminology, 27(4), 605-632. http://dx.doi.org/10.1111/j.1745-9125.1989.tb01048.x

Smart, C. (2002). Feminism and the power of law (1st ed., pp. 28-33). London: Routledge.

Stewart, F. (2014). German queer crime fiction (1st ed., pp. 21-24). Jefferson: McFarland.

Van Gundy, A. & Kappeler, V. (2014). Feminist theory, crime, and social justice (1st ed., pp. 1-5). Hoboken: Taylor and Francis.

Chapter 9
Integrating Criminology Theories

1. Introduction

The field of criminology is a very wide-ranging field and it takes a lot of theories from different streams of science into consideration, such as- law, anthropology, sociology and psychology (Cullen & Wilcox, 2010). Having high level of diversity in the combining theoretical structure of basic criminology is a poor presentation on the science of criminology and it depicts a lack of consistency in the industry. Despite large number of studies and research projects performed by scholars and criminology experts, the science of criminology still lacks a definitive or widely accepted unified theory of theatrical conceptual framework of criminology.

Various criminologists have worked towards establishment of integration among different theories of criminology, however, majority of these efforts include very critical and comprehensive literature reviews. These literature reviews certainly function as important resources and foundation of a much-needed integration of criminology theories, but are far from being a real integration of the theories. Many different studies have found suitable and reasonable links between different propositions argued in different types of criminology theories, however, each research study makes use of only a handful of criminology theories for integration efforts.

2. Criminal Behavior and Criminology: Theoretical Integration

The process of theoretical integration of criminal behavior theories can be performed in several different ways. Identification of different types of theoretical integration has been performed by Liska, Sanchirico, and Reed (1988). According to this categorization of types, the first type of theoretical integration is to integrate on basis of conceptual integration. In this approach, the concepts that are present in one theory are either matched with another theory for purpose of integration or the concepts between two theories are shown to have overlapping elements. The other type of theoretical integration is propositional integration. The mechanism of propositional integration is to establish relationship between the propositions used by two different criminal behavior theories. This relationship or link can be established by either identifying or showing that two or more theories of criminal behavior are making same kind of propositional predictions about crime, even if both theories begin with different assumptions or the different base concept. It is also possible to perform propositional integration of theories by developing explanation variables for all theories in consideration and then establishing a sequential relation between the variables. In this manner, the sequence of variables would include that the variable present in one theory would provide explanation of the variable change for another theory and so on (Liska, 1992). Using this approach, delinquency or criminal behavior can be established using combination of two or more theories, making it an integration of theories. It is possible to perform the process of theoretical integration process in either within-level (only macro or only micro) of the concept or in cross-level (structural process) manner.

The literature in criminology includes several different examples of criminal behavior theory integration, performed by use of propositional method or conceptual method as well as integration that is cross-level and integration that is within-level. Analyzing and explaining all the integrating efforts and integration theories would cover a very long chapter as there are hundreds of integration theories developed by integration of criminal behavior theories in different ways. A few of the most important and significant criminal theory integration models are presented in this chapter to illustrate the current state of integration in criminology literature. Nearly all the illustrations of theoretical integration criminal behavior theories that are present and analyzed in this chapter include the social learning theory in some manner and the theory of social bonding is also a quite common addition for integration (Akers, 2013). The reasons for which both theories are used are quite prominent and these reasons include- social learning theory is one of the most notable theories in criminal behavior theories and the social learning theory links to the social bonding theory in some respects. Both theories are used with high frequency in the criminology literature, making these two suitable additions for any integration project of criminal behavior theories.

Due to existence of many different criminal behavior theories and great possibility of combination across these criminal behavior theories, there exist a wide variety of integration theories. Many of the integration theories are designed for the sole purpose of achieving integration among the various types of criminology theories of criminal behavior and delinquency. However, some of the integration theories are resultant of efforts made to contrast and compare two or more criminal behavior theories with each-other. The variety of integration model represents the level of variety that is present across the literature in criminology studies and it also showcases the high interest of researchers in the field of criminology to identify the most approachable and suitable method of integrating the criminal behavior theories.

3.   Conceptual Amalgamation: Social Anomie, Conflict, Labelling, Bonding, and Deterrence

Akers (2013) attempted an integration of different types of criminology theory concepts in 1970s by identifying the overlapping concepts present in various social learning theories along with the propositions of social anomie, conflict, labelling, bonding and deterrence. In his later research studies, Akers claimed that an effective of integration would be to use the conceptual amalgamation approach. The conceptual amalgamation refers to the technique of seeing one specific idea of one criminology theory and then using it to explain a special case of some other criminology theory. An example of the conceptual amalgamation is that concept of 'belief' that exists in theory of social bonding and then using this theory in similar manner as constrain delinquency. The basic concept of belief is now usable with a wide variety of different social learning concept definitions to either positively or negatively link to criminal behavior or delinquency. Use of the broader definition of a single concept provides both specific and general-purpose beliefs that lead to delinquent behavior among criminals (Hale, 1996). In this approach, the belief of the person is evaluated that deems an action's justification for that specific person in certain specific circumstances.

Akers provides the argument that the concept of 'commitment', which is part of the social bonding theory is also worth absorption from the concepts of social learning theory. In this approach, the concept of commitment refers to the cost that a person would receive for committing a crime, for example- potentially losing the investments made in other tasks. This social bonding theory only links to half part of the social learning theory based concept that is 'differential reinforcement.' The concept of differential reinforcement adheres to the positive or negative results (rewards or punishments) that are linked to committing a crime. The social bonding theory concept of commitment only links to the part of losing the investments (punishment) and remains unaware of the other large factors associated with it. In this manner, the social bonding theory only reflects on only one part of the factors that are covered in the reinforcement balance concept. The concept of differential reinforcement in social learning theory can entirely absorb the concept of commitment from social bonding theory as there is nothing in commitment concept that is not already present in the differential reinforcement concept.

The research study conducted by Akers (2013) focused mainly on performing amalgamation of primary social theories of criminology and mostly included social bonding theory and social learning theory as a way of showcasing that integration of different criminology theories is possible with use of conceptual absorption. In the theory of social bonding based criminology approach, the 'attachment' concept is a measure of representing a person's closeness and affection for relationships with parents, colleagues and friends. Akers asserts that the same concept can be included within the 'intensity' measure that is part of social learning theory.

According to the research performed by Akers, all the areas of conceptual commodities in different types of criminology theories may not essentially result in similar propositions about the criminal behavior. This indicates that the technique of achieving conceptual integration of various criminology theories does not automatically equates to generation of proposition-level integration of all theories. For example- the theory of social bonding suggests that a person who has solid attachment with other people then it is more likely for the person to showcase delinquency in behavior, even in cases where the attachment is for people who are delinquent. On the other hand, the theory of social learning predicts completely opposite proposition for this situation.

4.   Social Support and Coercion: A Major Root of Criminal Behavior

In the field of criminology, there are certainly a wide variety of theories that attempt to explain criminology and criminal behavior among individuals. According to Colvin, Cullen and Ven (2002), there are two common themes that are visible across majority of these emerging new theories of criminal behavior and delinquency. These two themes include, coercion as one of the root causes of crime and that social bonds and support prevents criminal behavior. While in general sense of the argument, this statement is true, however, the research study by Colvin and Cullen identified some necessary cautions that must be part of this discussion about criminal behavior and criminal intent motivators. With this approach, the researchers outline the various nuances that exist between the complex combination of social bonds and coercion. Both themes in criminology are linked to each-other and offer the very basic framework for development of a fully integrated theory in criminology that is able to win consensus from public reception as well as from a theoretical standpoint. Their research firstly examines the case of coercion and its claim of a major root cause of criminal behavior. In basic terms, the term coercion can be referred to as a sense of force that individuals feel to either commit an act either in fear or in anxiety. The reasons behind committing an act because of coercion can vary from one case to another, such as- economic instability or lack of control on situation. Coercion may also derive from present lack of support from social bonds or from threat to existing social support (AGNEW, 1985).

Upon examining the cause of coercion in criminology, the aspect of social support is evaluated by the researchers and it is defined as a form of help of assistance by the community or social group of the person that allows the individual in achieving the expressive requirements of life. Like the theme of coercion, social support factor can also remain active in form of macro and micro level of society. The factor of social support does indeed contribute to the mental health of an individual and can play a very vital role in preventing criminal behavior among people. This factor is also very well supported by the recent research studies in the theory of social capital. The core concussion of this theory presented by Colvin, Cullen and Ven is that to reduce intensity of crime, it is imperative that societies and communities develop and improve on the sources of social support for all members of the community and actively take part in programs designed to reduce coercion.

5. Integrated Theory of Delinquent Behavior

Among the most comprehensive and sophisticated attempts of incorporating conceptual integration of different criminology theories, the efforts made by Elliott, Ageton and Canter (1979) are quite popular. His work makes efforts to integrate all of the different criminology theories across all micro and macro theories of delinquent behavior into one in order to develop a completely integrative framework. This approach of proposition based integration is popularly known with the name of strain, bonding and social learning theories. The integration model of criminology theories that is promoted by them utilizes the argument that any strain that is felt by the people functions to weaken the socially accepted conventional bonds and this results in stronger move towards delinquent behavior promoting peers. This theory suggests that it is the stronger link to delinquent peers that is responsible for the criminal behavior among people.

Elliott's Integrated Theory of Delinquent Behavior			
(i)	(ii)	(iii)	(iv)
Strain	Weak traditional bonding	Strong link to delinquent peers	Criminal or Delinquent behavior
Presence of some pressure or discrepancy in targeted goals or achievements or other types of strains in life.	Weakening of social bonds and commitment in family or among friends.	Increases exposure to criminal behavior having peers or delinquent people in comparison to people with non-delinquent behavior	Probability of engaging in delinquent behavior increases.

In his research study, Elliott proposes the argument that the theories of stain, bonding and social learning, there is an inherent sharing of some basic propositions, implications of propositions and assumptions for predicament of criminology theory. However, it is also reviewed there do exist several differences that are present in assumptions made across different criminology theories, therefore, it is important that these differences are addressed before any level of integration is performed. For example, the bonding theory suggests that delinquent behavior starts with the basic assumption of disposition by people that deviates from law. Due to this assumption, the social bonding theory makes it essential that the only source for delinquent behavior is the lack of social bonding that allows for prevention of criminal behavior (Nagin & Pogarsky, 2001). Contrary to this approach of social bonding theory, the strain theory does not have any inherent assumption about any criminal behavior motivations that is common among all of us. The strain theory has no point of reference to the strength of weakness of social bonding that may result in preventing or motivating a person to engage in criminal activity or delinquent behavior (Allatt, 1984). Unlike the strain theory, the assumptions that exist in the social bonding theory provide references to bonding factors that lead to both motivations of committing crime as well as factors that prevent offenses.

The social bonding theory makes use of the content and socialization approach that is based on traditional approaches; and suggests that any change occurs upon either weakening of the social bonding relations or the bonding failing to significant extent. The social learning theory indicates that the way an individual person moves in the direction of socialization. According to this theory, an individual can learn criminal behavior based on the socialization approach and it is the same way an individual learns conforming behavior.

In this research study, Elliott et al. (1979) addresses the differences in assumptions made by different criminology theories and the approach taken for the integration purpose is to take the side of assumptions made by strain and social learning theories. In this manner, the integration process eliminates the assumption of social bonding theory that there exists a natural and inherent motivation towards crime among all people, intensity of which is defined by association of non-delinquent and delinquent personnel.

6.   Network Analysis Theory and Its Effectiveness

To better explain the causes and motivations for delinquent behavior, Krohn (1986) proposed a conceptual explanation of the delinquent behavior that makes use of two different criminology theories, social bonding theory and social learning theory. This integrated theory is known as network analysis theory and from the structure of this theory, it is a cross-level integration theory which combines various different structural characteristics of interaction based processes and social networking approaches. The integrated theory presented by Krohn does not offer a complete integrating of the two criminology theories, as it was not the intention, but the resulting theory indeed provides a way of bridging the two theoretical theories for their propositions that contrast from each-other. These propositions do get integrated in a way by this new theory given by Krohn for aspects like differential association, criminal behavior motivators and criminal behavior contrasting effects.

According to this theory, the social network in the theory is a group of various actors or individuals who are linked to each-other on basis of social relationship. In this manner, the personal network that an individual person has refers to the various relationship links that the individual has with other people such as family members, relationship with friends, relationship at workplace, etc. In making observations like the theory of social control, the hypothesis proposed by Krohn indicates that 'the quality and behavior expectation of the social network for an individual function as a restraint on the behavior of the individual. Additionally, the individual becomes more probable to perform the type of behavior that is more consistent in the social group or network of the person.' In this manner, the theory presented by Krohn is quite like the theory given by Elliott et al., as it provides a contrast to the popular theory of social bonding that suggests that the constraints of social network only function towards conformation of the traditional values and norms. Rejecting the social bonding theory, Krohn provides results that are more consistent with the social learning theory and suggests that 'the social network is developed based on deviant activities performed by the individual and therefore, the restraining characteristics or effect of the social network is inherently towards motivation of delinquent behavior.'

In the network analysis theory, Krohn (1986) recognizes two primary structure specific characteristics of the social group or network, density of the group and its multiplexity. Multiplexity refer to the multiple number of different types of social relationships that two individuals have common between them. For example- two people who are friends with each-other, may also be neighbors and share the same school in the area as well as belonging to the same grade. The theory suggests that the higher the number of multiplexity in the social network of the person, the more impacting the constraint of social network is on the person (Bernard, 1992). The direction in which this factor works is usually towards reduction of the delinquent behavior, but this is because the probability of finding multiplexity is high in cases like family, school, church and other contexts where convention is given the priority. It is significantly less common to find presence of multiplexity in cases where delinquent behavior is the context. By making use of this approach in criminology integration theory, the network analysis approach integrates both commitment/involvement concept with the differential association concept.

The other factor, network density, is a reference to the ratio that provides a comparison between the numbers of social links present to the individual and the total number of social links possible for the individual. The level of network density would be very high in a smaller community where it is probable that most individuals have a social relationship with most other members of the community. It is argued in the network analysis theory that the higher level of network density results in lowered involvement in delinquent behavior. From a practical standpoint, the level of network density gets lowered upon increase in the population, sharing an inverse proportionality relation. If the population density in an area is high, the level of network density would move towards lower position, resulting in higher probability of delinquent behavior.

7.   Integration of Social Learning, Social Bonding, and Social Structure

A well-known integration of different criminology was performed by Thornberry (1987) and in this study, the researcher developed an 'interactional theory' that is based integration of different theories like social learning theory, social bonding and social structure theory. According to this integration of criminology theories, the elements that exist in the social learning and social bonding theories, the characteristics that impact these elements include neighborhood situation, community relations. Race and social class. This theory suggests that the primary cause of criminal behavior is presence of weakness in the bonding that exists for the society. Weakening of the social bonding leads to the individuals becoming more likely to engage in delinquency activities and criminal activities. However, the integration approach also adds that an individual will not be able to engage in criminal activities unless they have learned the delinquency behavior from their social links because of their association with other parts of delinquent peers (PRATT & CULLEN, 2000). If a person remains in close contact with other delinquent peers and stays in this situation for long term, criminal behavior becomes a stable and lasting part of individual's life.

The influences that a person receives from his or her peers are not entirely static as these may vary on basis of age of the individual and different factors like cessation of criminal behavior or continuation of it. In addition to this, it is not necessary that the relationship that is present among criminal behavior, learning and social bonding always flow in the same direction. For example- if an individual has low level of attachment to parents, it is possible for the individual to have lowered degree of commitment for school, which can then further reduce level of attachment to parents. In similar manner, low extent of attachment and commitment also leads to encouragement in delinquent behavior, which increases engagement in criminal behavior. Based on this process, it is likely that delinquent behavior will also lead to reduction of attachment towards parents as well as lowering commitment to school.

In their research studies, Thornberry et al. (1994) were not able to find any kind of evidence or support material to base the hypothesis of having reciprocal effects regarding commitment to school and attachment to parents. This research study did succeed in finding some degree of reciprocal effects, and these effects provided the information that the effect of delinquency is higher on the elements of commitment and attachment than the degree of effect made by attachment and commitment on presence of delinquent behavior. However, in these cases, the relationship that was obtained across the reciprocal effects was quite weak. In later studies on the same subject, Thornberry et al. (1994) found presence of reciprocal effects including delinquency effect combined with the variables of social learning theory. This research, along with some other research studies found that the various variables that are present in the theory of social learning provide a noticeable influence in all stages of delinquent behavior.

8. Synthesis Integration Process and Control Balance

Tittle (1995) proposed his own theory of integration that is named 'synthesis integration' process. In this process of integration, the mechanism of 'control balance' is provided as the unifying causal process that leads to presence of criminal behavior in an individual. According to this theory, the concept of 'control balance' refers to the ratio which exists for representation of how much control the individual is responsible to have control on and the actual ability for the same person to control. In this theory of integration, the control balance is presented as not just the motivation to engage in criminal behavior, but also as an inhibition to stay away from crime.

In the theory of control balance, the central idea is that an individual's probability to engage in criminal behavior is based on the level of control the person should have in their life decisions and the level of control that the person is able to exercise. If this balance of control deviates too much, it becomes likely that the person may engage in criminal or delinquent activity to restore the balance. In this theoretical integration approach, the criminal activity or delinquent behavior is a tool or device that is used by the individual with the aim of escaping low ratio of control and as a way of establishing or extending control on life factors that are defined by the control balance ratio. Presence of a control balance ratio that is unbalance and there is also a desire in the individual to have autonomy on own actions as well as on basic psychic and bodily needs, then these factors contribute to the high probability of that individual engaging in a criminal intent activity.

The theory of control balance in criminology functions with the context of balance derived from four primary variables in the situation: constraint (real or assumed restrain that the individual is likely to get from others in reaction to crime), opportunity (opportunity to commit the crime that is perceived to extend or restore balance), provocation (presence of some negative or positive stimuli in the situation) and predisposition (the motivation for delinquency act). All the main variables in the theory of control balance take elements from other popular theories of criminal behavior including the anomie theory, deterrence/rational choice theory, social learning theory and social bonding theory. The likelihood of the individual engaging in criminal activity gets higher in cases where the control balance is not balanced properly. The probability of delinquency increases in both cases of imbalance, positive or negative imbalance in control ratio. Probability of delinquent behavior from the individual is at its lowest when the control balance is balanced optimally. Individual who are currently in a situation with negative control balance are likely to engage in the activity of predatory or defiant type of delinquency (Cote, 2002). On the other hand, individual facing the situation of positive imbalance in control balance are likely to engage in exploitative behavior of crime.

The main argument that is made in the theory of control balance is that delinquent behavior is adopted by individuals as a response to imbalanced control balance ration with the aim of altering the control balance by some means of delinquent actions. A person who is currently facing an imbalance in control balance is very likely to commit criminal behavior if there is an opportunity to engage in activity that is probable to restore a favorable control balance and also if the counter opposition for the criminal activity is not adequately overwhelming for the individual. In his research, Tittle analyzed presence of a relationship between delinquency and crime with a number of different demographic and social elements such as gender, age, race, urban living status, parental status and social class.

9.   The Theory of Life-Course Criminology Approach

Life-course criminology is a theory that aims to explain intricacies of criminal behavior among people. The goal of this criminology theory is to have a better understanding of the reasons and factors of stability of changing nature of criminal and delinquent behavior among people through the course of their life, depending on various stages of life. A large number of different theorists and researchers have worked on the theory of life-course criminology approach across different time spans (Sampson & Laub, 1993; Farrington, 2005). By putting focus on individual aspects like variation in age, career choices and the trajectories followed by the person in different stages of criminal behavior. In the theory of life-course criminology, researchers pay most attention to the factors of age and life stage and keep it at the central focus of the research study observations.

The theory of life-course criminology makes the argument that the field of criminology should certainly adopt the concepts of life-course theory for the purpose of evaluating the cause and scope of a crime and criminal behavior. It is further argued that the basic principles of life-course criminology should reside at the center of the criminology researchers and these principles should be at the core of the study and other factors and research ideas should surround this central theme of delinquency theory (Laub, 2006).

Sampson and Laub (1993) make the argument that a number of different sudden and abrupt turning points in life (for example, getting married or obtaining a good employment) enhances the density and quality of social bonds for the person and these changes also combine with other gradual changes in life (such as gaining financial stability). With approach of this study and concept, the life-course criminology explains the reason behind a large number of young criminals leaving and discontinuing the life of crime after getting mature and older. Many of the young criminals still retain the life of crime upon getting older due to lack of turning point moments in life that provide stability, enrichment social bonds and responsibility with life. This theory claims that those individuals who do not witness similar positive stimuli events that help them get over the life of crime are more likely to continue offending and engaging in criminal activities. Stability of the factors that exist while the person is offending results in offering stability to the criminal behavior of the person, and change in the life-course (sudden and gradual) are capable of causing change in the criminal behavior of the person.

Warr (1998) also agreed with the arguments made by Sampson and Laub as well as with the explanation provided by the researchers about the transition in family relationship and friends throughout the life-course. According to Warr, work relationship and family relationship play a very vital role in the persistency or changing of the criminal behavior of a person.

10. Conceptual and Theoretical Integration of Criminology

In the field of criminology, majority of expert reviews and research studies point towards giving a certain degree of favor for the frugal and empirically proven integration of the explanations for criminal behavior. Theories that are based on integration in crime and criminal justice based empirical evidence are given the priority by researchers for purpose of integration. In this book chapter, a wide variety of different research studies are identified that have attempted to integrate a number of different criminal behavior theories together for a more comprehensive and thorough criminology theory. It is clear from the analysis of different integration efforts in this chapter that there has been some clear priority given to the approach of theoretical integration of the different theory of criminology (Cornish & Clarke, 2014). In current status of the industry, the momentum of criminology integration from a theoretical standpoint has received a significant boost because of a notable conference that was held in Albany at campus of the New York State University. From the number of different studies and integration efforts, it also becomes evident that integration of different criminology theories has remained a major topic of study and research in the literature field of criminology.

Nevertheless, the reception of different approaches of theoretical integration of criminology theories in an ideal scenario is positive, however, in actual real-industry practice scenario, the criminology integration models have obtained only mixed reception and acceptance in the industry of criminal justice. While some of the major integration theories have received support from the empirical data and evidence, other studies of criminology theory integration have either no support from the empirical data or have very little testing data to begin with, suggesting that many of the integration theories have received ignorance in practice. Focusing only on the positively reviewing climate of theoretical integration approach in the criminology element, it becomes evident that there is a continuous and significant indifference as well as a noticeable skepticism for the integration approaches and strategies used for integration theory development.

Even major supporters of the integration approach of different criminology theories from a conceptual aspect having a favorable opinion of the integration process, a good value is witnessed in the oppositional strategy. One of the most comprehensive and successful approach in this regard is to pit the theory of social learning based criminology against the various different and alternative theories that explain delinquent and criminally engaging behavior. One successful integration that has come out of this practice is the integration of social learning theory from the principle of differential association and reinforcement. This concept has remained well regarded among researchers as well as getting support from the empirical standpoint as well as receiving some significant level of attention in the criminology literature studies. Despite moderate success of some of the most renowned integration approaches and criminology theory integrations, there are still reservations among researchers about the future of the theoretical and conceptual integration of criminology theories. At the present state of theoretical integration, the problem of theory based competition between different theories against theory based integration of the theories has not been solved completely and efforts made so far have been unsuccessful.

On basis of the success measures that existing integration theories have received and the popularity of the integration approaches, it is likely that some more sophisticated and comprehensive integration approaches will be developed in the future. For most successful results with the integration theory, it is essential that the issue of competition versus integration is resolved first and foremost. Additionally, it is furthermore important that the integration theory performs a full integration of different theories rather than a case-by-case based integration.

11. Summary

Development of a theoretical integration process happens by means of explaining the process, testing the hypothesis developed in practice and making modifications to a single theory of criminology. The modifications process in the theoretical integration is performed in order to refine the theory and make it integrate more accurate elements. The modification process is completed on the basis of competition between two rival theories of criminology or by means of engaging in theoretical integration of multiple different criminology theories which are theoretical in nature. It is possible to perform a theoretical integration process on two different criminology theories by either using approach of propositional integration or by conceptual integration. It would include either the theories which are functioning on the same level of explanations or the theories which are functioning on the propositions on different levels of explanations. When it comes to the integrative model used in the field of criminology, the central component or the theory that is primarily used as the common theory is the social learning theory. Some of the most commonly used criminology theories which are taken for purpose of theoretical integration include strain theory, social bonding theory and social learning theory.

A single model of integration theory that encompassed all of the major macro and micro theories of criminology is a very difficult task due to variation in proposition and concepts, however, a functioning and well-designed framework for integration of all popular criminal behavior theories was given by Pearson and Weiner. In this framework of integration, the process used by the researchers was to make use of learning concepts. Akers performed a different approach for integration of the criminology behavior theory and proposed use of absorption of concepts as the basic theory of integration. In this theory of absorptions, the social learning theory is the base theory and it absorbs the concepts from other theories of criminal behavior for the purpose of integration. A separate theory of delinquency is proposed by Elliott who provides an integrated theory from the combination of three different criminal behavior theories, theory of strain, theory of social control and theory of social learning. Krohn developed the theory of network analysis, which takes elements from the theory of social learning and social bonding for the purpose of integration theory. An integration theory is given by Thornberry which is an interactive theory and it combines concepts and propositions from criminal behavior theories like social learning, social bonding and some other variables.

A thorough examination of theoretical integration of criminal behavior theories reveal that there have certainly been many integrative activities in the criminology field of literature over the years and there is a general positive attitude and orientation towards the approach of theoretical integration of criminal behavior theories. Despite this, there is major skepticism about success of such integration theories and there is also controversy on some of the most popular integrative theories as omissions of concepts is present for the purpose of streamlining the integration process. Primary source of skepticism comes from the approach of developing the integration theory by forcefully melding two or more different theoretical explanations or concepts of criminal behavior. Overall, presence of some well-received and successful integration models indicates that a comprehensive integration of criminal behavior theories is quite possible and careful examination of different theories is required in order to achieve the goal of a fully integrated criminology theory.

12. References

Agnew, R. (1985). Neutralizing the impact of crime. Criminal Justice and Behavior, 12(2), 221-239. http://dx.doi.org/10.1177/0093854885012002005

Akers, R: (2013). Criminological theories: Introduction and evaluation (2nd ed., pp. 208-210). Routledge.

Allatt, P. (1984). Fear of crime: The effect of improved residential security on a difficult to let estate. The Howard Journal of Criminal Justice, 23(3), 170-182. http://dx.doi.org/10.1111/j.1468-2311.1984.tb00504.x

Bernard, Y. (1992). North American and European research on fear of crime. Applied Psychology, 41(1), 65-75. http://dx.doi.org/10.1111/j.1464-0597.1992.tb00686.x

Colvin, M., Cullen, F., & Ven, T. (2002). Coercion, social support, and crime: An emerging theoretical consensus*. Criminology, 40(1), 19-42. http://dx.doi.org/10.1111/j.1745-9125.2002.tb00948.x

Cornish, D. & Clarke, R. (2014). The reasoning criminal: Rational choice perspectives on offending (1st ed., pp. 168-170). Transaction Publishers.

Cote, S. (2002). Criminological theories (1st ed., pp. 169-171). Thousand Oaks, CA: Sage Publications.

Cullen, F. & Wilcox, P. (2010). Encyclopedia of criminological theory (1st ed., pp. 201-202). Thousand Oaks, Calif.: Sage.

Elliott, D., Ageton, S., & Canter, R. (1979). An integrated theoretical perspective on delinquent behavior. Journal of Research in Crime and Delinquency, 16(1), 3-27. http://dx.doi.org/10.1177/002242787901600102

Farrington, D. (2005). Childhood origins of antisocial behavior. Clinical Psychology & Psychotherapy, 12(3), 177-190. http://dx.doi.org/10.1002/cpp.448

Hale, C. (1996). Fear of crime: A review of the literature. International Review of Victimology, 4(2), 79-150. http://dx.doi.org/10.1177/026975809600400201

Krohn, M. (1986). The web of conformity: A network approach to the explanation of delinquent behavior. Social Problems, 33(6), S81-S93. http://dx.doi.org/10.2307/800675

Laub, J. & Sampson, R. (1993). Turning points in the life course: why change matters to the study of crime*. Criminology, 31(3), 301-325. http://dx.doi.org/10.1111/j.1745-9125.1993.tb01132.x

Lechin, F. (2001). Asthma, asthma medication and autonomic nervous system dysfunction. Clinical Physiology, 21(6), 723-723. http://dx.doi.org/10.1046/j.1365-2281.2001.0382a.x

Liska, A. (1992). Social threat and social control (1st ed., pp. 103-105). Albany: State University of New York Press.

Liska, A., Sanchirico, A., & Reed, M. (1988). Fear of crime and constrained behavior specifying and estimating a reciprocal effects model. Social Forces, 66(3), 827-837. http://dx.doi.org/10.1093/sf/66.3.827

Nagin, D. & Pogarsky, G. (2001). Integrating celerity, impulsivity, and extralegal sanction threats into a model of general deterrence: Theory and evidence*. Criminology, 39(4), 865-892. http://dx.doi.org/10.1111/j.1745-9125.2001.tb00943.x

Pratt, T. & Cullen, F. (2000). The empirical status of Gottfredson and Hirschi's general theory of crime: a meta-analysis. Criminology, 38(3), 931-964. http://dx.doi.org/10.1111/j.1745-9125.2000.tb00911.x

Thornberry, T. (1987). Toward an interactional theory of delinquency*. Criminology, 25(4), 863-892. http://dx.doi.org/10.1111/j.1745-9125.1987.tb00823.x

Thornberry, T., Lizotte, A., Krohn, M., Farnworth, M., & Jang, S. (1994). Delinquent peers, beliefs, and delinquent behavior: A longitudinal test of interactional theory*. Criminology, 32(1), 47-83. http://dx.doi.org/10.1111/j.1745-9125.1994.tb01146.x

Tittle, C. (1995). Control balance: Toward a general theory of deviance (1st ed., pp. 112-114). Boulder: Westview Press.

Warr, M. (1998). Life-course transitions and desistance from crime*. Criminology, 36(2), 183-216. http://dx.doi.org/10.1111/j.1745-9125.1998.tb01246.x

Chapter 10
Marxist and Critical Theory

1. Introduction to Marxist Theory

Karl Marx (1818 – 1883), a German Philosopher, revolutionary socialist, journalist, sociologist, and economics, presented different theories about politics, economics, and society which are collectively famous as "*Marxism*" (Berlin, 2013). The literary world of Marx is far cry from the contemporary theories of his time since he spent most of his time analyzing and criticizing the domain of '*capitalism*' politically and theoretically. Hence, in a bid to move further with Marxist theory, it's important to get the drift of capitalism first.

Capitalism is termed as a free market economic system in a society where the private actors take full ownership, and control of the property best fits the mold of their own interests, and it serves the overall interests of the society based on the demand and supply mechanism (Schumpeter, 2013). "*At the core of Capitalism lies the fundamental motive to make a profit.*" Capitalism is best expressed by 18th century philosopher Adam Smith as *"It is not from the benevolence of the butcher, the brewer, or the baker that we expect our dinner, but from their regard to their own interest."*

Apparently capitalism seems to be the best system where the people own the tangible assets in shape of private properties, run their businesses in pursuit of their own self-interest, and drives the market through a sphere of healthy competition, healthy market mechanism, and good freedom for all with a limited role of the government. *Karl Marx, on the other hand, showed the bleak shades of capitalism which literally favors the capitalists at the expense of society* (Akers, 2013). He states that the capitalism only serves the capitalists and ignores the proletariat altogether, no matter in the democratic system or even in monarchy, the government takes very little interest in protecting the middle class, let alone the subdued poor class. Likewise, the Marxist theory sees capitalism as a favorable environment in which an owner takes liberty to buy the labor of another individual and utilize it to generate profits (McLellan, 1971).

2. Marxist Theory of Karl Marx and Criminal Justice Applications

Marxist theory of Karl Marx created quite a stir in the system since it was surely the very first of its kind. He explains that the law and criminal justice system is fully controlled by the ruling class i.e. capitalist elite. Marxist theory of law can be summarized as a triple treat for the ruling capitalist class i.e.

1. The evolving economic forces brings out a product which we call '*Law*'
2. The ruling class makes use of the '*Law*' to maintain its power and influence over the poor
3. Even the future communist society (*explained as the height of Marxism*) is likely to wither away 'Law' as a tool to maintain social control (Vago, 2015).

In a way, Marxist theory related to capitalism brings its notions into close contact of agreeable acceptance of *Conflict Theory* (explained in the previous chapters). Marx sees legal system and law as potent instruments to regulate and safeguard capitalist (*ruling class*) relations OR law is a tool that is misused by the ruling class, both for maintaining social control and domination over the poor labor class. Law is a servant of dominating class which flies in the face of the rights of poor class at large **(Marx, 2015)**. Since *the theory was born like a prism in the confused weather*, law, as a tool to breakdown the society into two classes, made numerous sociologists interested, specifically in criminal law, to investigate it further to date (Anderson, 2016). For instance, Quinney (1974) argued that law, in a capitalist society, gives ways and means to the powerful class to forcefully control the majority class i.e. poor class. In "*The Critique of Legal Order*" Quinney furthers the situation that in the wake of capitalism, criminal law would be frequently used in a bid to control and shape the domestic order; again, the poor class would be victimized since the ruling class will try their best to remain on the rising side.

The role of law and authority is crucial to bind individuals under the umbrella of complex socio-economic systems, yet in capitalism, the criminal law enforcement is a mere illusion of the restrictions enforced by the ruling class to preserve their own self-interest and gains. *In other words, law is nothing short of a way and means to continue the capitalist order*. This is what has been described by Quinney (1970; 1974a), after carefully examining the "ifs and buts" of capitalism. On the flip side, numerous theorists argued on the contrary with a view that the specs of Marxism have earned it a fine tag of "the most desirable theory", yet law is to be taken as an autonomous body in which barristers and judges work according to a set SOP's, which has been developed over a long period of time and there is nothing as such which relates law with the supposition of class struggle (Hirst, 1979; Thompson, 1990, Hay, 1975).

3. Challenges of Marxism and Types

Though Marxism was a difficult birth, yet theorists adopted the child; and despite the controversies, Marxism stood its ground for a long time. Marxism sees capitalism as an exploitative system which is nothing short of a class struggle (Engels, 2015). Through the lens of Marxism, the instrumentalist Marxism can be seen in between the following lines stated by Marx

"The executive of the modern state is nothing but a committee for managing the common affairs of the whole bourgeoisie" (Coco & Fedeli, 2014).

According to the above statement, *Instrumentalist Marxism* tags 'state' as a machine which supports the ruling classes (bourgeoisie) to rule over the poor working classes, hence extracting profits in shape of capitalist exploitation (Dunleavy & O'Leary, 1987; Gold et al., 1975). In a bid to tip the race in favor of ruling class, instrumentalist Marxism safeguards the capital interests of the bourgeoisie thus creating an unequal society at large. Marx wrote down instrumentalist Marxism as follows:

"The history of all hitherto existing society is the history of class struggles" (Tomaskovic-Devey, 2014). At the core of instrumentalist model, state is used as an instrument in a bid to fulfill the interests of the very ruling class of the society.

The *Structuralist Marxism* marks them as unsubstantiated claims and shore up the support in favor of the state in the sense that the role of the state should not be underestimated by the mere fact that who controls the state. The reason being, *the state doesn't act merely as a post-office*; the political state is not totally under the ruling class thus it can serve the interests of the working class (Poulantzas, 1968; 1978, Althusser, 1970). *The core of structuralist Marxism takes the bow of the constraints, that is, structural constraints on behalf of which state and the ruling class are not totally the hands down winners over the proletariats* (working class) (Milliband, 1977). Hence the role of the state is not to be considered in favor of capital interests, but in light of the structural constraints on behalf of societal economic requirements at large. Call it a capitalist system or any other system, state relies on the mode of production, and not purely on the vested interests of the ruling class. Antonio Gramsci (1999) takes it further by arguing that the domination of one class over another class in a capitalist society is not only because of capital interests, it's also because of the willing consent of the subordinates as follows:

"*The entire complex of practical and theoretical activities with which the ruling class not only justifies and maintains its dominance but manages to win the active consent of those whom it rules*" (Gramsci, 1999).

4. For and Against Marx's Understanding of Law

Marx ideas about law are primarily expressed in his work "*Communist Manifesto*" in which he says that the rational appearance of law rings hollow and unconvincing in his eyes for the reason that *law, alongside religion and morality are nothing short than bourgeois prejudices behind which the interests of the bourgeois lurk in ambush*. Marx also criticized the whole Western tradition which clearly shows that he held a strong opinion that the ruling class only toy with the laws to serve their own interests (Marx & Engels, 2014).

There is a mountain of evidence for and against Marx's understanding of law. Hans Kelsen (1955) said in "*The Communist Theory of Law*" that an essential element of Marx theory of law is anti-normative approach to social phenomena. Marx also disregarded the idea of communism since he deemed that the final stage of communism would lead to lawlessness and state would be merely acting as a revolutionary dictatorship of the poor class (Beverungen et al., 2013).

In conclusion, Marx adopted a rather cynical idea of law where there is literally no hope for a law that severs the common good of the people at large...till such time the revolution eradicates the distinctions of economic class...since law eventually fails to serve the common good, the legislators task is doomed to crash (Murphy, 2007).

To be very honest and accurate, there is very little space in the Marxist theory of law and justice which is empirically testable. Furthering this issue, it's important to get the drift that Marxist theory is born out of the inherent contradictions of capitalist society being the provider of law and criminal justice both, that's why its empirical validity cannot be endorsed by only testing it against the capitalistic systems. The point is, when it was tested against the pure capitalistic and socialist systems, Marxist theory fell short of a valid explanation of operation of the criminal justice system as well as the law. Even those empirical evidences run contrary to the claims postulated by the theory especially the argument that *"Crime is a problem of capitalism but not in socialism." Empirical evidences corroborate the fact that Crime is surely not a hands down winner in socialism as well* (Akers, 2013). The very example in this regard is of historical socialist societies both authoritarian or totalitarian, didn't make considerable progress where we can see it as a classless society with non-despotic system of criminal justice and law (Akers & Sellers, 2009). Even the historic social leaders such as Joseph Stalin had formulated a system in practice where the means of production were controlled by even very smaller elite as compared to the capitalist systems which surely jot down a line worthy of comment i.e. *is the cause of crime genuinely a capitalist system? and is socialism the very solution behind this*? The fact is, with regards to the tested socialist societies, ushering out capitalism in pursuit of a crime free society and legal justice system, is merely a utopian realm of thought (Lynch & Groves, 1986).

5.   Marxist Theory of Crime and Delinquent Behavior

Through the lens of Karl Marx, crime is not a stubborn thing except the fact that it changes its shape and appearance in various forms as an outgrowth of capitalism. Marx argues that the persons who make up the nations jail population are not actually the criminals; criminals are those who steal the very wealth from the nation (Marx, 2015b). For instance, if a person has 500 pair of clothes whilst another person doesn't have the capacity to go for even one *"is likely to trigger crime"*. In this regard, Marxist theory of crime advocates that *"crime stems in shape of a natural outgrowth of the capitalism"* (Parkin, 1981). This is what further translates into corporate capitalism vs corporate crime (Barnett, 1981).

Marxist theory of crime entails three distinct processes at large:

Capitalism is crimogenic because it instigates individuals to take a rain check from public duties and run for their own self interests

The role of the state and law making is nothing short of a puppet which stands tall to protect the interest of ruling class

Crime, in these societies is a mere reaction between the ruling classes and the poor classes due to class conflict, inequalities, poverty alongside circumstances favorable to high crime rates.

Marxist Sociologist David Gordon (1973) tagged capitalist societies as "*dog eat dog societies*" where each and every individual seeks out which side of the bread is buttered and this thinking literally overlaps the interests of other individuals and community at large. In fact, Marxist society pressurizes individuals that the only key to survival is to make more money, more profit, and be more successful. In such context, law breaking becomes secondary thing especially when people live in the gap between their dreams and the harsh realities of economics.

Secondly, in the wake of capitalism, the criminal law does exist, but merely to serve the interests of the ruling class and nothing else. It gives birth to poverty and what choice is there for the poor class because if they don't choose the slippery road of crime, how would they survive (Bonger, 1916)?

Third, Crime in capitalism is merely a struggle between the two classes. The reaction of the poor class against their superior class turns out to be a crime and the crime / legislation performs their roles as handy tools for the superior class against the poor class. These situations also give birth to corporate crimes committed on a mass scale in modern industrial countries (Snider, 1993). He also points out that the capitalist system makes hue and cry against the street crimes in which the criminals bear the brunt due to their weak position BUT ignores the huge corporate crimes altogether merely due to the fact that ruling class takes the line of least resistance at every corner. *The world has recently witnessed just a slice of corporate crime in shape of the disgraced financier Bernie Madoff who was sentenced to 150 years imprisonment for masterminding a huge corporate fraud of worth $65 billion dollars* (LeBor, 2009; Arvedlund, 2009).

Spitzer (1975) also produced a mountain of evidence favoring the fact that crime in capitalism is nothing short of a collision between two classes. For instance, the oft-quoted facts second that when certain working-class groups try to create eye-popping problems against the superior class, they are subjected to be taken under criminalization just to shore up the support and tip the race in favor of the ruling class. Snider (1993) corroborated the same fact by arguing that capitalist states are always hesitant to pass those laws which go against their capitalists related concerns. It is worth mentioning here that few theorists don't consider physical attack of a person from poor class a sin, on the score that it would be surely done in an effort to remove the social inequalities (Erickson, 1998).

6.   Quinney's Exceptions and Independent Space

From the time when Marx and Engels wrote down substantiated claims about capitalistic class, state, and crime in the shade of "*The Communist Manifesto*", numerous Marxian's were arguing about the phenomenon that the powerful "*ruling class*" rules over the "*working class*" and the so-called laws are in place for the mere cause of representing and protecting the ruling class.

Here is an exception presented by Quinney (1977) in his "*class, state, and crime*" that fly in the face of *instrumental position* and argues that the state does have an independent space away from the reach of ruling elite class. How much independence is there for the state is again a subject of debate. There are certain questions with regard to his literature like:

To what degree, state serves as a tool of repression

To what extent, the state can take the liberty of its own decisions

How far can state act in serving the interest of proletariat

Quinney assumes criminal justice system as a last resort for supporting the limping capitalist system and takes the works of many other theorists into account particularly Bonger, Engels, and Marx. He agrees with the notion of state's romanticism with the elite class, and crime being a mere struggle between the classes but he didn't resolve the much debated role of the state since he places the state role on a thin ice by arguing "*either state directly looks after the interests of the ruling class OR Indirectly serve the general interests of their specific members by bringing an environment where the individual members of the ruling class might not survive but the ruling class survives*. At the same time, he didn't provide a linkage between these two separate functions of the state (Hinch, 1884).

Quinney conforms to the bedrock of Marx theory that the law enforcement by the state is merely a screen-cover to hide and protect the ruling class and to control the members of the lower class. Crime itself is disguised in many capitalistic forms such as socialist injurious behaviors by the ruling class (economic exploitation, racism, sexism etc.), white collar crimes (pollution and price fixing), crime in shape of violating the civil rights (brutality by police force) (Vito, Maahs & Holmes, 1994). When it comes to the criminal acts perpetrated by the lower class, Quinney marks them as "*acts of survival*" and he argues that the acts of violence's committed by the lower class should be given a benefit of the doubt since these are the reactions of the inequalities in the capitalistic system (Vito, Maahs & Holmes, 1994).

7. Evolutionary Influences of Marxism

Beyond doubt, Marxism fills the void of evolutionary influences on humans, clears the ambiguity of the ruling system merely created for serving the interest of elite class, still it doesn't translate the theoretical influences into a practical track. *As a result, Marxism creates a secular utopia on planet earth which is always on a very thin ice* since the governments inspired by Marxism enjoyed bloody blood bath, killing millions of people, as a by-product of this theory (Zimmermann, 2017). One of the reasons might be that the reaction of class oppression turned out to be "*dictatorship of the poor class*".

When we try to explore the religious dimensions of Marxism, we see the deprivation of GOD from the very planetary system since Marxism sees poor class as the executioner and redemptive force of humanity and that's the direction where history is shaping its dimensions so that it achieves its perfection (Johnson, 1988). Marxism goes through a gamut of logics to finally land on a religious theme that the ultimate salvation and final stage of humanity will be achieved through class struggle and the prevalence of ultimate communism (Koyzis, 2003). With respect to religion, Boff, after paying a visit to former Soviet Union and Romania in 1987, brought Marxism into close contact of freedom of expression in these countries alongside an obvious air of ethical cleanliness (Page, 1996).

Just like Darwinism became a stepping stone in law of evolution, Marxist theory discovered the law of evolution in human history thus bent the history's arc in favor of the belief that the dominance of social classes is due to the alleged superiority of human races (Engels, 1848l; Marx et al., 1975). In this regard, Marx views about Jewish money and terms like *"Dirty Jew"* and *"Jewish Nigger"* created quite a stir since Marx pointed fingers over their supremacy yet he was himself a Jew as well (Marx, 2015c).

Describing Marxism through the lens of Law, it is explicitly described by David and Brieley (1978) as they rightfully connected the dots in a bid to expose the reality of Law:

"Law is only a superstructure; in reality, it only translates the interests of those who hold the reins of command in any given society; it is an instrument in the service of those who exercise their 'dictatorship' in this society because they have the instruments of production within their control. Law is a means of expressing the exploited class; it is, of necessity, unjust—or, in other words, it is only just from the subject point of view of the ruling class. To speak of a 'just' law is to appeal to an ideology—that is to say, a false representation of reality; justice is no more than an historical idea conditioned by circumstances of class."

8.   Crime vs. Capitalism

It might take a long time to connect the dots in understanding the relationship of capitalist economy and crime, yet first off, it's necessary to get the drift of capitalist society such as USA in which the people follow the capitalist ideology without even realizing that they are being exploited. Wolf (2005) fret his eyelids on the same issue that in capitalism, people are brought under conditions which put them under "*learn the teachings portfolio*" that relate to cultural etiquettes. In this way, they deem themselves as consumers and provide their laboring services to serve the capitalist economy with due consent. Althusser (1970) stated the same philosophy with a fair gamut of logics that a child, from an early age, gets training to become familiar with the ways of understanding the ideology of the ruling class such as philosophy of civic duties, sciences, arithmetic etc. which translates into the further production of blue collar workers (*laborers*), white collar workers (*petty bourgeoisie, low level managers*), and the managers of either dominated or the exploited class. Haddad Mousa (2012) referred to the statistical facts relevant with the same issue: UK is termed as a country with most unequal rich in the world, where the poorest 10 percentage of people are able to digest only one percent of the total income. On the flip side, the richest elites are destined to clutch thirty one percent of the total income.

All these facts and figures clearly corroborate the fact that crime is eventually triggered in capitalism mode because the mere objective to earn maximum profit and working in the pressured environment instigates strong inclination towards committing crime (Antonaccio, 2007). This economic inequality translates into cupidity since everybody revolves around the survival of the fittest; and an unrestrained economic system marks the eradication of all ethical concerns in a bid to purist the profit (Bonger, 1916). Theorists also argue that propagation of weak social institutions designed under the umbrella of capitalism is itself a crime (Bonger, 1916); and above all, *numerous oft-quoted figures also confirm that capitalistic economy perfectly fit the mold of criminal investigation since economic inequality translates into rising the levels of homicide* (Kick & LaFree, 1985; McDonald, 1976; Savolainen, 2000). *Capitalism, with such a rich history and lineage, alongside the findings produced by Bonger and other Marxian orientations, is surely connected with a connection to criminal significance.*

Important Note: In the wake of disastrous experiences of anti-Capitalism systems such as Former Soviet Union USSR, one shouldn't gamble the hope under the shadow of an entirely new anti-capitalist system; nor do one needs to wrap the current system altogether. At the very least, one should pinpoint the loopholes of capitalism in an effort to pin them down to keep the things straight.

9. What Is Critical Criminology and Its Emergence?

Critical Criminology purely focuses on analyzing the social attitudes in a society and crimes committed by delinquents from a cultural context. Critical criminology goes against the traditional criminological theories and digs deep into the fact that what are the kind of acts which the societies consider as delinquent acts and how to put a full-stop on future crossovers of delinquent acts in such societies (DeKeseredy & Dragiewicz, 2011). The fundamental thread which binds it together is the notion that social inequalities in a society influence crime while its rich history and lineage can be traced back Marx era which took the bow of early criminologists of that time. Let's get a slight drift of its emergence:

Bonger (1916) stated in his *"Criminality and Economic Conditions"* that crime takes the slippery slope where poor classes or lower classes people ought to be penalized much more and worse than the upper-class people.

Rusche & Kirchheimer (2003) spun a line in 1939 that the mode of production is to be hold accountable behind the patterns through which societies punish criminals. The subsequent works of Mills (1956) regarding *"The Power Elite"* and Sutherland's (1940) and (1945) works about the white-collar crime also confirmed the same inequality among classes.

Critical Criminology showed its offshoots during 1960's and 1970's when few criminologists revitalized Marxism and published their critical works particularly "*A sociological analyses of the law of vagrancy*" by Chambliss (1964), "*The child savers*" by Platt (1969), "*Defenders of order or guardians of human rights*" by Schwendinger (1970), "*The social reality of crime*" by Quinney (1970), "*The new criminology*" by Taylor, Walton & Young (1973).

The various strands of critical criminology solidified various new schools of thought in a bid to further answer the answered such as *Constitutive Criminology*, *Left Realism*, *Peacemaking Criminology* discussed as follows:

10. Reforming Criminal Justice System

Simply put, most of the other criminology theories make their center of attention upon the idea "*what triggers crime*"; on the other hand, Constitutive criminology opts for "*examining its production*". Through the very efforts of Stuart Henry & Dragon Milovanovic (1991), the world witnessed a pioneering effort towards constitutive criminology (Kanduc et al., 1997). This critical criminology's branch rejects the triggers of crime as an objective reality and screens it through the rational microscope of integrated elements like the discursive practices and ideology role in the society in an effort to understand the connection between society and individuals and how the crime is co-created in the society with the mutual connections of criminologists, the criminal justice system, victims, and the offenders (Akers, 2013).

As it stands, *Left Realism* takes the road exactly opposite to the constitutive criminology and rejects its logics as unrealistic and offers "*reforms in the criminal justice system*" as the only way to close the loopholes for crime (Akers, 2013). Left realism criminology voice concerns and a greater attention to the victim & offender, state as well as the community, and it also supports few conventional criminological research methods in order to turn the tide in favor of authentic criminal investigation (Miller, 2009). Left Realism took its offshoots in the United Kingdom, in the wake of ignorance of Marxist theorists over the issue of street crime. The reason being, Marxism was focusing on the broader aspect of capitalism thus completely ignored the anomalies in the criminal justice system in the first place; that's why the street crimes which were committed by the poor classes against the poor classes (inner-city crime) was indeed consigned to the bin (Young, Stenson & Cowell, 1991). This offered a desperate call (Left Realism) for reforms in the criminal justice system in a bid to bridge the gap between crime and its triggers.

Peacemaking Criminology took its roots through the very efforts of Richard Quinney and Harold Pepinsky (1991) with their great addition to criminology in shape of "*Criminology as Peacemaking*". The varieties in this theory doesn't suffice the requirements of a testable criminal justice system, nor does offer a testable theory of crime (Akers, 2013), still it offers its themes which advocates a reconciling, restitutive, and non-violent approach to understand and break the backs of criminal behavior.

Themes of Peacemaking Criminology

Sufferings of the people in this world are joined at the hip, always together, and literally inseparable.

We should not place a stigma on humans as reprehensible criminals or good citizens and derive false schemes through our very understandings.

We should see the other side of the coin i.e. our common humanity and attend to the very problem of crime through interacting the members of our own humanity.

Making the criminal alone suffer for his sins is throwing caution to the wind because we all need to take the responsibility for crime and suffer together.

On the whole, the peacemaking criminology tends to send waves for a thorough transformation of our way of thinking about criminal justice and the crime (Miller, 2009).

The branch of critical criminology has had a great impact on criminology's scope in the sense that the traditional criminology was exclusively focusing on violent acts committed by the criminals while critical criminology, on the other hand, focuses on a broadened category of illegal acts that are supposedly harmful to the society (Hillyard & Tombs, 2007). Critical criminologists also furrowed their eyelids that crime is socially and politically created in a society in which laws are created in the wake of social and political decisions (Quinney, 1970). Critical criminology moved the crime from an illegal act to the particular circumstances where harm is inflicted as a consequence regardless of the fact that the committed crime was legal or illegal (Miller, 2009). In other words, critical criminology has literally expanded the domain of crime by covering harms that are, at times, even not considered as illegal acts in criminal justice system. In the light of above facts and figures, the vast branch of critical criminology surely has the potential to investigate and change the directions and methods of criminal investigation in the time to come.

11. Summary

Capitalism is termed as a free market economic system in a society where the private actors take full ownership and control of the property best fit the mold of their own interests and it serves the overall interests of the society based on the demand and supply mechanism. *Marxist theory* explains that the law and criminal justice system is fully controlled by ruling class i.e. capitalist elite. *Instrumentalist Marxism* tags 'state' as a machine which supports the ruling classes (bourgeoisie) to rule over the poor working classes, hence extracting profits in shape of capitalist exploitation. The core of *structuralist Marxism* takes the bow of the constraints, that is, structural constraints on behalf of which state and the ruling class are not totally the hands down winners over the proletariats (working class). To be very honest and accurate, there is very little space in the Marxist theory of law and justice which is empirically testable. Marxist theory of crime advocates that *"crime stems in shape of a natural outgrowth of the capitalism"*. Here is an exception presented by Quinney in his *"class, state, and crime"* that fly in the face of *instrumental position* and argues that the state does have an independent space away from the reach of ruling elite class. Quinney conforms to the bedrock of Marx theory that the law enforcement by the state is merely a screen-cover to hide and protect the ruling class and to control the members of the lower class. Marxism fills the void of evolutionary influences on humans, clears the ambiguity of the ruling system merely created for serving the interest of elite class, still it doesn't translate the theoretical influences into a practical track. *Critical Criminology* purely focuses on analyzing the social attitudes in a society and crimes committed by delinquents from a cultural context. Most of the other criminology theories make their center of attention upon the idea "*what triggers crime*"; on the other hand, Constitutive criminology opts for "*examining its production*". *Left Realism* takes the road exactly opposite to the constitutive criminology and rejects its logics as unrealistic and offers "*reforms in the criminal justice system*" as the only way to close the loopholes for crime. Peacemaking criminology offers its themes which advocate a reconciling, restitutive, and non-violent approach to understand and break the backs of criminal behavior.

12. References

Akers, R. L. (2013). *Criminological theories: Introduction and evaluation.* Routledge.

Akers, R. L., & Sellers, C. S. (2009). *Criminological Theories: Introduction, evaluation, and application.* (5th ed.). New York, NY: Oxford University Press

Althusser, L. (1970) On ideology, 'Ideological state apparatuses', London, Verso.

Anderson, P. (2016). *Considerations on western Marxism.* Verso Books.

Antonaccio, O., & Tittle, C. R. (2007). A cross-national test of Bonger's theory of criminality and economic conditions. *CRIMINOLOGY-BEVERLY HILLS THEN COLUMBUS.*

Arvedlund, E. (2009). *Madoff: The Man who stole $65 billion.* Penguin UK.

Barnett, H. C. (1981). Corporate capitalism, corporate crime. *Crime & Delinquency.*

Berlin, I. (2013). *Karl Marx.* Princeton University Press.

Beverungen, A., Murtola, A. M., & Schwartz, G. (2013). The communism of capital? *Ephemera: theory & politics in organization.*

Bonger, W. A. (1916). *Criminality and economic conditions.* Boston: Little, Brown.

Chambliss, W. J. (1964). A sociological analysis of the law of vagrancy. *Social Problems, 12*(1), 67-77.

Coco, G., & Fedeli, S. (2014). Marxian public economics (with a comment by Massimo Florio). *A Handbook of Alternative Theories of Public Economics*, 60.

DeKeseredy, W. S., & Dragiewicz, M. (Eds.). (2011). *Handbook of critical criminology*. Routledge.

Dunleavy, P. and O'Leary, B. (1987) Theories of the state: The politics of liberal democracy, London, Macmillan Education Ltd.

Engels, F. (1848). Selected Works, 3 vols.

Engels, K. M. F. (2015). *The manifesto of the Communist Party*. Karl Marx Friedrich Engels.

Erickson, M. J. (1998). *Christian theology*. Baker Academic.

Gold, D. A., Lo, C. Y. and Wright, E. O. (1975) Recent developments in Marxist theories of the capitalist state, Monthly Review, 27 (5), pp. 29-43; (6) pp. 36-51.

Gordon, D. M. (1973). Capitalism, class, and crime in America. *Crime & Delinquency*, *19*(2), 163-186.

Gramsci, A. (Ed) (1999) Selections from the Prison Notebooks, London, The Electric Book Company

Hay, D. (1975), 'Property, authority and the criminal law', in D. Hay, P. Linebaugh and E. Thompson (eds), Albion's Fatal Tree. London: Allen Lane.

Henry, S., & Milovanovic, D. (1991). Constitutive criminology: The maturation of critical theory. *Criminology*, *29*, 293.

Hillyard, P., & Tombs, S. (2007). From 'crime' to social harm? *Crime, law and social change*, *48*(1-2), 9-25.

Hinch, R. O. (1884). *The analysis of class, state and crime: a contribution to critical criminology* (Doctoral dissertation).

Hirst, P. Q. (1979), On law and ideology. London: Macmillan.

Johnson, P., The intellectuals, Harper Perennial, New York, p. 55, 1988.

Kanduc, Z. (1997). Stuart Henry and Dragan Milovanovic constitutive criminology: Beyond postmodernism (London: Sage Publications, 1996), 288 pages. *European Journal of Crime, Criminal Law and Criminal Justice*.

Kelsen, H. (1955). The communist theory of law. New York.

Kick, E. L., & LaFree, G. D. (1985). Development and the social context of murder and theft. *Comparative Social Research, 8*, 37-58.

Koyzis, D. (2003). Political visions and illusions. *InterVarsity Press, Downers Grove, 101*, 174.

LeBor, A. (2009). *The Believers: How America fell for Bernard Madoff's $65 billion investment scam*. Hachette UK.

Lynch, M. J., & Groves, W. B. (1986). *A primer in radical criminology*. Harrow and Heston.

Marx, K., Engels, F., Lasker, I., & Ryazanskaya, S. (1975). Selected correspondence.

Marx, K., & Engels, F. (2014). Manifesto of the Communist Party (1848) and alienated labor (1844). *The Globalization and Development Reader: Perspectives on Development and Global Change*, 549.

Marx, K. (2015). *On the question of free trade*. Arsalan Ahmed.

Marx, K. (2015b). *A Dictionary of Thought*. Open Road Media.

Marx, K. (2015c). *A world without Jews*. Open Road Media.

McDonald, L. (1976). The sociology of law and order. Boulder, CO. *Westview Press. Messner, SF (1989). Economic discrimination and societal homicide rates: Further evidence*

339

on the cost of inequality. *American Sociological Review*, *54*, 597-611.

McLellan, The thought of Karl Marx (1971)

Miliband, R. (1977) Marxism and politics, Torfaen, The Merlin Press Limited.

Miller, J. M. (Ed.). (2009). *21st century criminology: a reference handbook* (Vol. 1). Sage.

Mills, C. W. (1956). 77ie power elite.

Haddad, M. (2012). The perfect storm: Economic stagnation, the rising cost of living, public spending cuts, and the impact on UK poverty.

Murphy, M. C. (2016). Philosophy of law: The fundamentals'. *Malden/MA: Blackwell, 2007), p,196*.

Page, J. A. (1996). *The Brazilians*. Da Capo Press.

Parkin, F. (1981). Marxism and class theory: A bourgeois critique.

Pepinsky, H. (1991). Peacemaking in criminology and criminal justice. *Criminology as peacemaking*, 299-327.

Poulantzas, N. (1968) Political power and social classes, London, New Left Books.

Poulantzas, N. (1978) State, power, socialism, London, New Left Books

Quinney, R. (1970), The social reality of crime. Boston Mass.: Little, Brown and Co.

Quinney, R. (1974a), Criminal justice in America: A critical understanding. Boston: Little, Brown and Co.

Quinney, R. (1974). *Critique of legal order: Crime control in capitalist society*. Boston: Little Brown.

Quinney, R. (1977). Class, state and crime: On the theory and practice of criminal justice. *New York: David McKay*.

Quinney, R. (1991). The way of peace: On crime, suffering, and service. *Criminology as peacemaking*, 3-13.

Rusche, G., & Kirchheimer, O. (2003). *Punishment and social structure*. Transaction publishers.

Savolainen, J. (2000). Inequality, welfare state, and homicide: Further support for the institutional anomie theory. *Criminology*, *38*(4), 1021-1042.

Schumpeter, J. A. (2013). *Capitalism, socialism and democracy*. Routledge.

Schwendinger, H., & Schwendinger, J. (1970). Defenders of order or guardians of human rights. *Issues Criminology*, *5*, 123.

Snider, L. (1993). The politics of corporate crime control. *Global crime connections: Dynamics and control, University of Toronto Press, Toronto*, 226.

Spitzer, S. (1975). Toward a Marxian theory of deviance. *Social problems*, *22*(5), 638-651.

Sutherland, E. H. (1940). White-collar criminality. *American Sociological Review*, *5*(1), 1-12.

Sutherland, E. H. (1945). Is "white collar crime" crime? *American Sociological Review*, *10*(2), 132-139.

Taylor, I., Walton, P., & Young, J. (1973). The new criminology: For a social theory of deviance.

Thompson, E. P. (1990), Whigs and Hunters. Harmondsworth: Penguin.

Tomaskovic-Devey, D. (2014). The relational generation of workplace inequalities. *Social Currents*, *1*(1), 51-73.

Vago, S. (2015). *Law and society*. Routledge.

Vito, G. F., Maahs, J. R., & Holmes, R. M. (1994). Criminology: Theory. *Research, and Policy. Belmont, CA: Wadsworth*.

Wolff, R. D. (2005). Ideological state apparatuses, consumerism, and US capitalism: Lessons for the left. *Rethinking Marxism*, *17*(2), 223-235.

Young, J. (1991). Left realism and the priorities of crime control. *The politics of crime control.*

Zimmermann, A. (2017). *Marxism law and evolution – creation.com. Creation.com.* Retrieved 18 January 2017, from http://creation.com/marxism-law-and-evolution

Chapter 11
Strain, Anomie, and Social Disorganization

When everybody gets the trophy, no one actually wins; but this isn't the case with social disorganization theory since it investigates crime on a broader scale (*Everybody in the neighborhood or one can say the entire neighborhood*) rather than on individual level and provides a cumulative crime effect in response.

Shaw and McKay (1942) generated a true recipe of a systematic and non-random pattern of crime in Chicago which is commonly regarded as "*Social disorganization theory*". Chicago's population was merely a few thousand upon its incorporation in the United States. Between the mid 1800's and early 1900's, its population grew to 2 million plus in the wake of immigrants' arrival from European countries due to heavy industrial growth in Chicago region (Palen, 1981). The enormous growth in population instigated a backfire later on in shape of crime and disorder and that's how Shaw and McKay (1942) attempted to explain crime scenarios in Chicago neighborhoods and shaped up the classic formulation of "*social disorganization theory*". The theory was a bit trickier than its sounds since it wasn't focused on an individual's involvement in crime; rather it was focused towards the explanations that "*what makes or instigates a neighborhood susceptible to crime*" (Miller, 2009).

While investigating the distribution of crime in Chicago neighborhood, they mapped the criminal data with respect to the youth residential locations that were referred to juvenile court and drew upon the following results:

1) A systematic pattern of high rate crime was observed in lower class neighborhoods that was adjoined with the industrial area

2) These lower class neighborhoods exhibited very long tails of tuberculosis, alcoholism, addiction of drugs, prostitution, and infant mortality rates.

3) Over the period of many decades, there had been a significant change in their ethnic and racial compositions.

4) The correlation did exist between high rates of delinquency with respect to African American heads and foreign-born households yet Shaw and McKay didn't find a well-wrought explanation against their ethnicity brands including both white and black.

The conclusion reflected by the investigation resonated from all corners with the following verbatim:

"In the face of these facts it is difficult to sustain the contention that, by themselves, the factors of race, nativity, and nationality are vitally related to the problem of juvenile delinquency. It seems necessary to conclude, rather, that the significantly higher rates of delinquency found among the children of Negroes, the foreign born and more recent immigrants are closely related to existing differences in their respective pattern of geographical distribution within the city" (Jonassen, 1949).

Important Point: This is what the *"social disorganization theory"* is all about i.e. neighborhood is the mere brand of this theory AND the neighborhood circumstances are actually behind the crime rates rather than the individual factors.

1. Park and Burgess's Theory of Human Ecology and Social Disorganization

In a bid to formulate the said theory, they heavily relied on Park and Burgess's *"theory of human ecology* (1925) in which they subdivided the Chicago into 5 zones and Zone 2 was regarded as the zone *in transition* i.e. the most socially disorganized area, the oldest part of the city, the poorest as well as the least wanted area to live. This was the zone investigated by Shaw and McKay (1942) and *they derived the factual, hard and ominous realities in the said zone which translate beyond the "No Crime" scenario* as follows:

The socially disorganized areas show no regards to the common values of the people living there and these areas are incapable to handle the problems related to their community, mostly because it entails a significant shortage of communication as well as the shared values.

The three indirect fertile indicators of the said social disorganization are residential instability, poverty, and ethnic-racial heterogeneity (Miller, 2009). With all these factors in place, a strong sense of inability to perform and handle the community problems prevail in these areas.

The only shortfall that points toward the scenario of *"shot in the wrong direction"* is *"the conclusions were drawn merely on the proxies such as residential inability or poverty that's why few theorists wagged fingers against the authenticity of the theory, calling it a theory showing no regards to facts and zero direct testability against the said factors"* (Sampson and Grooves, 1989).

2. Development of Social Disorganization Theory:

From the era of 1970's, this piece of puzzle was further explored by the theorists in a bid to fill the void of gaps in the said theory (Kornhauser, 1978; Bursik, 1988, Sampson, Morenoff & Raudenbush, 2005, Jencks & Mayer, 1990). For instance, Sampson and Grooves (1989) further subdivided the neighborhood indicators as:

Networks of weak local friendships

Organizational participation at a low rate.

Teenage group without any supervision

The findings were relevant with the findings observed from "*British Crime Survey*" data from 238 neighborhoods in Wales and England. After a decade, the results were replicated again, and the findings again corroborated the previous results from the original study as well (Lowencamp, Cullen & Pratt, 2003). Lander (1954) *also tried to provide a logical red meat to the theory* by investigating 8464 criminals who were all tried in the Baltimore Juvenile Court in three years period 1939-1942. The bedrock of his observation was "analyzing the juvenile criminals against the variables of median years of school life completion, median monthly rental, non-white and foreign-born residents alongside a few other variables. Interestingly, the findings coincided with those of Shaw and McKay (1942) with respect to the concentric ring pattern. Later on, Bordua (1958) also investigated part of the Landers findings by utilizing the criminals' data from Detroit, Michigan juvenile court for the time period between 1948 and 1952 and found an interesting indicator "*overcrowding*" with respect to criminality. Chilton (1964) also replicated the findings of both Lander and Bordua by using the juvenile court data from Indiana, Indianapolis from the period 1948 to 1950 alongside the data from the US. Consensus1950. He again found out that the physical characteristics and criminality by previous theorists were "*shots in the right direction*" since his findings corroborated the original findings in the earlier studies. What's more, a significant correlation between criminality and overcrowded circumstances (> 1.5 persons per room) was observed.

Many theorists arrayed with an argument that *the broader horizon of the social disorganization theory is might be a futile investigative journey into greater degrees of cluelessness BUT the facts represent something very opposite to this school of thought*. Numerous theorists put their share in researching the social disorganization theory by using different variables in a bid to fill the vacuums presented in previous findings (Quinney, 1964; Bursik & Webb, 1982; Schuerman & Kobrin, 1986). When it comes to critically reviewing the social disorganization theory, *one cannot rollback the significance of its statistical findings nor can abandon its existence on the basis of continued fertile resistance against this theory*. At the very least, within the domain of criminal justice system and criminology, neighborhood plays a crucial role in determining the delinquency. Apart from testing this theory close to its original configuration, it needs to be explored with new methodologies in a bid to further its investigation and broaden its horizon. It should be kept in consideration that "*a single theory cannot turn off the crime in a jiffy, nor is there a quick fix to criminal delinquency*", yet the social disorganization theory can open doors to the unanswered areas of delinquency with regards to neighborhood conditions.

3. What Is Strain or Anomie Theory?

Anomie theory which is sometimes also referred as Strain theory indicates that a human mind is itself locked inside its own small bubble which is nothing short of his emotions towards his goals and life objectives. And the strains of inability to achieve one's goals might provide a red meat to crime. In other words, the natural inclination of an individual is towards the standard norms of the society but he can fall prey towards the slippery road of crime if the social structure fails to provide him with valid chances to succeed (Miller, 2009). Individuals who undergo the social stresses like verbal or physical abuse (negative stimuli) or financial loss or death of a close one (positive stimuli), are likely to show inclination towards delinquency in a bid to cope with the strain (Agnew, 1992). *It's like putting delinquency on steroids* where an individual doesn't feel and see the possible consequences of his criminal actions because the only thing which matters to him is "*to cope with the strain*". For instance, if an individual is fed up from the continuous abuses from his parents, he might get a chance to steal all the valuables at home and run away. An individual might beat someone who used to harass him. Likewise, in an effort to cope up with the strain, he might indulge in drugs, making himself a drug addict.

In the light of above facts, it can be stated that the strain, in numerous shapes, leads to negative emotions, making an individual vulnerable to get indulged in a criminal act. In fact, the negative emotions inflict pressure for a corrective action where crime might be the one possible outcome to get away with the stress, especially when the individual is deprived of comprehending the possible consequences of committing a crime and he possesses favorable characteristics with a strong tendency for criminal coping (Agnew, 2013).

The very first fundamental theory of crime was presented by Merton (1938) in the 1930's in the midst of the Great Depression. He presented the key idea of *why numerous milestones of USA citizens run through the slippery crossovers of criminal junctions*. He put forth an argument that every citizen of United States of America, irrespective of the standing of his class, is persuaded to make every single effort to pull off the goal of financial success. The flip side of the coin shows the bleak picture because most of the low-class individuals are prevented such achievements through proper legal means. The reasons could be many, such as their parents might not be better off putting their children in good schooling environments or they might fail to provide them a good atmosphere at home, to get them admission in good colleges or their funds doesn't suffice the requirements to start their business on a good scale (Miller, 2009). These circumstances are likely to instigate strain, negative emotions, and the gloomy circumstances are likely to bend their brain's arc towards income generating crime such as prostitution, drug selling, and theft.

However, Merton (1938) held a strong opinion that crime is not merely the only option for these individuals to cope up with their strains.

Some individuals will simply bear the strain with an eye popping display of logics

Some individuals will mark them as unsubstantiated desires resulting in lowering down their thirst for money

Some individuals will place a full stop to the unachievable goals and turn towards other goals that they deem achievable.

4. Development of Merton's Strain Theory

Newton's third law of motion states that "for every action, there is always an equal and opposite reaction". Merton's theory paved the way for developing other strain theories where his student Albert Cohen's (1955) theory of strain is worthy of comment that seems to beef up the logics pertaining to the class status deprivation and crime. Deriving his arguments on the blue-print of Merton theory, he explained that the lower-class individuals demand respect and money from others which is quite understandable. However, *both things (respect & money), despite their eye glazing attributes, prove to be anything but an unattainable idea through legal channels.* This creates another point of tension when the children from lower class enter their schools and get mistreatment both from their middle-class teachers as well as from their middle-class fellows. The fact is, money can be stolen but middle-class status cannot be snatched like the money. Hence, these strains get under their skin and they develop an alternative reactive status system in which they tend to soften the blow of strain by valuing and accepting all those things which middle class rejects at large (*Remember Newton's third law*). For instance, if the middle-class values polite behavior and private property, as a reaction, they would take a harder line of action by valuing and accepting value theft (opposite to property) and aggression (opposite to politeness) (Cohen, 1955). This is what eventually turns out to be juvenile gangs according to Cohen whilst many theorists pitched a fit against this assumption with an argument that whether the lower class gangs embrace the crime from all corners by completely rejecting the traditional values or what (Agnew, 2000).

In a bid to unfold more possibilities flirting with crime by lower class juvenile gangs, Cloward and Ohlin (1960) presented another version of Strain theory. They followed the same blueprint "*the incapacity to pull off traditional success objectives through legal ways and means triggers the creation of gangs*". But what distinguishes them from earlier studies was the point i.e. "the understanding of crime should not be based solely on one's opportunities to strike traditional success goals but also on the basis of illegal opportunities available to the individual as well". In other words, *the roots of delinquency should be traced back to the illegal opportunities available that are favorable to get them engaged in delinquent crimes* such as drug use and sale, theft, and violence etc.

All the aforementioned theories of Merton, Cohen, Cloward and Ohlin strain theories have one idea in common i.e. *the entity of strain has metastasizing properties* which entails the incapacity to achieve traditional success goals using legal means. Being inspirational and all-time hit theories of crime in the periods of 1950 and 60's, these theories helped shaping up the public policy of those times by targeting a severe war over the issue of poverty (Agnew, 2000). On the flip side, these classical strain theories of crime fall prey to enough criticism and almost faced an ax by 1970's and 80's (Agnew et al., 1996; Kornhauser, 1978). For instance, a few theorists counter-attacked and echoed the arguments with suggestions that juvenile's related goals do have a broader horizon that's why they chase a wide variety of goals which includes but not limited to friendly relations with parents, self-sufficiency and independence from adults, and recognition with peers etc. (Greenberg, 1977; Elliott, Huizinga & Ageton, 1979). In this regard, Baron (2004) also argued that homelessness also serves as a catalyst for crime since one is always wary to make its both ends meet and homelessness instigates enough pressure upon an individual to get indulge in criminal activities.

5. Opposing Interpretation of Delinquent Subcultures

Correct anticipation and quick fixing the crime is like promising the moon that's why the results of every second theory places itself at odds with the findings provided by the first theory. This is what we witness in the findings provided by Miller (1958) as opposed to Cohen (1955).

The interpretation of delinquent subcultures described by Albert Cohen is in contrast with the findings provided by Walter B. Miller (1958; 1959). Miller is at odds with Cohen's reactive nature phenomenon of the lower-class juveniles, and he also doesn't see their deviant behavior as a consequence of their inability to pull off success through legitimate means. *One couldn't help saying that Miller sees Cohen's triggers of delinquency as a "weapon of mass distraction".* He set off a debate in the air that Cohen's conclusion exhibits more show than substance because, according to Miller, it is not due to the reactive nature of the lower-class BUT it is because of the different culture of the lower class itself that is literally different from the higher classes in every sense of the word and this fundamental culture has not been just passed on from one generation since there have been arrays of generations from which this culture has been transcended to the later generations. In other words, *delinquency and crime of lower-class cultures stem from their own value system within their own culture which grew and developed with integrity of its own rather than a reactive subculture.*

Here comes a moot; what is that lower-class structure and where it is situated that Miller speaks of? In this regard, Miller provided the attributes of the hard-core group in this lower class that has been fed through a series of shaking down progressions through cultural streams and diverse population and finally came out in shape of complex patterned social structural elements which Miller highlighted as *"focal concerns"* by the names trouble, toughness, smartness, excitement, fate, and autonomy (Miller, 1958; Brotherton, 1996; Bordua, 1961; Clark & Wenninger, 1963; Hagedom, 2004). Here is a brief drift of each as follows:

➤ Trouble

The focal concern that talks about what worldly life and environment gets you into i.e. the young working class accepts the bald-faced truth that their life would definitely be accustomed to violence and they will fight back the violence without any runaway theory.

➤ Toughness

The focal concern that is connected with bravery, masculinity, physical prowess, and fearlessness in the face of physical threat. This fertile bravery related attribute can trigger or result into a crime such as an assault in a bid to keep up the repute.

➤ Smartness

The focal concern which is tagged with an inherent capability to manipulate people and things to personal advantage. This capability to outfox others creates personalities of pickpockets, pimps, petty thieves, conmen, and the hustlers.

➤ Excitement

The focal concern which has the propensity of losing fair grounds in search for 'thrills' such as booze and sexual adventures, gambling in a bid to stir emotional stimulus. All these quests can spin out of control thereby creating the risk of trouble and fighting.

➤ Fate

The focal concern which draws a red line against their lives and fortune. They believe that their life, without a grain of salt, is like a rolling cycle without the paddles. They have no control on their lives and there is literally nothing or very little which they can do with their life. This sullen attitude itself fuel concerns about *"when things break for me"*.

➤ Autonomy

The focal concern which makes them think ambivalently about the severity of control by the others. As a response, they seek freedom and independence from external constraints which is likely to turn their behavior against the social norms.

6.   Anomie / Strain Theory and Recent Research Findings

The 'strain' imprint with respect to the longtime research done, clearly paved its way to reach out the blueprint *"strains do have the ability to enhance the probability of committing crime"* (Agnew, 2006). In a bid to secure a reason for the said argument, Spano, Riveria, and Bolland (2006) drew upon a conclusion that the propensity of getting involved in violence was much more in those juveniles who underwent violent victimization. In Canada, Baron (2004) also investigated the homeless juveniles and found out that homelessness was a deep rooted problem among juvenile criminals who were reportedly homeless for several months in the previous year. Various types of strains tend to box-in the individuals and later bring them on the brink of delinquency as investigated by Jhang and Johnson (2003). They analyzed numerous individuals and found out that they underwent different types of strains such as criminal victimizations, family pressures, financial troubles and the like. They also established an argument that individuals who underwent more strain fall prey to anger, which, in response, directed them toward crime later on. *Lest one be tempted into thinking that anger is the only emotion*, Agnew (2006) also explained certain other emotional drivers in the said context such as fear, frustration, and depression.

Research on strain theory also revealed the fact that strain has the perfect propensity to promote the social learning of crime as well (Cohen, 1955; Coward & Ohlin, 1960). They observed that crime send the shockwaves to lead individuals to connect with other individuals who strongly favor the criminal pathways. The research on strain theory clearly shows that "*strain, although not being the only but one of the major champions of crime, which has the flair of increasing the probability of committing crime to considerable extent*" (Peternoster & Mazerolle, 1994).

7. Empirical Investigations of Class-Crime Connection

If we remove the Lower-Class and Minority groups from the theory, does the math fails!! This is questionable since the middle decades of early 20th century tagged crime with the lower-class group at large (Cohen, 1955; Miller, 1958; Cloward & Cohen, 1960). This has been challenged recently when theorists sweat the details through empirical investigations, yet further research needs to be done to determine the class-crime connection. There is a bit of debate equally for and against this comprehension. For instance, surveys done in the USA jails on criminal offenders revealed that most of the criminals belonged to lower class, less educated, and unemployed (Bureau of Justice Statistics, U.S. Department of Justice, 2004). It was also observed by Wright et al. (1999) that the lower educational goals coupled with lower occupational objectives alongside triple threat of alienation, aggression, and financial strain put a considerable impact upon instigating lower class individuals towards delinquency. The minority groups, on the other hand, are unfairly victimized since police and law enforcement agencies unfairly target them merely on the belief that because they belong to a minority group, they are more likely to be indulged in criminal activities (Miller, 2009). Even this practice is not limited to the police alone; the minority groups are also victimized in the operations of asset protection and scrutiny of private sector as well (Meeks, 2010; Lundman & Kaufman, 2003; Glover, 2007; Kowalski & Lundman, 2007; Dottolo & Stewart, 2008; Higgins & Gabbidon, 2009).

Still it remains controversial with arguments afoot that *this is due to the disparity of criminal justice system which slides knife into poorest of the poor (the same is true for minority groups) while leave the white sharks' unattended* (Parkin, 1981; Bonger, 1916). Another argument in this regard has been swirled by Barnet (1981) who gave specific evidences of corporate crimes committed by the wealthiest of the wealthy people. Similar results were observed by Tittle, Villemez and Smith (1978) when they went through around 35 research studies and found a very minor connection between lower class and crime.

8. Crime and Other Relevant Factors

Crime has never been at a loss for structural correlates since the moment it started breathing" that's why it entails bunch of correlates described briefly as below:

• Age and Crime

The relationship between age and crime is one of the hard facts in criminology (Hirschi & Gottfredson, 1983). *The age crime curve cemented its authenticity and popularity long ago* (Steffensmeier, Allan, Harer, & Streifel, 1989) still its resistance has also gained momentum since there has been a sharp disagreement on its meaning and comprehensions (Miller, 2009).

• Education and Crime

Education has an authentic correlation with crime since there is an overwhelming consensus among the society that prevention of crime is directly linked with the promotion of education (Miller, 2009).

• Families and Crime

The role of families and parental behavior can either negatively assault on children (increasing crime in response) or positively progress and put an impact on children (decreasing crime in response). The best examples in this regard are social control theory of Hirschi (1969), the life course perspective presented by Sampson & Laub's (1990), Social learning model formulated by Akers (1973), and the General theory of crime proposed by Gottfredson and Hirschi (1990).

The list is necessarily wide since the aforementioned correlates are nothing short of just a brick in the wall and there is a wide list of correlates of crime which includes but not limited to citizenship and crime, gender and crime, guns and crime, neighborhood influences, employment perspective, the peers, ethnicity and race, the religion, social class, immigration and so on.

9. Theoretical Explanations: Delinquent Sub-Cultures and the Existence Of Gangs

The objective research on gangs and delinquent subcultures is an assault on basic math. That's why Cultural criminologists prompt a groundswell of criticism from time to time that the objective research procedures on gangs do not suffice the information needed about gangs and their cultures at large (Kontos, Brothern, & Barrios, 2003). Without mincing words, formation of gangs and their operations is a reality nobody can deny (Lyon & Thrasher, 1927; Miller, 1958; Spergel, 1964). The existence of gangs and their prominent role in local social orders has also been observed by criminologists (Vigil, 2010; Venkatesh, 2008, 2009). The flip side of the coin also shows that understanding and controlling the gangs is a complex task and it needs greater attention with regards to the social change at different levels like local, national, and on global scales (Miller, 2009).

It has been observed that school dropout is a criminogenic factor for the reason that a typical school dropout would be able to snatch only a low-quality job in the market, no need to explain further exploitation by the employer or company alike (Staff and Uggen, 2003). Even a few theorists also suggested that solely the attribute of youth employment is tagged with delinquency with a few noteworthy exceptions (Good et al., 1986). More than half of high school dropout black individuals gained a prison record in their early 30's according to US Bureau of Justice Statistics Website. Factors contributing to crime and delinquency do vary, but high school dropouts remain the most important factor since these youths are likely to get indulge in delinquent behaviors due to not completing their education and ending up in low quality and low-profile jobs at large (Miller, 2009).

10. Psychological Implications of The Theory

There is a sharp disagreement between aspirations and expectations with respect to crime on the score that when crime went on with a rapid pace during the period of 1960's in the United States, there was no sign of economic loss since economy was booming and there had a been a considerable effort to reduce poverty from all corners (Miller, 2009). In a bid to make a bulwark against the crime scenario, several researches attempted to examine the relational connection between ideal goals (aspirations) and expected level of achievement of goals (expectations). The research was done with respect to occupational and educational goals in general. Based on the strain theory calculations, the results should be conforming like there should be high criminal activities among those who were having relatively high aspirations but low expectations. Surprisingly, the results showed very much to the contrary "crime was highest among those who had low aspirations and low expectations (Kornhauser, 1978; Agnew et al., 1996, Agnew, 2000).

This discrepancy was unsolved till the research conducted by Passas and Agnew (1977) put forth an argument that success goals are not absolute, they are relative. Individuals do see other people in their reference groups when deciding about their aspirations and expectations. Consequently, those who are close to high class societies undergo strain because they decide their aspirations and expectations by comparing their positions with those more privileged than them. This also justifies the high crime rate during 1960's because those who didn't fetch economic progress as compared to their closed ones might undergo strain which translated in delinquency in response.

11. Few Conducive Strains and Delinquent Behavior

Agnew (1985, 1989, and 1992) proposed a general strain theory of crime and delinquency (GST) *and stretched out a much broader horizon and boundaries of strain*. He used the same blueprints of social learning and social control theories presented by Akers (1985) and Hirschi (1969), and utilized their fundamental concepts to figure out the motives of crime. According to Agnew (1992), strain is nothing short of circumstances and events which are normally disliked by people especially when it comes to explaining the incapacity to accomplish their goals. Furthering this research, strain theory broadened its horizon by entailing a wide list of strains conducive to crime. Below is the list of few strains that are conducive to crime and delinquency according to Agnew's General Strain theory of crime and delinquency:

• Parental Rejection

The children experience strain due to the fact that their parents don't give them much support, time, and affection as per their genuine requirements.

• Child Abuse and Negligence

This entails emotional, sexual, and physical abuse and the disappointment in terms of gaining enough medical, shelter, and food.

• Work in a Bad Environment

This includes working in a bad environment with little to zero prestige, zero or little chances for growth coupled with job insecurity.

• Bad School Days

bad school experience is also conducive to crime that includes humiliation from school fellows and teachers, low grades, unfair treatments, and the like.

The list is long and much research is needed in order to answer the unanswered such as abusive peer relations, unemployment, marital difficulties, victimization, racial discrimination, homelessness, failure to achieve objectives, and so on.

12. Summary

Shaw and McKay (1942) generated a true recipe of a systematic and non-random pattern of crime in Chicago which is commonly regarded as *"Social disorganization theory"*. It was focused towards the explanations that *"what makes or instigates a neighborhood susceptible to crime.* Anomie theory states that the strains of inability to achieve one's goals might provide a red meat to crime. The very first fundamental theory of crime was presented by Merton (1938) in the 1930's in the midst of the Great Depression. He presented the key idea of *why numerous milestones of USA citizens run through the slippery crossovers of criminal junctions.* Albert Cohen (1955) theory of strain is worthy of comment that seems to beef up the logics pertaining to the class status deprivation and crime. In a bid to unfold more possibilities flirting with crime by lower class juvenile gangs, Cloward and Ohlin (1960) presented another version of Strain theory i.e. *the roots of delinquency should be traced back to the illegal opportunities available that are favorable to get him engaged in delinquent crimes*, drug use and sale, theft, and violence etc. Miller is at odds with Cohen's reactive nature phenomenon of the lower-class juveniles, and he also doesn't see their deviant behavior as a consequence of their inability to pull off success through legitimate means. *Crime has never been at a loss for structural correlates since it started breathing"* that's why it entails bunch of correlates. Agnew (1985, 1989, and 1992) proposed a general strain theory of crime and delinquency (GST) *and stretched out a much broader horizon and boundaries of strain.*

13. References

Akers, R. L. (1973). Deviant behavior: A social learning approach (Belmont, CA: Wadsworth, 1977). *An upper level text written from a cultural transmission perspective. Evaluates major theories of deviance and examines a wide variety of deviant activities.*

Akers, R. L. (1985). *Deviant behavior: A social learning approach.* Wadsworth Publishing Company.

Agnew, R. (1985). A revised strain theory of delinquency. *Soc. F., 64,* 151.

Agnew, R. (1989). A longitudinal test of the revised strain theory. *Journal of Quantitative Criminology, 5*(4), 373-387.

Agnew, R. (1992). Foundation for a general strain theory of crime and delinquency. *Criminology, 30*(1), 47-88.

Agnew, R., Cullen, F. T., Burton Jr, V. S., Evans, T. D., & Dunaway, R. G. (1996). A new test of classic strain theory. *Justice quarterly, 13*(4), 681-704.

Agnew, R. (2000). Sources of criminality: Strain and subcultural theories. *Criminology: A contemporary handbook,* 349-371.

Agnew, R. (2006). Pressured into crime: An overview of general theory of crime. *Los Angeles, CA: Roxbury.*

Agnew, R. (2013). When criminal coping is likely: An extension of general strain theory. *Deviant Behavior, 34*(8), 653-670.

Barnett, H. C. (1981). Corporate capitalism, corporate crime. *Crime & Delinquency.*

Baron, S. W. (2004). General strain, street youth and crime: A test of Agnew's revised theory. *Criminology, 42*(2), 457-484.

Bonger, W. A. (1916). *Criminality and economic conditions.* Boston: Little, Brown.

Bordua, D. J. (1958). Juvenile delinquency and "anomie": An attempt at replication. *Social Problems, 6*(3), 230-238.

Bordua, D. J. (1961). Delinquent subcultures: Sociological interpretations of gang delinquency. *The Annals of the American Academy of Political and Social Science, 338*(1), 119-136.

Brotherton, D. C. (1996). "Smartness," "toughness," and "autonomy": Drug use in the context of gang female delinquency. *Journal of Drug Issues, 26*(1), 261-277.

Bureau of Justice Statistics, U.S. Department of Justice. (2004). Survey of inmates of state prisons. Washington, DC: U.S. Government Printing Office.

Bursik Jr, R. J., & Webb, J. (1982). Community change and patterns of delinquency. *American Journal of Sociology, 88*(1), 24-42.

Bursik, R. J. (1988). Social disorganization and theories of crime and delinquency: Problems and prospects. *Criminology, 26*(4), 519-552.

Chilton, R. J. (1964). Continuity in delinquency area research: A comparison of studies for Baltimore, Detroit, and Indianapolis. *American Sociological Review*, 71-83.

Clark, J. P., & Wenninger, E. P. (1963). Goal orientations and illegal behavior among juveniles. *Soc. F., 42*, 49.

Cloward, R. A., & Lloyd, E. (86). Ohlin. 1960. Delinquency and opportunity: A theory of delinquent gangs.

Cohen, A. K. (1955). Delinquent boys; The culture of the gang.

Dottolo, A. L., & Stewart, A. J. (2008). "Don't ever forget now, you're a black man in America": Intersections of race, class and gender in encounters with the police. *Sex Roles*, *59*(5-6), 350-364.

Elliott, D. S., Ageton, S. S., & Canter, R. J. (1979). An integrated theoretical perspective on delinquent behavior. *Journal of Research in Crime and Delinquency*, *16*(1), 3-27.

Glover, K. S. (2007). Police discourse on racial profiling. *Journal of Contemporary Criminal Justice*, *23*(3), 239-247.

Good, D. H., Pirog-Good, M. A., & Sickles, R. C. (1986). An analysis of youth crime and employment patterns. Journal of Quantitative Criminology, 2, 219–236.

Gottfredson, M. R., & Hirschi, T. (1990). *A general theory of crime*. Stanford University Press.

Greenberg, D. F. (1977). Delinquency and the age structure of society. *Contemporary crises*, *1*(2), 189-223.

Hagedorn, J. M. (2004). Gang. *Encyclopedia of Men and Masculinities*, 329-330.

Higgins, G. E., & Gabbidon, S. L. (2009). Perceptions of consumer racial profiling and negative emotions an exploratory study. *Criminal Justice and Behavior*, *36*(1), 77-88.

Hirschi, T. (1969). Causes of delinquency Berkeley: University of California. *Press.-386.*

Hirschi, T., & Gottfredson, M. (1983). Age and the explanation of crime. *American Journal of Sociology*, *89*(3), 552-584.

Jang, S. J., & Johnson, B. R. (2003). Strain, negative emotions, and deviant coping among African Americans: A test of general strain theory. *Journal of Quantitative Criminology*, *19*(1), 79-105.

Jencks, C., & Mayer, S. E. (1990). The social consequences of growing up in a poor neighborhood. *Inner-city poverty in the United States*, *111*, 186.

Jonassen, C. T. (1949). A re-evaluation and critique of the logic and some methods of Shaw and McKay. *American Sociological Review*, *14*(5), 608-617.

Kontos, L., Brotherton, D. C., & Barrios, L. (Eds.). (2012). *Gangs and society: Alternative perspectives*. Columbia University Press.

Kornhauser, R. (1978). Social sources of delinquency. Chicago: University of Chicago Press.

Kowalski, B. R., & Lundman, R. J. (2007). Vehicle stops by police for driving while Black: Common problems and some tentative solutions. *Journal of Criminal Justice*, *35*(2), 165-181.

Lander, B. (1954). *Towards an understanding of juvenile delinquency: A study of 8,464 cases of juvenile delinquency in Baltimore* (Vol. 578). Columbia University Press.

Lowenkamp, C. T., Cullen, F. T., & Pratt, T. C. (2003). Replicating Sampson and Groves's test of social disorganization theory: Revisiting a criminological classic. *Journal of Research in Crime and Delinquency*, *40*(4), 351-373.

Lundman, R. J., & Kaufman, R. L. (2003). Driving while black: Effects of race, ethnicity, and gender on citizen self-reports of traffic stops and police actions. *Criminology*, *41*(1), 195-220.

Lyon, F. E., & Thrasher, F. M. (1927). The Gang. A Study of 1,313 Gangs in Chicago.

Meeks, K. (2010). *Driving While Black: Highways, shopping malls, taxi cabs, sidewalks: How to fight back if you are a victim of racial profiling*. Broadway Books.

Merton, R. K. (1938). Social structure and anomie. *American Sociological Review*, *3*(5), 672-682.

Miller, W. B. (1958). Lower class culture as a generating milieu of gang delinquency. *Journal of Social Issues*, *14*(3), 5-19.

Miller, W. B. (1959). Implications of urban lower-class culture for social work. *Social Service Review*, *33*(3), 219-236.

Miller, J. M. (Ed.). (2009). *21st century criminology: a reference handbook* (Vol. 1). Sage.

Parkin, F. (1981). Marxism and class theory: A bourgeois critique.

Passas, N., & Agnew, R. (Eds.). (1997). *The future of anomie theory*. Northeastern University Press.

Paternoster, R., & Mazerolle, P. (1994). General strain theory and delinquency: A replication and extension. *Journal of Research in Crime and Delinquency*, *31*(3), 235-263.

Quinney, R. (1964). Crime, delinquency, and social areas. *Journal of Research in Crime and Delinquency*, *1*(2), 149-154.

Sampson, R. J., & Groves, W. B. (1989). Community structure and crime: Testing social-disorganization theory. *American journal of sociology*, *94*(4), 774-802.

Sampson, R. J., & Laub, J. H. (1990). Crime and deviance over the life course: The salience of adult social bonds. *American sociological review*, 609-627.

Sampson, R. J., Morenoff, J. D., & Raudenbush, S. (2005). Social anatomy of racial and ethnic disparities in violence. *American Journal of Public Health*, *95*(2), 224-232.

Spergel, I., & Ohlin, L. E. (1964). *Racketville, slumtown, haulburg: An exploratory study of delinquent subcultures*. Chicago, IL: University of Chicago Press.

Staff, J., & Uggen, C. (2003). The fruits of good work: Early work experiences and adolescent deviance. *Journal of Research in Crime and Delinquency, 40*(3), 263-290.

Steffensmeier, D. J., Allan, E. A., Harer, M. D., & Streifel, C. (1989). Age and the distribution of crime. *American Journal of Sociology, 94*(4), 803-831.

Schuerman, L., & Kobrin, S. (1986). Community careers in crime. *Crime and justice, 8,* 67-100.

Shaw, C. R., & McKay, H. D. (1942). Juvenile delinquency and urban areas.

Palen, J. J. (1981). *The urban world.* McGraw-Hill Companies.

Park, R. E., Burgess, E. W., McKenzie, R. D., & Wirth, L. (1925). The City (The University of Chicago Studies in Urban Sociology). *The City (The University of Chicago Studies in Urban Sociology).*

Spano, R., Rivera, C., & Bolland, J. (2006). The impact of timing of exposure to violence on violent behavior in a high poverty sample of inner city African American youth. *Journal of youth and adolescence, 35*(5), 681-692.

Tittle, C. R., Villemez, W. J., & Smith, D. A. (1978). The myth of social class and criminality: An empirical assessment of the empirical evidence. *American Sociological Review,* 643-656.

U.S. Bureau of Justice Statistics (BJS): http://www.ojp.usdoj .gov/bjs

Venkatesh, S. A. (2008). *Gang leader for a day: A rogue sociologist takes to the streets.* Penguin.

Vigil, J. D. (2010). *Barrio gangs: Street life and identity in Southern California.* University of Texas Press.

Wright, B. R. E., Caspi, A., Moffitt, T. E., Miech, R. A., & Silva, P. A. (1999). Reconsidering the relationship between

SES and delinquency: Causation but not correlation. *Criminology, 37*(1), 175-194.

9 781788 236249